In the Shadow of Florence

IN THE SHADOW
OF FLORENCE

Provincial Society in Renaissance Pescia

JUDITH C. BROWN

New York   Oxford
OXFORD UNIVERSITY PRESS
1982

Library of Congress Cataloging in Publication Data
Brown, Judith C.
In the shadow of Florence.
Bibliography: p.   Includes index.
1. Pescia (Italy)—Economic conditions.
2. Pescia (Italy)—Social conditions.   I. Title.
HC308.P43B76   330.945'52   81-38377
ISBN 0-19-502993-3   AACR2

Printing (last digit): 9 8 7 6 5 4 3 2 1
Printed in the United States of America

To Shannon

Acknowledgments

This book began as a doctoral dissertation submitted to The Johns Hopkins University. Most of the research for it was made possible by a Fulbright Fellowship which enabled me to spend the academic year 1973–74 in Florence.
Many people have been of valuable assistance in the preparation of this study. I owe a special debt to Richard Goldthwaite, whose dedication as a teacher and scholar inspired me throughout the years. I am also grateful to Robert Forster and Giuliano Pinto for their critical reading of the manuscript during its early stages, and to E. A. Wrigley for my first lessons in demographic history and for his comments on the demographic analysis in this book. In gathering archival materials I benefited from the generosity of David Herlihy and Christiane Klapisch who shared their catasto data in machine-readable form. For their help in the various archives I consulted, I thank Rolando Anzilotti, Guglielma Paoli, Michele Sansoni, and Paola Peruzzi.
Finally, I wish to give special recognition to my husband Shannon to whom I dedicate this book. His constant encouragement, his willingness to share the burdens as well as the joys of family responsibilities, and his rigorous inquiry at every step of the way helped make this book a reality.

Baltimore, Maryland   J.C.B.
April 1981

Contents

Figures

Weights and Measures

1 quartiere	= .247 acres	= 10.02 are
1 staio	= .686 bushels	= 24.36 liters
1 barile of wine	= 10.74 gallons	= 40.6 liters
1 barile of oil	= 33.42 liters = 28.86 Kg.	= libre 8 "di misura"
1 libbra	= .74 pounds	= 339.54 grams
1 lira	= 240 denari "di piccioli"	= 20 soldi

In addition to the lira, a silver based currency, several gold based currencies were in use. These generally rose in value with respect to the lira. A few equivalences are given below to serve as reference points.

Ratio of gold currencies to soldi

Year	Florin	Ducat	Scudo
1351	68		
1400	77		
1450	96		
1500	134	140	
1550	150	167	144
1600	200	200	192

Sources: ASPe, 1424. Tavole di ragguaglio per la riduzione dei pesi e misure che si usano in diversi luoghi del Granducato di Toscana al peso e misura vegliante a Firenze (Florence, 1782); C. M. Cipolla, Le avventure della lira (Milan, 1958); R. de Roover, The Medici Bank: Its Organization, Management, Operations and Decline (New York, 1948), pp. 19, 61; A. Galleotti, Le monete del Granducato di Toscana, 2d ed. (Bologna, 1971); A. Martini, Manuale di Metrologia, ossia misure, pesi e monete in uso attualmente e anticamente presso tutti i popoli (Turin, 1883); A. Molho, Public Finances in the Early Renaissance, 1400–1433 (Cambridge, Mass., 1971), app. D.

Abbreviations

AC	Archivio Capponi
ASF	Archivio di Stato di Firenze
ASL	Archivio di Stato di Lucca
ASPe	Archivio di Stato di Pescia
ASPi	Archivio di Stato di Pisa
BCatPe	Biblioteca della Cattedrale di Pescia
BComPe	Biblioteca Comunale di Pescia
BNF	Biblioteca Nazionale di Firenze
CC	Camera del Comune—Provveditori—Entrata e Uscita
Del	Deliberazioni
Monte	Provveditori del Monte—Entrata e Uscita del Camarlingo per la Diminuzione del Monte

Introduction

The development of the Renaissance state and its territorial expansion is one of the most fundamental themes in Renaissance historiography. Since the publication of Jacob Burckhardt's *The Civilization of the Renaissance in Italy* over one hundred years ago, it is difficult to find many works on the history of the Italian city-states that do not touch at least peripherally on this subject. Emerging out of the struggle between popes and emperors, the communes of the Italian peninsula began to implement programs of territorial growth that culminated in the creation of territorial states by the last half of the fourteenth century. The causes, progress, and cultural implications of this development for the dominant cities have been examined at length. Yet, despite this interest, or perhaps because it has focused on the dominant cities themselves, the economic, fiscal, and political consequences of the development of territorial states for subject areas have scarcely been studied.[1]

This has not hindered the growth of heated polemics that are part of a larger and ongoing debate about imperialism in general. When applied to the policy of Renaissance city-states, the term

1. For Tuscan history this omission was first noted by Marvin Becker, whose own work, however, is concerned precisely with a dominant city; Marvin Becker, *Florence in Transition* (Baltimore, 1968), 2:188. More recently, Michael Mallett has also called attention to the need for further work in this area: "Review of David Herlihy and C. Klapisch, *Les Toscans et leurs familles," Economic History Review*, 32 (1979), 291.

imperialism only adds to the diversity of opinion because in this context, as in most others, it incorporates a variety of value-laden and ideologically determined meanings that mostly serve to obscure rather than to clarify debate.[2] If we take it to refer, at its most general, to a relation of active dominance and subjection between states, there can be no doubt that the Renaissance state was imperialistic.[3] Disagreement, however, does not center so much on this point as on two related ones: what were the causes of imperialism and what were its effects? Were Renaissance states forced to acquire subject areas in order to ensure their own economic and political survival? And once incorporated were these areas exploited to their detriment for the benefit of the rulers?

The questions are not new. Public opinion was divided about the benefits of territorial expansion at the very time it was taking place. In the late fourteenth and early fifteenth century there was much criticism over the needs and desirability of territorial acquisitions. Some thought that the creation of ever larger territorial states would bring to the dominant cities greater political and military security as well as economic gains in the form of greater tax revenues and control over larger trading areas; others, especially among the lower segments of society, were fearful both of the animosity such wars raised among neighboring powers and of the expenses of territorial conquests. The costs, they feared, would far outweigh any possible benefits. Commenting on Florentine policy in the midst of a war with Genoa in the early fifteenth century, one Florentine spokesman argued with his peers: "And note how much damage we have suffered because of the war with Genoa, for each year we have lost a million florins in com-

2. Richard Koebner and Helmut Schmidt have found at least twelve meanings in the past 120 years: R. Koebner and H. Schmidt, *Imperialism: The Story and Significance of a Political Word, 1840–1960* (Cambridge, 1964). The literature on the subject of imperialism is vast. Useful bibliographies and general surveys may be found in William Becker, "Imperialism," *Encyclopedia of American Economic History*, Glenn Porter, ed. (New York, 1979); also see Benjamin J. Cohen, *The Question of Imperialism: The Political Economy of Dominance and Dependence* (New York, 1973); D. K. Fieldhouse, *Economics and Empire, 1830–1914* (London, 1973); David S. Landes, "The Nature of Economic Imperialism," *Journal of Economic History*, 21 (1961), 497–512.
3. This definition is adopted from Cohen, *The Question of Imperialism*, pp. 15–16.

munal revenues and mercantile profits. . . . Our city was feared
by all before we possessed Arezzo, Pistoia, San Miniato, the
Valdinievole, the Valdarno, Colle, San Gimignano, and other
places. We were in better condition then than now, after we have
gained all of these cities and Pisa too."[4]
Machiavelli took up this theme in the sixteenth century. To
make subjects of a conquered people was for him the most coun-
terproductive method of aggrandizement: ". . . to make a conquered people subjects has ever been a source of weakness and of
little profit, and . . . when carried too far it has quickly proved
ruinous to the conqueror. And if this system of making subjects
is disadvantageous to warlike republics, how much more perni-
cious must it be for such as have no armies, as is the case with the
Italian republics of our day?"[5]
Machiavelli's great contemporary, Francesco Guicciardini, like
most Renaissance policy-makers, disagreed with this view. "Who
can doubt that the city of Florence and the republic of Venice
would be weaker and less powerful than they are if they had en-
closed their territory between narrow limits. Now they have sub-
jugated neighboring cities and enlarged their jurisdiction, it is
not easy for every neighbor of theirs to attack them. . . . Having
many subjects increases public revenues in many ways, and private wealth also increases in the dominating city."[6]
Such emphasis on the economic and political imperatives of
imperialism has been shared by many modern scholars, and especially by Marxist historians writing at the turn of the century.[7]

4. Cited in Gene Brucker, *The Civic World of Early Renaissance Florence*
(Princeton, 1977), p. 344. Criticisms of the imperialist policies pursued by
Florence are cited throughout his book.
5. Niccolò Machiavelli, *Discourses on the First Ten Books of Titus Livius*,
Modern Library edition (New York, 1950), bk. 2, ch. 4.
6. Francesco Guicciardini, *Considerations on the "Discourses" of Machiavelli*, in *Selected Writings*, Cecil Grayson, ed. (London, 1965), ch. 19.
7. According to Romulo Caggese, for example, "In Toscana, come nel resto
dell' Italia comunale, le libertà repubbliche fioriscono quasi contem-
poraneamente; e, siccome esse sono da per tutto conseguenza e risultato
di interessi economici e sociali in conflitto, nella fase prima e più torbida
della loro formazione, avviene che gli stessi interesse e le stesse disposizioni
d'animo spuntano fuori e si determinano in tutte le città. Ciascuna di
esse quindi, e portata inevitabilmente ad urta e contro i vicini ed i
lontani, spesse volte contro tutto e contro tutti per conquestare ciò che i
vicini ed i lontani vogliano, anch'esse, conquistare, cioè il territorio, la

But even recent studies written by historians of different ideological persuasions have adopted similar positions. According to Marvin Becker, for example, the rise of empire was the product of economic needs: "This search for revenue," he states, "led to the integration of Florentine territory, the rise of empire, and a strenuous program of mercantilism."[8]

Because they attribute economic motives to Renaissance imperialism, most historians have depicted it as exploitative of subject areas. Even Machiavelli, who felt that the dominant powers lost more than they gained from their acquisitions, argued that the relation between dominant cities and their dependencies was ininherently one of conflict and exploitation: "In free countries . . . we see wealth increase more rapidly, but the contrary of all this takes place in countries that are subject to one another; and the more rigorous the subjection of the people, the more will they be deprived of all the good to which they had previously been accustomed."[9]

Modern scholarship has tended to support the exploitation thesis. Marxist historians like Gaetano Salvemini were convinced that the winning cities in the struggle for territorial supremacy established regimes of ruthless oppression over the vanquished: "In general, rural communes became simple organs subordinated to the central power and charged with distributing and collecting taxes, maintaining order, and making sure that the land was worked. . . . Pitilessly oppressed, the rural communes ended up failing and bankrupt; the peasants fell into misery, hating the city dwellers; at times, reduced to the extremes of patience, they revolted."[10]

Although such conclusions were successfully challenged two decades ago by Enrico Fiumi, who stressed the mutually beneficial relations between subject communes and dominant cities, the

libertà di movimenti, il predominio su gli elementi feudali, una posizione privilegiata nei rapporti col Papato e con l'impero." Romulo Caggese, *Firenze dalla decadenza di Roma al risorgimento d'Italia* (Florence, 1912), 1:141–42.
8. M. Becker, *Florence in Transition*, 1:4.
9. Machiavelli, *Discourses*, bk. 2, ch. 2.
10. Gaetano Salvemini, "Un comune rurale nel secolo XIII," in *Opere di Gaetano Salvemini*, Ernesto Sestan, ed. (Milan, 1961), 1:2, 287–88.

exploitation thesis has been modified rather than eradicated.[11] Because Fiumi's case rests primarily on data from the late thirteenth and the first half of the fourteenth century, scholars writing more recently have argued that exploitation did take place but only in the centuries following the onset of the Black Death. Marvin Becker claims that after mid-fourteenth century, Florence embarked on a ruthless program of exploitation from which "were forged the links of empire."[12] The Renaissance state, he believes, was not so much a work of art, as Burckhardt would have it, as it was a product of economic and political imperialism over subject areas.[13]

Similarly, Anthony Molho in his study of Florentine public finance asserts that "There are sufficient indications . . . to lead an historian to the conclusion that the basically symbiotic and harmonious relation between Florence and her subject lands, which Fiumi so convincingly delineated, was gradually transformed into a harsh and oppressive rule that tended to erode the economic prosperity of the Tuscan countryside."[14] This exploitation, according to Molho and Julius Kirshner, became more firmly entrenched with the creation of the dowry fund in the 1420s. The payment of dowries to investors in the fund "depended on the government's collection of taxes and the tax burden, in Florence and elsewhere in Trecento and Quattrocento Italy, rested disproportionately on those who did not invest in the Monte and who could not profit from its operations: residents of the *contado* and *distretto,* as well as the urban working classes. The dowry fund became the central institution through which the ruling class of Florence in the fifteenth century was able to expropriate wealth from the lower and disenfranchised orders of the territorial state."[15]

11. Enrico Fiumi, "Sui rapporti economici fra città e contado," *Archivio storico italiano,* 94 (1956), 18–68.
12. Becker, *Florence in Transition,* 1:16; 2:181–82.
13. *Ibid.,* 2:73.
14. Anthony Molho, *Florentine Public Finances in the Early Renaissance, 1400–1433* (Cambridge, Mass., 1971), 24.
15. Julius Kirshner and A. Molho, "The Dowry Fund and the Marriage Market in Early *Quattrocento* Florence," *Journal of Modern History,* 50:3 (Sept. 1978), 436. Similar views on the taxes of subject areas and the role of the Monte not just in Florence but in other Italian states as well, can

A more ambivalent but on the whole still negative view of the effects of territorial expansion on subject areas emerges from the recent study of Tuscany undertaken by David Herlihy and Christiane Klapisch. On the one hand they argue that the vastness of the Florentine market and of Florentine capital investments encouraged the economic integration and the prosperity of Tuscany. On the other, the fiscal system of Florence and the unequal distribution of wealth between the dominant city and its subjects put severe limits on the economic development of the region. The wealth of Tuscany, they feel, tended to solidify in the hands of the Florentine patriciate.[16]

Among recent scholars, only Gene Brucker seems to cast a skeptical eye on the validity of the exploitation thesis. The relations between dominant cities and subject areas, he claims, were not inherently exploitative but were influenced primarily by short-term fiscal and military pressures. In the Renaissance, as in previous times, the economic burden of subject areas varied in direct proportion to the fiscal and military needs of the dominant cities.[17]

The variety of opinion that has emerged on this subject suggests that a new approach may be needed. To resolve the questions about the effects of Renaissance imperialism on subject areas historians will have to examine the development of the territorial state from the perspective of the subject areas themselves. This book is a study of one such place—the town of Pescia, incorporated into the Florentine state in mid-fourteenth century. It is hoped that an examination of the social, economic, and political structure of this small town, before and after integration into the Florentine dominion, will help clarify the relations that obtained among the various members of the Florentine territorial state.

Such a study necessarily takes us into the realm of local history and raises certain inevitable questions. The first has to do with the validity of a case-study approach. How can we be sure that

be found in Lauro Martines, *Power and Imagination: City-States in Renaissance Italy* (New York, 1979), pp. 184–85.

16. David Herlihy and Christiane Klapisch-Zuber, *Les Toscans et leurs familles: Une étude du catasto florentin de 1427* (Paris, 1978), pp. 259–60.

17. Gene Brucker, "Review of Marvin Becker, *Florence in Transition*, vol. 1," *American Historical Review*, 73 (1968), 795.

our results are representative of more general conditions? The answer is that we cannot. What we can do is simply to show the types of socioeconomic and political relations that did take place in one town, and provide a model for the analysis of similar problems in other places. In this task every effort was made to select a subject area that did not appear to have been singled out for special treatment by the dominant city. The town of Pescia was selected because it fit this criterion, because it was a dependency of Florence, a city whose historiographical tradition is richer than that of any other Renaissance city, because it was incorporated into the Florentine state at the beginning of the Renaissance after a lengthy period of self-rule, and finally because of the quality of surviving sources.

The second question raised by a study such as this has to do with the desirability of yet one more local study. Beginning with Gregorio Dati's *L'istoria di Firenze dal 1380 al 1405,* written in the early fifteenth century, the history of Italy has been the history of its cities. Why then add one more to the collection? One reason is that most of these histories, especially for the smaller cities of the Italian peninsula, tend to be antiquarian chronicles whose aim is to glorify the history of a particular town. Depending on the proclivities of the authors, the brilliance of the chosen locality could be found either in the achievements of an autonomous communal past, when only local notables were responsible for the town's great deeds, or alternatively it could be found in those local accomplishments that contributed to the greatness of the ruling cities of the Renaissance states.[18] Either way, the emphasis on the unique achievements of each community has tended to create a type of discrete local history from which little can be learned about the relations between the small town and the world around it.

More analytical works frequently share this problem. Scholars who have studied changes in demographic structure, in the economy, or in the political structures of local areas have seldom treated the performance of their subject within the context of a wider regional or interregional system. Rural-urban as well as

18. An enjoyable book of the former type is M. Cecchi and E. Coturri, *Pescia ed il suo territorio nella storia nell'arte e nelle famiglie* (Pistoia, 1961). An example of the latter type is P. Anzilotti, *Storia della Val di Nievole dall'origine di Pescia fino all'anno 1818* (Pistoia, 1846).

inter-urban linkages have been left unexplored, as have those
between economic, social, and political structures. What has
emerged generally is a collection of studies on specific localities
whose only relationship appears to be geographic propinquity
rather than mutual interdependence.[19]

One notable exception has been the work of David Herlihy,
who has endeavored to analyze the development of local regions
within a broader socioeconomic, political, and cultural framework.[20] But Herlihy's work, like that of most other scholars, has
centered on the late medieval and early Renaissance period, the
formative years of the "Renaissance state." Consequently, the
political economy of most of the fifteenth and sixteenth centuries
is still unexplored.

The present study, then, will focus primarily on the changes
that took place in Pescia's society between mid-fourteenth and
the early seventeenth century. Changes in the size and structure
of the population, in the economic life, and in the public administration of the town will be explored with a view toward understanding how they contributed to and were in turn the product
of a new political, economic, and social structure—the territorial
state. Such a study hopes to differ from other local studies not
only by dealing with a longer and different chronological period
than most, but also by a more rigorous application of analytical
tools. It also plans to address itself to the question of how Pescia
fit into a broader regional and European framework. The significance of this study, it is hoped, will transcend the local setting. In
the fourteenth through the sixteenth century, the economic, social,
and political integration of autonomous areas into larger territorial units was not confined to Tuscany. Throughout Europe

19. Even works that set out to analyze a local area in terms of a wider setting
do not always succeed, as can be seen in Fiumi's discussion of the decline
of San Gimignano: Enrico Fiumi, *Storia economica e sociale di San
Gimignano* (Florence, 1961), ch. 5–6. Italian studies have not availed themselves of central place or urban network analysis which emphasize the
relation between urban development and regional or national setting.
Examples of the application of such theory to urban studies are listed in
David Herlihy, "Urbanization and Social Change" in *Four "A" Themes:*
[paper delivered at the] *Seventh International Economic History Congress*
(Edinburgh, 1978), pp. 68–74.

20. David Herlihy, *Medieval and Renaissance Pistoia: The Social History of
an Italian Town, 1200–1430* (New Haven, 1967).

the territorial state, whether at the level of principalities or of monarchies, was beginning to take on a life of its own. An analysis of the new social, economic, and political bonds that tied Pescia to a larger world may contribute to a better understanding of analogous transformations in other European societies of the Renaissance.

In the Shadow of Florence

1
Origins

The commune of Pescia, located in the Valdinievole, lies at the mouth of a narrow river valley inserted in a fold of the Apennines forty miles northwest of Florence. The Valdinievole is an area approximately twenty miles long and six miles wide, and is made up of two distinct zones. To the north is a series of hills jutting out from the Apennines and separated from one another by roughly parallel river valleys. To the south is an alluvial plain that drains into the swamp of Fucecchio and ultimately into the lower Arno valley. The whole is separated from the rest of Tuscany by mountains on three sides and by swamplands on the fourth.[1]

Pescia, like most towns of the Valdinievole, is situated in the zone of low hills near the alluvial plain. Its development was profoundly influenced by its location in the Valdinievole and by the configuration of the land itself. Its location between the plain of the Valdinievole and the foothills of the Apennines gave it relatively easy access to the outside world and protection from some of that world's dangers. At the same time, its location at the mouth of the Pescia river valley ensured its importance vis-à-vis the small mountain towns located farther upstream in the direction of the Apennines.

The town is sheltered on three sides by low, steep hills which

1. For a description of the Valdinievole as a geographic unit, see Maria Puccinelli, "La Valdinievole," *Memorie della Società Geografica Italiana*, 29 (1970), 3–130; also, Roberto Almagià, ed., *Le regioni d'Italia*, 8 (Turin, 1964), 68–69.

provide a lush green backdrop for the yellow stucco houses with
their red tile roofs. The houses crowd together along the banks
of the Pescia river and are hemmed in by hills on the east and
west. On the south they border on the plain of the Valdinievole.
As population grew, settlement took place primarily on the flat
floor of the Pescia river valley, just above the plain, where building was relatively easy, and agriculture as well as rudimentary industry could benefit from the river's proximity. As a result, the
town grew in the form of two long, narrow rectangles, parallel to
the river and running on a north-south axis.

Approaching along the old Roman road, the Via Cassia, that
skirts the plain of the Valdinievole, the visitor enters Pescia by
way of the eighteenth-century Florentine gate. The main impres-
sion is of a late Renaissance and Baroque city. Here and there
traces of an older architecture may be found—a medieval gate is
embedded in the wall of an eighteenth-century home, a thirteenth-
century bell tower rises under a baroque cupola; the vicar's
palace, a thirteenth-century construction, presides over the six-
teenth- and seventeenth-century palaces that flank the main piazza. The predominant architectural style thus captures the most
vital period of Pescia's history. At the same time, fragments of
older building forms bear witness to the achievements of the medieval past and serve to remind the viewer that the prosperity of
the late Renaissance and early modern period rested in critical
measure on the social and economic foundations of the Middle
Ages and the early Renaissance.

The construction of the Via Cassia by the Romans is inextricably
related to Pescia's growth and development. By the last decades
of the second century, the Via Cassia, linking Rome to Pistoia,
was extended across the northern end of the Monte Albano into
the Valdinievole, along the foothills of the Apennines and into
Lucca, from where it continued up the coast to Liguria and eventually to Gaul.[2] Rome and Gaul were also connected by other
roads, namely the Via Emilia along the Tyrrhenian coast, and the
Via Francigena which followed the northern coast of Italy, turned
inland toward Lucca and once more turned south across the
swamps of Fucecchio toward Siena and Rome. After the collapse

2. Puccinelli, "La Valdinievole," p. 50.

Figure 1-1. Sixteenth-century Pescia

of the Roman Empire in the West, these two roads became increasingly dangerous. Travelers on the Via Emilia were easy prey to pirate raids along the coast and, as agricultural lands were abandoned, those on the Via Francigena were exposed to malarial fevers on the swampy stretch across the alluvial plain of the Valdinievole between Fucecchio and Lucca. As a result, the Via Cassia became a frequently traveled road and before long the foothills in its vicinity began to be dotted with small settlements like Montecatini, Borgo a Buggiano, Stignano, Uzzano, and Pescia—all less than half a day's foot journey from each other.

The origins of these settlements are lost in the upheavals and disorders of the early Middle Ages, but there is little doubt that they grew under the impetus for trade provided by the road. Indeed, the first historic notice of Pescia, going back to the year 742, suggests the presence of merchants and of commercial activity in the area. That year, a certain Crispinulo, "merchant of Pescia," bought some lands and vineyards from a resident of Pi-

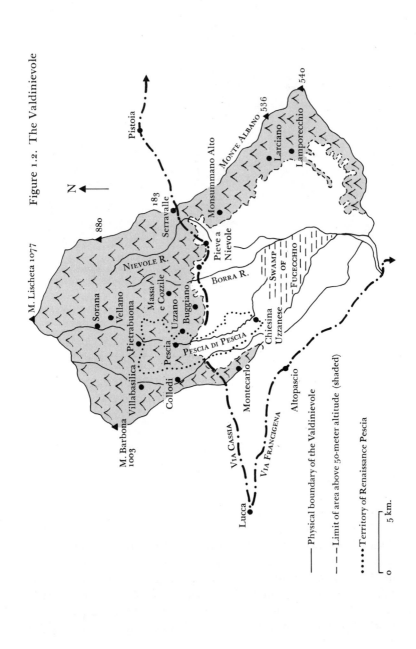

Figure 1.2. The Valdinievole

N

M. Lischeta 1077

880

M. Barbona 1003

Sorana
Vellano
NIEVOLE R.
Pietrabuona
Villabasilica
Massa
e Cozzile
Uzzano
Pescia
Collodi
Buggiano
183
Serravalle
Pieve a
Nievole
Monsummano Alto
MONTE ALBANO 536
Larciano
Lamporecchio 540

Pistoia

BORRA R.

SWAMP OF FUCECCHIO

PESCIA DI PESCIA

Chiesina
Uzzanese

Montecarlo

Altopascio

VIA CASSIA

VIA FRANCIGENA

Lucca

——— Physical boundary of the Valdinievole

– – – Limit of area above 50-meter altiude (shaded)

•••••• Territory of Renaissance Pescia

0   5 km.

stoia.[3] The transaction was a modest one, and Pescia should not be mistaken for anything more than a hamlet. Nonetheless, the presence of merchants at Pescia and the ability of people from different settlements along the Via Cassia to engage in routine transactions underscore the importance of the road and the economic activity it engendered.

Although for the next few centuries Pescia remained a hamlet in which several feudal lords, among them the bishops of Lucca and Pistoia, and the Cadolinghi family, vied for temporal jurisdictions, a number of events suggest that it and the region around it continued to grow. By 938 the hamlet had grown sufficiently to constitute a parish with several dependent villages.[4] By 1018, other small settlements such as Vellano, seven miles north of Pescia, on a mountain road branching off the Via Cassia, followed suit.[5] As density of population increased, the settlements grew not only along the Via Cassia, but also along the Apennine passes linking the plain of the Valdinievole with Modena and Bologna.

A quickened pace of economic activity and population growth in the area is also suggested by developments in the plain. By the eleventh century the Cadolinghi family began to engage in drainage efforts that would allow agriculture to spread to the plain.[6] Population pressure on the land may have encouraged these efforts, and to the extent that they succeeded they, in turn, contributed to higher population densities as the impact of land reclamation on the local agricultural economy was probably considerable. The rich alluvial soil of the plain was much better

3. Emmanuele Repetti, *Dizionario geografico, fisico, storico della Toscana*, vol. 4 (Florence, 1841), p. 114.
4. Nori A. Galli, *La grande Valdinievole* (Florence, 1970), p. 35. The villages of Civigliano, Chiari, and San Pietro di Ceule with its church (later called San Pietro di Fornace) formed part of the parish by the tenth century; BCatPe, *Memorie di Pescia raccolte da Francesco Galeotti nel 1659*, pp. 21–24. Unfortunately, none of the documents pertaining to the parish of Pescia lists all the villages that were part of the parish. This makes it impossible to trace the exact boundaries of the parish. E. Coturri, "Le pievi della Valdinievole alla fine del secolo X," *Bullettino storico pistoiese* (1968), p. 20.
5. The church of S. Martino of Vellano had formed part of the parish of S. Maria di Burra. Coturri, "Le pievi della Valdinievole," p. 30.
6. In the eleventh century the Cadolinghi began to construct the Canale Arme, later called Canale Usciana, to help drain the plain of the Valdinievole into the Arno. Puccinelli, "La Valdinievole," p. 53.

suited to cereal cultivation than the soil of the foothills, and its incorporation into the agricultural economy of the region meant that a larger population than before could now be supported.

The drainage schemes that were undertaken in the Valdinievole as in the rest of Tuscany at this time profoundly altered the possibilities for trade, communications, and human settlement along the lowlands. Indeed, one scholar has argued that these changes led to a "road revolution."[7] Their consequences for Pescia were undeniable. By the second half of the eleventh century the town had a flourishing market which soon became the focus of regional trade.[8] Its operations, therefore, became a matter of regional concern, and several towns in the area attempted to promote trade conditions that would be favorable to it. Standards of weight and quality were imposed as well as penalties against merchants found cheating their customers. Anyone found disturbing the peace of the market was to be permanently expelled.[9] With the aid of such legal sanctions, the economy of the region continued to grow. When a tax list (estimo) of the diocese of Lucca was compiled by the bishop in 1260, the parish of Pescia was the wealthiest of the Valdinievole and one of the wealthiest of those located outside the city of Lucca itself.[10]

The economic development of the Valdinievole was thus encouraged by technological changes in agriculture as well as by favorable legal arrangements. The latter, in turn, were the product of political institutions that were supportive of trade and of the social class that engaged in entrepreneurial activity. At Pescia, as elsewhere in the Italian peninsula, the establishment of a

---

7. J. Plesner, "Una rivoluzione stradale nel Dugento," *Acta Jutlandica*, 10 (1938), 3–101.

8. A notarial act of 1068 states that the church of Santo Stefano and Niccolao "est constructa prope mercato longo"; cited in BCatPe, *Memorie Galeotti*, p. 30.

9. ASF, *Diplomatico*, Pescia, 29 July 1202.

10. The purpose of the *estimo* was to draw up an inventory of the wealth of all the parishes in the diocese of Lucca. The parish of Pescia, with its twenty dependent churches, hospitals, and monasteries, had an assessed wealth of over 3,733 lire. This assessment placed it as the fourth richest parish of fifty-three located outside the city of Lucca. Pietro Guidi, *Rationes Decimarum Italiae nei secoli XIII et XIV, studi e testi* (Vatican City, 1932), 58.

communal regime in the twelfth century helped to create conditions favorable to economic development.[11] Originating as private associations of townsmen organized to protect their own interests, the communes gradually assumed public functions. Foremost among these were the administration of justice, military defense, and the protection of trade and property. At Pescia a consular system of government, probably resembling others in Italy, had emerged by 1163.[12] Little is known, however, about the institutions of government at Pescia and the extent of their power other than the fact that the consuls exercised some of the most important attributes of sovereignty, namely, that of making treaties and alliances, and of determining who could enjoy the protection of communal life. It is also evident from the measures instituted for the protection of the market that the political power of the consuls was used to further the economic activity of Pescia and the surrounding region.[13]

Although it is impossible to chart the territorial jurisdiction of Pescia's government in the Middle Ages, there can be little doubt that efforts to extend the power of the commune over an increasing sector of public life were paralleled by efforts to extend the commune's power over an ever larger share of territory. Such efforts involved Pescia in conflict with nearby communes engaged in similar expansionary activity. One such dispute, in 1202, led to an agreement between Pescia, Uzzano, and Vivinaia to elect representatives who would settle boundary disagreements and establish firm territorial boundaries among the three parties. The treaty's success, however, was temporary, since by 1298 the boundary between Pescia and Uzzano was under dispute once

11. Gino Luzzato, *An Economic History of Italy from the Fall of the Roman Republic to the Beginning of the Sixteenth Century*, trans. P. J. Jones (London, 1962), pp. 91–98.

12. M. Cecchi and E. Coturri, *Pescia ed il suo territorio nella storia, nell'arte e nelle famiglie* (Pistoia, 1961), p. 61.

13. The agreement of 1202 among Pescia, Uzzano, and Vivinaia (the present-day Montecarlo), as well as later agreements with other towns in the area, suggests that the consuls of Pescia felt free to enter into treaties with officials of other jurisdictions. For a discussion of some of these treaties, see Giuseppe Calamari, "Leghe e arbitrati tra i comuni della Valdinievole nel secolo XIII," *Bolletino di ricerche e di studi per la storia di Pescia e di Valdinievole*, 1 (1927), 6–9; 2 (1928), 20–29.

more, and that between Pescia and Vivinaia remained a source
of friction until the mid-fifteenth century.[14]

It is not until mid-fourteenth century that there begins to
emerge a fairly precise picture of the communal territory, and by
that time Pescia had pretty much reached the size and shape it
retained until the early modern period. The *estimi* of Pescia,
compiled periodically after 1353, together with the statutes of
1339 and several border treaties of the fourteenth and fifteenth
centuries, indicate that by mid-Trecento the territory of the commune extended over an area of approximately twenty-three square
miles in the shape of a long, narrow rectangle straddling both
sides of the Pescia river.[15] The rectangle was seven miles long,
and reached as far north as the fortress of Romita in the region
of hills leading into the Apennines. To the south, the commune
extended into the plain past the Via Cassia and up to the Fosso
di Montecarlo and Chiesina Uzzanese. By the early Renaissance,
then, the commune had gained control over territory on both
sides of the most important road across the Valdinievole as well
as of several strategic heights guarding the mountain passes to
Lucchese territory and to Modena and Bologna.

At the heart of this territory, in a process that remains shrouded
in obscurity, the town of Pescia itself expanded along the lines
prefigured by the settlement patterns of the tenth and eleventh
centuries. On the east side of the river, surrounding the parish
church, there appeared an agglomeration of houses. On the west
side and slightly to the north, there developed another agglomeration around the market square with its town hall and vicar's pal-

14. ASF, *Diplomatico,* Pescia, 29 July 1202; Pescia, 14 March 1298; Pescia,
    26 June 1409; Pescia, 22 February 1413; Pescia, 8 December 1465.
15. Although numerous thirteenth- and fourteenth-century documents refer
    to Pescia and its district, none define the precise territorial boundaries
    involved. Consequently, these must be derived indirectly from sources
    such as boundary treaties (see footnote 14 above) and *estimi.* The latter
    were tax records compiled by the government of Pescia for the purpose
    of taxing all land located within the district and city of Pescia. All per-
    sons owning land in that area declared the number of properties they
    owned, the location of these properties, their size, and type of crop cul-
    tivated. For the purpose of determining the territory of the commune
    the only useful information is the place-name identifying the location of
    each piece of property. Since many of the place-names survive to this day,
    modern maps of the area can be used to trace a fairly accurate boundary
    of the Renaissance territory.

ace. The civic and ecclesiastic centers of the town, each sur-
rounded by its own set of walls, were thus separated from each
other by the river. Only a bridge tenuously linked the two halves
together—a vivid reminder that despite the friction that undoubtedly existed between the ecclesiastic and secular powers, a minimum degree of cooperation was needed for mutual survival.

The political and military developments that influenced the
territorial configuration and legal jurisdiction of the commune
of Pescia are perhaps more easily identified than the actual process by which the commune gradually asserted itself over the
land and the people of the region. The declining power of the
papacy and of the empire over the Italian peninsula in the eleventh century and the struggle of the Italian cities for political
autonomy and territorial expansion helped to provide both an
impetus for and a constraint upon the communal development of
Pescia. The long-standing rivalry between the pope and the emperor had by the twelfth century left the two greatly weakened,
so that, while the Italian cities recognized the sovereignty of one
or the other, they gradually pursued their own independent
courses. The inability of either pope or emperor to consolidate
his power over Italy left, moreover, a political vacuum that the
communes of Tuscany and other regions tried to fill by strengthening their own political institutions and territorial claims. The
wars that ensued were to last the better part of two centuries.
Florence fought Pistoia, Pistoia fought Prato, Genoa fought Pisa,
and even the smallest rural settlements, including Pescia and its
neighbors, fought each other in a system of rapidly shifting alliances for the control of their surrounding territories.[16] For the
smaller communes of Tuscany, the result of these wars was two-
fold: on the one hand, the competing claims of the large cities
facilitated the development of autonomous political institutions
in the smaller ones; on the other, the competing claims of the
small cities for territorial expansion, in the long run, weakened
their ability to resist the expansionist schemes of large cities like
Lucca, Pisa, and Florence. Nowhere are the effects of these con-

16. An account of the Tuscan wars and military alliances beginning at the
    time of the investiture conflict and continuing for the next few centuries
    may be found in Robert Davidsohn, *Geschichte von Florenz* (Berlin,
    1896–1927); Italian translation, *Storia di Firenze* (Florence, 1956–1965),
    1:7–11.

flicting tendencies so clearly seen as in the history of Pescia and
the other towns of the Valdinievole in the late Middle Ages and
early Renaissance.[17]

With the death of Count Ugo, the last of the Cadolinghi, in
1113, Pescia had come under the jurisdiction of the Countess
Matilda, who died two years later, also without heirs. Since Matilda's feudal holdings reverted to her suzerain, the emperor, and
her allodial lands were bequeathed to the pope, Pescia came under the jurisdiction of the former. Henry V's effective rule over
the area, however, was brief. He came to Italy in 1116 to take
over his Italian possessions but was forced to leave in 1118 without accomplishing his task. Upon his departure, both the cities
of Italy and the pope began to divide the spoils. One of the first
armed conflicts occurred when Lucca occupied Pescia and Fucecchio. Ostensibly the reason for the occupation was to compensate for the wrong perpetrated by the emperor, who had
given the archbishop of Pisa certain Valdinievole lands of the
Cadolinghi patrimony which Lucca thought should have gone to
its own bishop.[18] The records do not allow us to make an assessment of the immediate impact of the occupation on the area, but
Lucca's claim did not go unchallenged for long. Other Tuscan
powers continued to make incursions in the area despite the fact
that finally, in 1194, the emperor himself gave the *curtis Piscie
cum mansis et manentibus* to the bishop of Lucca.[19]

The Valdinievole's location, between Pistoia to the east and
Pisa and Lucca to the west made it an easy target for troops from
all three cities as well as from Florence. Consequently, Lucca's
sway over the area fluctuated with the course of military conflict
in the Valdinievole and Tuscany in general, as well as with its
own ability to finance military campaigns. Endemic warfare was
costly, and on at least one occasion Lucca was willing to grant
free jurisdiction for one year to Fucecchio and the communities

---

17. For a detailed account of political and military affairs in the Valdinievole
    in the late Middle Ages, see: Giuseppe Ansaldi, *La Valdinievole illustrata*
    (Pescia, 1879); P. Anzilotti, *Storia della Valdinievole dall'origine di Pescia
    fino all'anno 1818* (Pistoia, 1846); P. O. Baldasseroni, *Istoria della città
    di Pescia e della Valdinievole* (Pescia, 1784); Cecchi and Coturri, *Pescia
    ed il suo territorio*.
18. Davidsohn, *Storia di Firenze*, 1:573–74.
19. Repetti, *Dizionario*, 4:115; BCatPe, *Memorie Galeotti*, p. 411.

of the Valdarno, Valdinievole, Val di Lima, and Valdariana, in exchange for the sum of 2000 lire and jurisdiction over cases involving high justice.[20] There is no evidence that this arrangement was repeated after the expiration of the year, but the paucity of records does not rule out the possibility. Moreover it is not clear to what extent the arrangement differed from the status quo since Pescia and the other communities in the Valdinievole all had consular governments which, as we have seen, exercised considerable powers as early as the beginning of the thirteenth century. Finally, the treaty itself suggests that local institutions were sufficiently developed to be capable of self-government, and if perchance they were not, they surely would be before the year's experience was over. Thus, the inability of Lucca or any other major power to establish itself firmly over the Valdinievole must have contributed to the growth of autonomous political institutions and strengthened local claims for expanded legal and territorial jurisdictions.

That these claims and aspirations left the small rural communes particularly vulnerable to the ambitions of their larger neighbors was perceived by Pescia and the other Valdinievole towns. They made several attempts to weaken Lucca's hegemony by forming regional political leagues. The underlying principle behind these leagues was that with some degree of unity and cooperation the towns of the Valdinievole might preserve the local autonomy they cherished in the face of outside threats. The first such league, formed in 1202 in the wake of border disputes that had plagued the area, established the office of prior to head the consuls of Pescia, Uzzano, and Vivinaia.[21] The functions of the prior were not spelled out in the treaty, and the office is never heard of again. Presumably the creation of the office was intended to minimize conflict between the three governments, but more than likely the realization of the need for unity was not strong enough to overcome the strength of *campanilismo* (parochialism) in the Valdinievole.

The boldest attempt to break free from the designs of Lucca and the other Tuscan powers occurred in the 1280s. The scheme may have been prompted by the realization that, as the largest

20. ASL, *Capitoli*, 28, 4 March 1258.
21. ASF, *Diplomatico*, Pescia, 29 July 1202.

Tuscan cities consolidated their authority over their immediate hinterlands, it was only a matter of time before communities like Pescia would have to surrender even the limited autonomy they had heretofore enjoyed. Pescia, Borgo a Buggiano, Vellano, Fucecchio, and several other towns consequently banded together and put themselves under the protection of the emperor, Rudolf of Hapsburg. Rudolf freed them from the authority of Lucca in exchange for an oath of fealty that was to be a prelude to his recovery of all his imperial rights in Italy. The members of the league gladly consented to the oath since they perceived that Rudolf was too weak actually to impose effective authority over them. The problem was that if this was the case, he was also too weak to offer effective protection. The Guelph forces in Tuscany were not about to tolerate a resurgence of imperial power and they acted quickly to nip the scheme in the bud. Lucca, with the help of Florence and Prato, attacked the Valdinievole in a savage punitive expedition designed to be a deterrent to similar schemes in the future. On August 20, 1281, Pescia was pillaged and burned. The devastation was so great that even the pope admonished Lucca never again to engage in such barbarous acts.[22] Florentine troops, who had participated in the expedition, were also shocked at the ferocity of Lucca's attack and tried to help the destitute survivors of the onslaught. Lucca interpreted these gestures as attempts by Florence to increase its influence in the Valdinievole; and perhaps this cynical interpretation was not completely unwarranted. Within a year after the destruction of Pescia, Florence was attempting to extend its influence in the Valdinievole by inserting clauses favoring its commercial expansion in the region at Lucca's expense in a military pact signed by Lucca, Siena, Pistoia, Prato, Volterra, and Florence.[23]

Despite these cautious probes in the Valdinievole on the part of Florence, the region remained under Lucca's hegemony even

22. Davidsohn, Storia di Firenze, 3:260–65. There is some disagreement among scholars about the extent of the damage but all agree that it was very serious. Cf. Giuseppe Ansaldi, Cenni biografici dei personaggi illustri della città di Pescia e dei suoi dintorni (Pescia, 1872), p. 32; and Gigi Salvagnini, Pescia, una città: proposta metodologica per la lettura di un centro antico (Florence, 1975), pp. 75–76.

23. "Lega fra Siena, Firenze, Lucca, Pistoia, Prato, Volterra," in Gino Arias, I trattati commerciali della repubblica fiorentina (Florence, 1901), pp. 409–10.

as the dominant city itself became subject to the successive rule of two Ghibelline tyrants, Uguccione della Faggiuola (1314–16) and Castruccio Castracane (1316–28). Indeed, the factional strife and the subsequent establishment of Ghibelline rule in Lucca was paralleled by similar developments in the Valdinievole. These were difficult years for Pescia, not only because of internal dissension and the forced exile of the leading Guelph families, but because of the protracted and bloody wars that took place in the Valdinievole, as the Guelph forces, led by Florence, struggled to defeat the Ghibelline lords of Lucca.[24] When Castruccio died on September 3, 1328, the Guelph forces were once more on the ascendant in Tuscany, and Florence did not lose much time before making its influence felt on the Valdinievole. Although at first the communities in the area, still ruled by Ghibelline factions, tried to preserve their newly acquired independence by forming a regional league for their common defense, the Florentine presence could not be ignored.[25] By June 1329, the Valdinievole towns entered into a peace treaty with Florence that provided economic and political arrangements very favorable to that city. The towns agreed to obey the Roman church and the pope, and to give to Florence and its allies free access in the Valdinievole. They also agreed to supply Florence with troops in return for stipulated payments. In addition, they pledged to respect the free flow of people and merchandise through the Valdinievole and to encourage freedom of trade and exchange. Enemies of Florence were not to be given hospitality in the area, and all exiles regardless of faction (but mostly Guelphs) were to be readmitted to their homes.[26]

24. BCatPe, *Memorie Galeotti*, pp. 65–68. Antonio Torrigiani, *Le castella della Valdinievole* (Florence, 1865), pp. 95–97.
25. The league, consisting of Pescia, Buggiano, Montecatini, Uzzano, Massa, Monsummano, Vellano, Sorico, Pietrabuona, S. Piero in Campo, Vivinaia, Collodi, and Veneri, met at the church of S. Francesco in Pescia, on 28 September 1328, and agreed to improve the fortifications of the Valdinievole. By 24 May 1329, however, the Ghibellines at Pistoia made peace with Florence, and the towns of the Valdinievole realized they could not hold out any longer. For details regarding the pact, see G. Calamari, "La lega dei comuni di Valdinievole e la loro pace con Firenze (1328–1329)," *Bullettino storico pistoiese*, 28 (1926), 9–10.
26. ASF, *Capitoli*, 32, 21 June 1329, fol. 12; reprinted in Calamari, *ibid.*, pp. 12–18.

The treaty was a combination of military aid and trade agreements showing recognition of the military instability that still obtained in Tuscany and awareness of the need for favorable economic conditions after the return of peace. Yet, despite the provisions for peaceful commercial exchange, peace eluded the Valdinievole. Within a month, Ghibelline forces led by Gherardino della Spinola successfully overran the Valdinievole and Lucca. Pescia once more returned under the hegemony of Lucca as that city came to be ruled by a score of petty tyrants and soldiers of fortune who nominally adhered to the Ghibelline cause.[27] In the meantime, Florentine attempts to recapture the area continued throughout the 1330s, and as now one army and now another laid waste to the countryside the prize they were fighting over became increasingly impoverished and ravaged by war. Eventually, Pietro and Marsilio de' Rossi gained control of Lucca and its subject areas in the Valdinievole and sold them to Mastino della Scala. The latter, in turn, had secretly promised to sell his purchase to Florence, but changed his mind as political ambition got the better of him. As a result, Florence sent an army into the Valdinievole, led by Pietro de' Rossi, who proceeded to encamp outside of Pescia and to loot and pillage what little was left. Mastino was thus persuaded to give up his possessions in the Valdinievole, and a peace agreement was concluded on January 20, 1339.[28]

Shortly thereafter, on February 17, 1339, Pescia formally submitted to Florence.[29] Ambassadors previously elected by the community at a general meeting granted Florence complete dominion and jurisdiction over the town, its court, district, inhabitants, and descendants for all time.[30] The ambassadors also promised

27. For a brief and humorous account of the rapid changes that took place in Lucca's government, see Ferdinand Schevill, *Medieval and Renaissance Florence* (New York, 1963), 1:216–17.
28. Torrigiani, *Le castella della Val di Nievole*, pp. 154–55.
29. ASF, *Capitoli*, 2, fols. 1–2, 17 February 1339.
30. "Ser Riccardus Bigori de Barelia, Ser Galvanus ser Orlandi, Ser Landus Lippi . . . , sindici et procuratores et nuptii speciales terre, communis, universitatis et hominum de Piscia eiusque curia et districtu . . . omni modo, jure et via quibus melius potuerint, ex certa scientia et non per errorem et ipsorum spontanea voluntate subicierunt, supposuerunt et submiserunt communi et populo Florentie . . . dictam terram, commune, universitatem dicte terre de Piscia eiusque curiam, districtum et per-

that Pescia would obey Florentine officials. The penalty for non-compliance was a fine of 10,000 silver marks levied on the town. Despite the stipulation that this submission was made by the ambassadors of their own free will, the relation that was established between Pescia and Florence was not a contractual one between equals, but one of master and subject. Pescia granted Florence full sovereignty and promised obedience. Florence neither gave nor promised anything in return. Whatever its previous juridical status, Pescia, having given up its sovereignty, was no longer the equal of Florence. Its status within the Florentine state would henceforth be defined by the dominant city.

Yet the fiction of a contractual arrangement, implying as it does the relation between equals, persisted in the set of privileges that Florence granted Pescia and its neighbors, Buggiano and Uzzano, in April 1339. Ostensibly, the reason for issuing the privileges was that the three communities deserved special treatment because they had submitted freely and of their own volition.[31] As the term "privileges" implies, however, the relation between the two sides was inherently unequal, and this was symbolically depicted each year when, according to the terms of the privileges, each town was to pay homage to the dominant city by lighting a wax candle offering to St. John, the Florentine patron saint, in the Florentine cathedral.[32]

To understand the rhetoric of the treaty of submission and the privileges of 1339, it is essential to remember the strength of republican ideas in Florentine political life. The language of free-

---

tinentias et homines et personas omnis dicte terre, . . . eiusque curie et districtus et pertinentiarum, ipsorumque hominum et personarum filios, posteros et descendentes in perpetuum." *Ibid.*

31. ". . . considerantes et attendentes quod Communia Piscie et Bugiani, Collis, Stignani et Burgi curie et districtus Bugiani, et Uzani provincie Vallis Nebule . . . libere et absolute se per eorum legictimum sindicum submiserunt dominio et jurisdictioni communis Florentie, propter que magnas prerogativas merentur et privilegiis et immunitatibus sunt digni . . ." (*ibid.*).

32. ". . . quod in signum jurisdictionis et dominii communis Florentie predicta tria communia et quodlibet eorum teneantur et debeant, singulis annis in festa beati Johannis Batiste de mense junii, offerre seu offerri facere in civitate Florentie, apud dictam ecclesiam beati Johannis civitatis Florentie, unum honorabile cerum pro quolibit dictorum trium communium . . ." (*ibid.*).

dom was aimed not so much at deceiving its new subjects, as at reconciling the Florentine image of itself as the defender of Tuscan *libertas* with Florentine territorial policy. For Florence, *libertas* meant both republican self-government and political independence from foreign rule. The two, moreover, were inextricably related. Florentine expansion into Tuscany therefore presented difficult problems of identity, problems which could be solved only if Florentine territorial policy could be justified in terms of the defense of republican liberty in Tuscany. And this is in effect what Florentines argued. The areas that came to be incorporated into the Florentine dominion were said to have submitted of their own volition in order to escape the rule of tyranny and exist under conditions of freedom within the Florentine dominion.[33]

To what extent did this ingenious, if self-serving, theory apply to the realities of Pescia's incorporation into the Florentine state? That Pescia and the Valdinievole submitted freely to Florentine rule is at best a moot point. Under existing political and military circumstances they were hardly in a position to do otherwise. But the other conditions that accompanied the establishment of Florentine rule were less obviously deceptive. It cannot be denied that for several decades Pescia had been ruled by a series of petty tyrants. It was therefore quite natural for Florentines to believe they were freeing their neighbors from the yoke of tyranny. Moreover, since the tyrants were for the most part Ghibellines from northern Italy, the notion of helping Pescia and the other communes of the Valdinievole escape tyrannical rule could be applied with even greater facility. For by mid-fourteenth century, Florence, with some justification, had come to identify the establishment of despotism with the geographic region north of the Apennines and with the Ghibelline cause.[34]

33. For the meaning of *libertas* within the Florentine republican tradition and the attempt to reconcile Florentine foreign policy with a republican ethos, see the excellent essay by Nicolai Rubinstein, "Florence and the Despots: Some Aspects of Florentine Diplomacy in the Fourteenth Century," *Transactions of the Royal Historical Society* (1952), pp. 21–46; also D. M. Bueno de Mesquita, "The Place of Despotism in Italian Politics," in *Europe in the Later Middle Ages*, ed. John R. Hale (London, 1965), pp. 301–31; Quentin Skinner, *The Foundations of Modern Political Thought* (Cambridge, 1978), 1:3–84.
34. Rubinstein, "Florence and the Despots," pp. 31–32.

As for the freedom enjoyed under Florentine rule, quite apart from the Florentine notion that Florentine rule was inherently the rule of *libertas*,[35] the communes of the Valdinievole were in fact left with a considerable degree of autonomy.[36] In the first place, the institution of the "commune" was not abolished. Pescia and its neighbors retained their corporate identity. Second, and most important, they retained many of their self-governing functions. They were allowed to make their own laws with the proviso that the lawbooks be approved by Florence once a year.[37] They were allowed to elect their own communal officials (priors, councilmen, and others) so that the only officials appointed by Florence were the vicar of the Valdinievole and the *podestà* under him.[38] The latter had full jurisdiction over civil and criminal cases but his powers were limited by both Florence and the local communes. Florence reserved for itself jurisdiction over cases involving the death penalty or mutilation. The government of Pescia shared with the *podestà* the powers of ban and executive, and

35. Tuscan liberty, according to Florentine writers, was inherited from Roman liberty, and was shared by all the communes of Tuscany (*ibid.*, p. 3).
36. For a similar conclusion see Ronald Witt, "Coluccio Salutati and the Political Life of the Commune of Buggiano," *Rinascimento*, 17 (December 1966), 27–55; also Giorgio Chittolini, "La formazione dello stato regionale e le istituzioni del contado: ricerche sull'ordinamento territoriale del dominio fiorentino agli inizi del secolo XV," *Egemonia fiorentina ed autonomie locali nella Toscana nord-occidentale del primo Rinascimento: vita, arte, cultura,* 7th International Congress, Centro Italiano di Studi di Storia e d'Arte, Pistoia (Bologna, 1978), pp. 17–70.
37. "Item ad hoc ut dicte terre salubrius et melius gubernentur, teneantur et debeant rectores dictarum terrarum Piscie, Buggiani et Uzani, singulis annis, in principio mensis maij, transmictere ad dominos Priores artium et Vexilliferum justitie civitatis Florentine eorum statuta, ordinamenta et provvisiones et leges, que omnia possint per ipsos dominos Priores et offitium duodecim bonorum virorum . . . approbari, corrigi et emendari et alia addi et de novo fieri . . ." ASF, *Diplomatico*, Pescia, 14 April 1339. An examination of the books of statutes submitted by Pescia to Florence over the next two centuries, however, reveals that Florence did not usually exercise its prerogative to change the local laws and almost always accepted the statutes submitted. ASF, *Statuti dei Comuni Soggetti,* vols. 565–70.
38. ASF, *Diplomatico*, Pescia, 14 April 1339. The vicar administered the entire Valdinievole and Val d'Ariana. The *podestà*, whose office was abolished in 1424, was the administrative officer for the *podesteria* of Pescia, which consisted of the town of Pescia and its *contado*, Vellano, Castel Vecchio, Sorana, and Pietrabuona.

jurisdiction over civil cases.[39] The imposition and collection of
taxes were also the responsibility of the communal government,
subject only to the stipulation that taxes imposed by Florence
also be paid.[40] In addition, local officials were responsible for the
maintenance of public property and public roads and for the
routine administration of the commune. If on the one hand their
power was limited by the requirement that neither the priors nor
the city council of the subject communes could meet without the
consent of the *podestà,* on the other hand, the *podestà* could not
issue judicial decisions except in the presence of the local city
council.[41] Finally, local independence was encouraged by defining one of the functions of the local priors as that of supervising
the conduct of the *podestà,* the vicar, and the city council.[42] The
Florentine government encouraged the local communes to report
malfeasance in office on the part of Florentine officials and to appeal unpopular decisions made by the *podestà* or the vicar. For
this purpose, the Florentine government established the practice
of sending a syndic to hear such complaints before the termination of each *podestà's* and vicar's term of office.[43] That such complaints were heeded is evident from the fact that Pescia and its
neighbors felt free to complain and from the measures taken by
Florence to curb abuses.[44]

39. The *podestà* had "merum et mistum imperium" and could "cognoscere
et sententiare de omnibus questionibus in civilibus et criminalibus" ex-
cept for those cases reserved for Florence; BComPe, *Statuti, 1340,* Bk. 1,
R. 2–3. The powers of ban and executive were shared by the priors;
BComPe, *Statuti, 1340,* Bk. 1, R. 4. The city council of Pescia, called the
Consiglio Generale, had "omnem et totam baliam et auctoritatem et
potestatem quam habet totum comune et universitas comunis et terre
Piscie . . . ," BComPe, *Statuti, 1340,* Bk. 1, R. 5.
40. BComPe, *Statuti, 1340,* Bk. 1, R. 4; BComPe, *Statuti, 1339,* Bk. 1, R. 24.
According to the privileges of 1339, Pescia, Buggiano, and Uzzano were
to be subject to the Florentine *estimo,* but during the first years of
Florentine rule they were exempt from this tax because of the poverty
that the previous decades of war had brought to the area; ASF, *Diplomatico,* Pescia, 14 April 1339.
41. BComPe, *Statuti, 1339,* Bk. 2, R. 69; BComPe, *Statuti, 1340,* Bk. 1, R. 5.
42. *Ibid.,* Bk. 1, R. 4.
43. *Ibid.,* Bk. 2, R. 1.
44. As a result of numerous complaints on the part of the subject communes,
the Florentine government imposed heavy fines on Florentine officials
who abused their powers and extorted money from the inhabitants of the

This then was the basis of Pescia's status within the Florentine state—the loss of sovereignty to the dominant city, the retention of a corporate identity, and the continued exercise of a limited autonomy. Thus came to an end the effort of more than two centuries to retain political independence. After incorporation into the Florentine dominion there is no evidence that Pescia attempted to regain its independence. How this new status affected the people, economy, and political life of Pescia during the first two centuries of Florentine domination remains to be seen.

Valdinievole. For several examples, see C. Guasti and A. Gherardi, *I capitoli del comune di Firenze: inventario e regesto* (Florence, 1866–93), 2:32; 2:36; 2:39; ASF, *Diplomatico*, Pescia, 23 February 1385.

2

The People

One of the effects of Florentine territorial expansion, it has been argued, was to reduce the population of subject areas.[1] Allegedly, as the inhabitants of the *contado* and district sought to escape the exploitative rule of the dominant city, towns like Pescia were drained of large proportions of their populations, and especially of their most affluent members. Long-run changes in Pescia's population, as we will see, do not support this hypothesis. This is not to say that Florentine rule had no impact on Pescia's demography, but to suggest instead that it was one of the many factors that influenced and were in turn influenced by changes in the population. To understand these changes is to perceive the complexity of the relations between population and economic, social, and political structures—relations which are particularly significant in the context of a pre-industrial rural economy where the basic demographic unit, the family, was also the basic unit of economic and social activity. For this reason, a study of the people of Pescia—of the cycles of birth, marriage, and death they experienced—is an appropriate place to embark upon a study of the town's economic, social, and political life under Florentine rule.

1. Anthony Molho, *Florentine Public Finances in the Early Renaissance, 1400–1433* (Cambridge, Mass., 1971), pp. 23–28. David Herlihy also argues that Florentine policies were "a major factor in initiating the great depopulations of the fourteenth century" in the Florentine countryside. He adds, however, that "those same depopulations inevitably brought about improved social conditions for the peasant." D. Herlihy, "Santa Maria Impruneta: A Rural Commune in the Late Middle Ages," in *Florentine Studies: Politics and Society in Renaissance Florence,* ed. Nicolai Rubinstein (London, 1968), p. 276.

SIZE OF POPULATION

Fluctuations in the size of Pescia's population from the Middle Ages to the end of the Renaissance can be divided into three main periods: growth from the tenth to approximately the early fourteenth century; decline from that time until mid-fifteenth century; and renewed growth from mid-fifteenth century until 1630 (see Table 2–1).

The size of Pescia's medieval population is difficult to estimate but (as noted in Chapter 1) there are indications that from at least the tenth century population was growing. The appearance of hamlets such as Chiari and San Pietro di Ceule, on the outskirts of Pescia, the building of monasteries and *spedali* as well as of separate baptismal churches throughout the Valdinievole, the development of roads, and the intensification of agriculture, all indicate a growing community.[2] Historians have frequently relied on other types of indirect evidence such as lists of arms-bearing men, numbers of adult males taking oaths of fealty, or chronicle accounts of the size of field armies to derive estimates of population size. Unfortunately, even such crude population indicators are lacking for Pescia until 1331, when 733 adult and able-bodied men participated in a meeting to elect representatives who would swear the town's fealty to King John of Bohemia.[3] To extrapolate the total population from the list of participants, one must know what proportion of the population such a sample

2. See above, pp. 5–8.
3. Several histories of Pescia claim that the town's medieval population was 15,000—and inordinately large figure that is completely out of line with what is known about Tuscan populations. P. Anzilotti, *Storia della Val di Nievole*, p. 101; Giuseppe Ansaldi, *La Valdinievole illustrata*, pp. 125–26. The claim is based on a statement originally made in a no longer extant *Giornale della comunità* for the year 1432, in which the city council allegedly issued this figure in a report to Florence. The report asked for tax relief and contrasted the poverty and depopulation of Pescia at that time with the town's past splendor. The seventeenth-century historian Francesco Galeotti cited this incident and his source in his *Memorie di Pescia*. Unfortunately, other historians accepted the figure without question. There is no reason to doubt the veracity of Galeotti's account. He was a remarkably accurate and careful chronicler of Pescia's history. What is suspect is the veracity of the city council of 1432 in making its report. The circumstances surrounding the drafting of the report speak for themselves about the motive for a deliberate distortion. BCatPe, *Memorie Galeotti*, p. 161.

represents.[4] The document recording the event states that the men represented three-quarters of the male (presumably adult male) population of Pescia, and if it is assumed that the ratio of males age eighteen and older to the total population was 1 to 3.3, as it was one century later when we have the statistics for the 1427 catasto, the total population of Pescia in 1331 can be estimated at over 3,225 inhabitants.[5] This is probably close to the peak of the town's medieval population.

The decade that followed was one of war, devastation, famine, and epidemics. These reached a high point in 1339 and 1340 when grain scarcity, famine, and epidemic throughout Tuscany were aggravated at Pescia because of military activity.[6] By 1346, when another meeting was held to decide which families were faithful Guelphs, and hence eligible to hold political office, only 421 Pesciatines and their descendants were qualified. We can assume that efforts were made to restrict political power to a small

4. In addition to the *podestà* and six members of the city council, the participants, whose signatures are part of the document recording the election, are described as "ipsi idem Pesciatini infrascripti qui sunt maior et sanior pars et ultra quam tre partes de quatuor partibus omnium et singulorum hominum dicti Comunis. . . ." The document is transcribed in *Memorie Galeotti*, p. 347 ff. *Maior et sanior* should not be taken as a statistically exact reference, as the expression was used loosely in the Middle Ages to refer roughly to all the men that mattered in a community. In this instance it will be interpreted as all males age eighteen and over because that was the age at which a male was legally considered an adult; BComPe, *Statuti 1339*, Bk. 1, R. 51.

5. The estimate is based on the following calculation:

$$P_p = 733 \times 4/3 \times 3.3.$$

6. In 1334, Beltramme del Balzo, a mercenary hired by the Florentine government, entered the Valdinievole with 800 men and laid waste to the countryside of Pescia and Buggiano; Baldasseroni, *Istoria di Pescia*, pp. 180–85. Pescia's *contado* was again devastated in 1337; Giovanni Villani, *Cronica di Giovanni Villani* (Florence, 1823), 2:87; and was the scene of many skirmishes in 1338–39. Because of the damage caused by war Florence made special provisions for the area in the privileges of 1339: "Set considerantes quod predicta communia (Pescia, Buggiano, and Uzzano) et quodlibet eorum fuerunt jam diu in maxima guerra et pessimo statu, dederunt dictis tribus communibus . . . privilegium et immunitatem, quod hinc ad tre annos proxime venturos non teneantur nec cogi possint per commune Florentie . . . solvere aliquam gabellam impositam vel imponendam, excepta gabella portarum civitatis Florentie." The epidemic of 1340 is vividly described by Villani, *Cronica*, 11:114.

group, making accurate population estimates difficult, but probably the population had fallen to about 2000 inhabitants.[7] From the descriptions of Florentine officials, there is little doubt that the political upheavals of the 1330s and early 1340s, together with the famines and epidemics that accompanied them, contributed to a marked decline in population.

The demographic contraction continued for over the next half-century. The Great Plague of 1348–51, followed by repeated onslaughts of epidemics and grain scarcities in the last half of the fourteenth and first decades of the fifteenth century, caused severe population losses in all of Tuscany.[8] By 1407 the population decline occasioned by these crises as well as by emigration became a matter of concern to Pescia's city council.[9] Two decades later the town had no more than 1800 inhabitants.[10]

In the course of the fifteenth century the demographic tide turned. Plague and famine were still experienced at times, yet Pescia's population grew considerably.[11] The town's baptismal

7. The number of faithful Guelphs is cited in BCatPe, Memorie Galeotti, pp. 94, 146. Using the same ratio of adult males to total population as above we arrive at a population figure of 1,389. To this we must add the number of Ghibellines in the town, about which we have no accurate information.

8. It has been estimated that in the city of Florence and some other parts of the state as much as two-thirds of the population perished. See Herlihy and Klapisch, Les Toscans, pp. 165–81.

9. For the relation between Florentine fiscal policy and emigration see p. 215. Only a partial list of famine and epidemic years at Pescia can be derived from the sources. From 1349 to 1427 grain scarcities occurred in 1356, 1359, 1374, 1375, and 1386–89. Epidemics struck in 1363–64, 1374, 1383, 1399–1400, 1404, and 1423. Cecchi and Coturri, Pescia ed il suo territorio, p. 127; BCatPe, Memorie Galeotti, pp. 100, 145; ASPe, Del., 7, f. 24v; 9, f. 22v; 10, f. 77v; 11, f. 30v; ASF, Catasto, 258.

10. This figure is based on the 1427 catasto and was derived by adding the members of religious institutions to the secular individuals residing at Pescia. An additional 10 percent was added to this total to compensate for the estimated underreporting, which is discussed in Appendix 1. Accordingly, the population estimate is based on the following formula:

$$P_p = 1,573 + 52 + .10(1,573 + 52).$$

11. Again, it is impossible to compile a complete list of famine and epidemic years for the fifteenth century. The two most serious incidents of plague seem to have occurred in 1470 and 1496–97. Galeotti cites a letter in his possession, written by Jacopo Montalati on 12 November 1497 in which he laments the death of over 1000 people due to plague; BCatPe, Memorie

registers show an average of 181 baptisms annually in the 1490s[12] which, if we assume a crude birth rate of approximately 45 per 1000, conforms to a population of over 2900 inhabitants.[13] In 1552 the population reached approximately 4400, and forty years later 6,192. The average annual rate of growth came to 0.75 percent between 1427 and 1552, and increased to 0.90 percent in the second half of the sixteenth century. Growth continued into the first decades of the seventeenth century, although at a slightly reduced rate of 0.77 percent, and probably did not cease until halted abruptly by the Tuscan-wide epidemic of 1630–31, which struck Pescia later but with greater intensity than most other places in Italy. In a few months the town lost about half of its population, many to plague and some to flight. In 1632 there were only 4,399 people left.[14]

Galeotti, p. 176. The high mortality associated with the plague outbreak of 1497 was related to a Tuscan-wide grain shortage in 1496–97; *ibid.*, pp. 184–85.

12. This figure is based on the mean of three-year moving averages. For a description of the baptismal registers see Appendix 2.

13. The basis for this estimated birth rate is discussed in the section on births. It should be noted, however, that there are several problems in deriving population estimates from the average number of annual baptisms. The first has to do with establishing a crude birth rate, and the second with equating the number of annual baptisms with the number of actual births. The birth rate adopted here is consistent with probable birth rates for other years (see the section on births). The second problem is somewhat more difficult. Undoubtedly the number of births was greater than the number of baptisms, but there is no good way of estimating the extent of the discrepancy because most of our information comes from the upper classes of Tuscany. This has considerable bearing in a preindustrial context in which many infants died shortly after birth. At Pescia several family diaries indicate that infants were usually baptized within a day of birth. A possible clue to the extent of this pattern is that in the 1490s, the only decade for which we can determine the date of baptisms, these took place in a random fashion throughout the year. On the other hand, females were generally under-registered. At birth the male-female ratio should be 105 to 100, yet at Pescia in eight out of twelve years there were anywhere from 112 to 122 boys baptized for every 100 girls, a ratio that casts doubt on the reliability of the registers as an index for births. BComPe, I.B.19, *Libro di ricordanze di Ottavio del Capitano Bastiano Galeotti;* I.B.52, *Libro di ricordi di Giuliano di Lorenzo di Guiliano Ceci da Pescia.*

14. Population figures for 1552, 1622, and 1632 were derived from census data reporting a population of 4,002, 7,142 and 3,999 respectively; BNF,

Table 2-1. Estimated size of Pescia's population 1331–1632

Year	Number of people
1331	3,225
1346	2,000
1427	1,800
1490	2,911
1552	4,400
1591	6,192
1622	7,850
1632	4,399

Sources: see pages 23–26 and footnotes 3–14.

For these fluctuations in the size of Pescia's population to be viewed in perspective, they must be seen within a Tuscan, and to some extent within a European, context. The direction of Pescia's demographic trends conform to the larger European and Tuscan patterns, but the strength of the direction and some of its timing set Pescia apart from its wider setting. The decline that took place from the 1330s to mid-fifteenth century was in the range experienced elsewhere, that is, population losses amounted to about 40 percent. Pescia, however, appears to have lost close to this proportion of its population even before the pandemic of 1348–51. The onset of demographic decline was most closely related to local political and military upheavals of the 1330s and 1340s which caused grave socio-economic dislocations and undoubtedly weakened the population's defenses against the epidemic of 1340. Significantly, these population losses also occurred before the imposition by Florence of a strenuous program of fiscal

Magliabechi, II.I.120; II.I.240; E.B.15.2. Because the catasto of 1427 and population survey of 1590 under-report the actual population by at least 10 percent (see Appendix 1), I have assumed the same error in the other censuses. The only exception is the census of 1591, which is probably accurate because it represents a correction of the census taken a few months earlier. The towns of the Valdinievole, faced with a grain shortage, asked the Florentine government to help by sending extra grain to feed the population. In so doing, they reported a much larger population than was recorded in 1590. Understandably, the Medici administrators were skeptical and ordered another survey, hence the Pescia census of 1591 with its 6,206 inhabitants, compared to the 5,443 reported half a year earlier. Archivio Capponi, IV.2.24; population figures for 1632 are from BNF, EB.15.2.

Figure 2-1. Estimated population of Pescia, 1331–1632

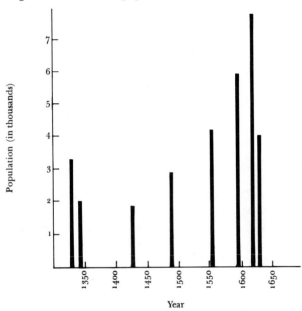

exactions. This is not to deny that Florentine taxes had an impact on the town's population but to suggest that they were neither the initial nor, as we will see, the principal cause of the depopulation of the early Renaissance.

Pescia also differed from the rest of Tuscany in its recovery. Whereas the Florentine state as a whole grew at an average annual rate of 0.53 percent between 1427 and 1552 and 0.15 percent between 1552 and 1622, Pescia grew at an average annual rate of 0.75 and 0.88 percent respectively. By modern standards these growth rates may not seem very substantial, but in a preindustrial society whose long-run growth rates generally remained well below 1 percent, Pescia's growth was impressive. Obviously, subject areas could grow under Florentine domination, and could do so at a faster rate than the city of Florence itself.[15]

15. The city of Florence itself grew at an average rate of 0.37 between 1427 and 1552 and 0.27 between 1552 and 1622. Tuscan and Florentine growth data are from Herlihy and Klapisch, *Les Toscans*, pp. 181–88; and Lorenzo del Panta, *Una traccia di storia demografica della Toscana nei secoli XVI–XVIII* (Florence, 1974), pp. 53–62.

How Pescia fit into the Tuscan demographic picture of the Renaissance can be seen best by looking at maps of the area (Figures 2–2 and 2–3).[16] From mid-fifteenth to mid-sixteenth century all parts of the Florentine state grew, albeit at slightly different rates, with the district, especially in its eastern half, growing somewhat faster than the old Florentine *contado*. At this time Pescia grew more rapidly than most other areas but its relative expansion was not nearly as remarkable as in the subsequent period. Starting in mid-sixteenth century, different parts of the Florentine state began to experience quite different rates of demographic growth. In response to economic changes, Tuscany was undergoing a massive shift in its population in favor of the northwestern half of the state. Located in this area, Pescia both benefited from and contributed to the general demographic expansion. Only Livorno, where the Medici grand dukes had sent convicts and other "undesirables," exceeded Pescia's expansion.

To understand why these changes took place we must remember that in any society a change in total population occurs through changes in birth, death, and migration. At Pescia, as elsewhere in Tuscany, the interplay of these demographic features is difficult to follow, although from the fifteenth century on there are enough data available to permit rough calculations of some vital rates.

A crude model of Pescia's demographic development under Florentine domination can be developed from these and from inferences about the demographic behavior of populations in general and Renaissance Tuscany in particular. The decline that took place from mid-fourteenth to mid-fifteenth century is the most difficult to explain because so little is known about births. Nonetheless, it does seem certain that a combination of rising rates of mortality and emigration were important determinants of the fall in population. The considerable growth that took place thereafter resulted from declining death rates and, more importantly, from sustained high birth rates and increased immigration. Before turning to an analysis of these factors, however, it will be necessary first to analyze some of Pescia's marriage patterns, both because of their importance for birth rates and because more than any other demographic feature they reveal the intricate links between demography and society.

16. The map is adapted from map 1 in L. Del Panta, *Una traccia,* unnumbered page.

Figure 2-2. Population growth in the Florentine State, 1427–1552
(vicarates)[a]

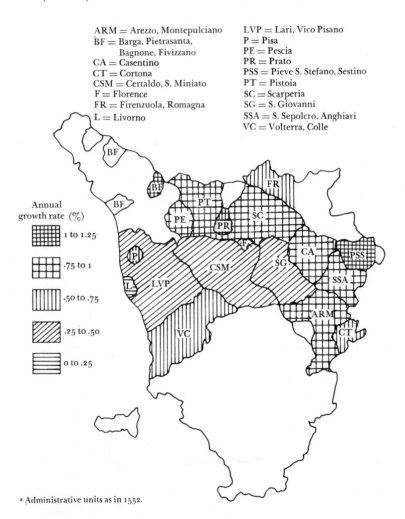

ARM = Arezzo, Montepulciano
BF = Barga, Pietrasanta,
     Bagnone, Fivizzano
CA = Casentino
CT = Cortona
CSM = Certaldo, S. Miniato
F = Florence
FR = Firenzuola, Romagna
L = Livorno

LVP = Lari, Vico Pisano
P = Pisa
PE = Pescia
PR = Prato
PSS = Pieve S. Stefano, Sestino
PT = Pistoia
SC = Scarperia
SG = S. Giovanni
SSA = S. Sepolcro, Anghiari
VC = Volterra, Colle

Annual
growth rate (%)

1 to 1.25

.75 to 1

.50 to .75

.25 to .50

0 to .25

[a] Administrative units as in 1552.

Figure 2-3. Population growth in the Florentine State, 1552–1622 (vicarates)

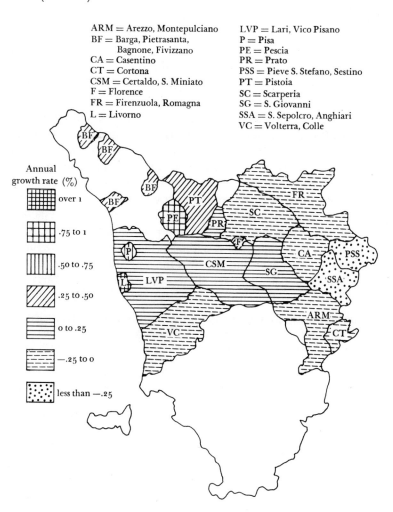

ARM = Arezzo, Montepulciano
BF = Barga, Pietrasanta,
    Bagnone, Fivizzano
CA = Casentino
CT = Cortona
CSM = Certaldo, S. Miniato
F = Florence
FR = Firenzuola, Romagna
L = Livorno

LVP = Lari, Vico Pisano
P = Pisa
PE = Pescia
PR = Prato
PSS = Pieve S. Stefano, Sestino
PT = Pistoia
SC = Scarperia
SG = S. Giovanni
SSA = S. Sepolcro, Anghiari
VC = Volterra, Colle

Annual
growth rate (%)

over 1

.75 to 1

.50 to .75

.25 to .50

0 to .25

—.25 to 0

less than —.25

MARRIAGE

A detailed discussion of marriage patterns at Pescia is possible only for the year 1427, but the record for one year suffices to suggest the complex relations between socio-economic and demographic developments and their effect on fertility.[17] This is not to say that the precise causal relations that obtained in 1427 remained unchanged throughout the Renaissance, but simply that the social and economic influences on the demographic patterns of the early Renaissance continued into the late fifteenth and sixteenth century.

In 1427 almost all adult females listed in the catasto were either married or widowed.[18] Assuming that the cross-section pattern is representative of longitudinal trends in the first quarter of the fifteenth century, virtually all females who were not members of religious institutions were married by the time they reached their late teens. Of twenty-three females of ages 16 to 19, only four were single and three of these were sixteen years old.[19] The concentration of female marriages in such a small age category suggests that female age at first marriage was not greatly influenced by wealth. Among the laity, marriage was a social ideal attained by virtually all females at a fairly young stage in the reproductive cycle.

The male age at marriage shows considerably more variation (see Table 2–2). Pesciatine males, like their Tuscan neighbors,

17. Unfortunately, in the catasto survey, Pescia's countryside (Castellare, Cerreto, Sorico, Collechio, Monte di Pescia, Monzone) was included but not listed separately from the town proper. Consequently, it is not possible to analyze differences in demographic patterns according to residence, as can be done for some other parts of Tuscany. In a commune of Pescia's limited size, however, this gap is probably less serious than for larger towns.

18. At Pescia, only some of the female members of religious institutions are listed in the catasto. These make up less than 2 percent of the female population. On the basis of similarly incomplete listings, the total female population in Tuscan religious institutions has been estimated at 2 to 3 percent; see Herlihy and Klapisch, Les Toscans, pp. 151–58.

19. Because of inexact reporting of ages in the catasto, it would be misleading to run correlations between age and marital status. In order to minimize the distortion, ages have been lumped in such a way as to distribute as evenly as possible the favored ages, namely, ages ending in 0 and 5 as well as even numbers. The age group selected in this instance is simply the late teens. There were no married females less than fifteen years of age.

married later and the age at marriage was spread over a longer time span. In 1427 only 19.5 percent of men of age 18 to 22 who were not members of religious institutions were married. The proportion increased over the next few years, but by the age of 28 to 32 almost one-third were still single.[20]

To a larger extent than among females, the age at marriage of men was influenced by wealth. The relation, however, was not strictly linear. Table 2-3 shows the marital status of males in three age and three wealth categories—the latter defined as roughly the lowest, the middle, and the highest third of the wealth distribution.[21] With all categories the chances of being married or widowed increased with age, but among the poor the likelihood of being or having been married rose less rapidly than among the wealthy. By the age of 28 to 32 barely more than half the males in the lowest wealth category were married.[22] The rich, on the other hand, after a late start in marriage, caught up by their late twenties and early thirties, when over 85 percent were married.

20. As well as using the above criteria for lumping age categories, in the case of males the age categories that were chosen were those used by Herlihy and Klapisch so as to make the results comparable to the entire region. See Herlihy and Klapisch, *Les Toscans*, p. 403.

In addition, a few remarks should be made regarding marital status categories. I have assumed that males up to age 32, living in their parents' household and having no wife or children listed, were single. I have dropped this assumption after age 32 because widowers or separated males would have been more common. Table 2-2, however, presents the data as in the catasto, with males 18 and over listed as unknown if no marital status was mentioned even if they did not appear to have a wife or children. This way the reader may judge the possibility of error himself, though probably most males under 33 who were listed as unknown were in fact single.

21. The categories of assessed wealth are not based on the total assessed wealth of the household, but rather on the assessed per capita wealth of each household (excluding servants and others who were household residents but not dependents). Most of the households with the greatest wealth were also households that consisted of large extended families with more than one conjugal unit. By adopting per capita wealth of households as the measure of wealth it was hoped to reduce the distorting effects of total assessed wealth. In these extended families the total assessed wealth is the wealth of more than one "houschold." For a different approach, see Herlihy and Klapisch, *Les Toscans*, pp. 476–79.

22. Because of the small size of the sample, a Chi Square statistic would be an inappropriate measure for the data in Table 2-3.

Table 2-2. Marital status of Pescia's population, 1427

	Males				Females			
Age	Percent married	Percent widowed	Percent single	Percent[a] unknown	Percent married	Percent widowed	Percent single	Percent unknown
0–17	0.0	0.0	100.0	0.0	4.3	0.0	95.7	0.0
18–22	19.5	0.0	4.5	76.0	93.8	0.0	4.1	2.0
23–27	58.0	0.0	2.0	40.0	96.2	0.0	1.9	1.9
28–32	66.6	8.3	0.0	25.0	94.9	0.0	2.6	2.5
33–37	83.3	2.4	0.0	14.2	93.0	7.0	0.0	0.0
38–42	92.6	2.4	0.0	5.0	90.6	9.3	0.0	0.0
43–47	80.0	0.0	0.0	20.0	92.8	7.1	0.0	0.0
48–52	97.9	0.0	0.0	2.1	78.7	21.2	0.0	0.0
53–57	55.1	0.0	0.0	44.9	53.8	46.1	0.0	0.0
over 57	82.8	7.9	0.0	9.3	42.5	52.5	0.0	5.0

a See footnote 20.

Source: ASF, Catasto, 258.

Table 2–3. Marital status of males distributed by age and by wealth

Per capita wealth of households[a]	Age 18–22		Age 23–27		Age 28–32	
	Married or widowed	Single	Married or widowed	Single	Married or widowed	Single
0–30	4 (23.5)[b]	13 (76.5)	7 (36.8)	12 (63.2)	10 (58.8)	7 (41.2)
31–80	5 (33.3)	10 (66.7)	14 (73.7)	5 (26.3)	11 (91.7)	1 (8.3)
over 80	0 (0.0)	1 (100)	7 (50.0)	7 (50.0)	6 (85.7)	1 (14.3)

[a] Expressed in florins. Households not established at Pescia have been omitted. In determining per capita assessed wealth of a household, individuals such as servants or apprentices, who are not recognized as dependents by the head of the household, were omitted.
[b] Numbers in parentheses are raw percentages for that particular age category.

Source: ASF, Catasto, 258.

With all three age categories, the greatest tendency to marry appears among the middle wealth group. By the time men of this group reached their mid-thirties, however, differences in marital status among males seem to have disappeared. As with females, marriage was attained by most of the laity, albeit at a more measured pace.

The desirability of marriage among males is reflected not only in its widespread incidence but also in the small number of widowers. Only 2.4 percent of males listed in the catasto were widowed, compared with 14.3 percent of females. One of the reasons for this is that widowers remarried soon after the death of their wives. Such freedom of action was more difficult for widows, whose deceased husbands often sought to control their actions from the grave with wills stipulating that their wives were to receive a stipend so long as they remained unmarried and continued to lead chaste lives.[23] Moreover, since widowers usually remarried women much younger than themselves they contributed further to the high incidence of widowhood. Among husbands of age 58 and over the mean age difference between spouses was 16 years.

The large age difference between spouses, however, was not confined to marriages where the husband was an old man. Indeed, it has been noted as one of the most striking characteristics of Tuscan marriage patterns in general.[24] At Pescia the age difference averaged 11.9 years, with considerable variations both by age and by wealth categories. Among the young, age differences were less pronounced than among the old, reaching only 8.12 years in couples where the husband was the age of 28 to 32. The

23. "Stando viduam et vitam viduilem et honestam servando"; ASF, *Notarile Moderno*, 4033, Vincenzo Piero Gialdini, will of Bartolomeo Benedetto Framinghi, fols. 156r–157v. Numerous other instances may be found in the notarial records.

24. Although age differences between husband and wife were large throughout Tuscany, the range was from a low of five years in the eastern part to about ten years in the western part where Pescia was located. In the city of Florence itself the difference was 11.9 years. See Herlihy and Klapisch, *Les Toscans*, pp. 532–33. There is some evidence that elsewhere in Europe large age differences may also have been common. One such place was the French village of Montaillou in the late Middle Ages; Emmanuel Le Roy Ladurie, *Montaillou: The Promised Land of Error* (New York, 1979), see pp. 190–91.

difference was also smaller among the middle class than among the poor, who tended to marry later. Not surprisingly, the largest age difference was among the rich, probably because the men in this group married later than others, and also because their wealth enabled them to attract younger wives if they remarried. Of men the age of 58 and over who lived in households with the greatest per capita wealth, the mean age difference between husband and wife was 19 years.

The explanation for these marriage patterns lies in the complex interplay of demographic and cultural variables, of which the most obvious is the sex composition of the town (see Appendix 3). In the age group 18 to 47, the ratio of males to females was 100 to 106. The smaller number of males their own age would lead women to seek marriage partners among men older (or younger) than themselves. But large age differences between husband and wife were a Tuscan-wide phenomenon, even though the sex ratio was generally favorable to males in all age categories, so that the effect of Pescia's sex composition was only to reinforce the pattern. The result was an average age difference higher than elsewhere in Tuscany with the exception of the city of Florence itself.

Of greater significance for understanding marriage patterns is the economic role of the family as well as broader cultural norms regarding inheritance and family life. Females were usually excluded from the system of inheritance, being provided instead with a dowry, and since they joined their husband's family upon marriage, their own families had strong motives to marry them off at a young age or place them in a convent.[25] The dowry of a

---

25. The amount of money required to place a girl in a convent was smaller than that needed for a dowry. In 1464, for example, the notary Piero di Giorgio paid the nuns of San Michele 60 florins for allowing his niece to enter the convent. That same year his daughter's dowry cost him 200 florins. BComPe, I.A.60, *Libro del Notaro Piero di Giorgio*, f. 51v. Justifying the smaller bequests to three of his daughters destined for the convent, Francesco Filippo Berrectari of Pescia tells us "perchè al seculo bisognia più dote che alla religione"; ASF, *Notarile Moderno*, 4035, Vincenzo Piero Gialdini, fols. 166v–170r. Either way, however, the share of the patrimony going to females was smaller than that reserved for males. Occasionally, wills stipulated that if male heirs were lacking, females should receive the bulk of the patrimony on condition that they pass it on to their future male offspring and that these in turn adopt the testa-

young woman was smaller than that of an older one and her family could avoid the costs of clothing and feeding her once she left home. For men, on the contrary, marriage was a burden to be delayed. Young men seldom had the income to support a family. Although some instances may be found of fathers' allotting part of their patrimony to a son who was living under the same roof, generally the *pater familias* kept control of the family's wealth until his death, especially in a rural society where wealth was tied to the land.[26] A young man wishing to marry was therefore dependent on the wishes and economic resources of his family.

tor's family name and coat of arms. The most notable example of this practice at Pescia involves the Cardini and Orlandi families. Giovanni Berto Cardini of Colle Valdelsa died childless. In a will of 1474 he left his property to his sister, Albiera, who had married Bartolommeo Michele Orlandi of Pescia with the stipulation that her two sons become the inheritors if they adopted the Cardini name. BComPe, I.A.3.3, *Elenco delle famiglie che godono degli onori.* Bonds of affection and solidarity among the women of a family sometimes led to small bequests being passed along the female branches. The will of Filippo Alessandro Lemmi de Buonagrazia, for example, includes a bequest of 100 scudi to his niece, Artemisia, which had been left to her by her paternal grandmother. ASF, *Notarile Moderno*, 4330, Antonio Forti, fols. 8r–12r. Similarly, in 1590 Beatrice di Bastiano Galeotti willed 500 scudi of her dowry to her brother's daughter. In the event that Beatrice died before her husband, he could use the money until his death, when it would revert to her niece. BComPe, I.B.19, *Libro di ricordanze di Ottavio del Capitano Bastiano Galeotti,* fols. 40r–41v. For a fuller discussion of dowries in law and in practice, see Stanley Chojnacki, "Dowries and Kinsmen in Early Renaissance Venice," *Journal of Interdisciplinary History,* 5 (Spring 1975), 571–600; also Herlihy and Klapisch, *Les Toscans,* pp. 532–33.

26. The economic control fathers could exercise over their sons even after the latter were grown and married is illustrated by the plight of Giuliano di Lorenzo Ceci, a notary and schoolteacher who married in May 1553 and brought his wife to live with him in the paternal home the following year. He wrote in his diary that by taking an extra job he was able to save a little money in 1556, enough to buy his wife some cloth, and this was the first clothing he bought her because his father collected all his salary as a schoolteacher and spent it. Four years later, the son finally summoned enough courage to keep his own salary, not without considerable explanations. He recorded the momentous event in his diary: "Ricordo come del mese di nov. 1560 cominiciai a resquotere i denari del salario mio della schola che per il tempo passato l'havevo sempre lassato risquotere a mio padre . . . dicendo a lui che havessi patienza perchè

Among Pescia's small professional class this often meant the
postponement of marriage until the completion of one's training.
In 1427 five out of fourteen males of age 18 to 22, for example,
were studying outside of Pescia or undergoing an apprenticeship.
All were single and would probably remain so until they could
establish their own careers.[27] The notion that one should not
marry until well established was best expressed by Ottavio di
Bastiano Galeotti, who on December 26, 1584, was told by a kins-
man that his recently widowed sister-in-law was secretly trying to
marry her eighteen-year-old son, Giuseppe, to a daughter of Antonio Buonvicini. "I answered him," he tells us in his *ricordanze,*
"that I was displeased that Francesca, Giuseppe's mother, made
such a resolution, which I attributed to her being out of her
senses because it was only seven days since the death of Messer
Martio [her husband] . . . and that I do not like it at all that
Giuseppe who is only 17 or 18 years old should marry because he
is too young and this will cause him to abandon his studies, but
that my opinion would be that he should study another four or
three years, which . . . will lead to Giuseppe's greater reputa-
tion, and that in the present course he will go to his downfall
and ruin. . . ."[28]

Marriage plans among men dependent on the land were also
limited because of the conflicting roles of the family in an agricultural setting—that of producers on the one hand and consumers on the other. In the early Renaissance the agricultural
economy of Pescia forced concern to focus on the role of consumers because they far outnumbered the producers in the working economic unit—the family farm.[29] Consequently, all men,
but poor ones in particular, tended to delay marriage until their
own fathers were too old and weak to work effectively or until

---

volevo risquoterli da me, e da me spenderli, e che stessi sicuro che non
li manderei a male, anzi li metterci e spenderci per la casa . . . ,"
BComPe, I.B.52, *Libro di ricordi di Giuliano Lorenzo Ceci da Pescia,* fols.
9r–v, 12r, 16v. Examples of a less frequent pattern, that of grants made
during the father's lifetime may be found occasionally among the Florentine patriciate. Francis W. Kent, *Household and Lineage in Renaissance
Florence* (Princeton, 1977), p. 71.
27. Scarcity of data on professions, unfortunately, does not allow an extended
     study of age at marriage by occupational categories in the catasto.
28. BComPe, I.B.19, *Ricordanze di Ottavio Bastiano Galeotti,* fols. 18r–19r.
29. See below, pp. 78–80.

Table 2–4. Relation between marital status and heading a household, 1427

Age	Total number of males	No. of married or widowed males	Married and widowed males who were also heads of households
18–22	46	9	4
23–27	50	28	17
28–32	36	27	14
TOTAL	132	64	35

Source: ASF, Catasto, 258.

one or both parents were dead. The presence of older married brothers also discouraged additional marriages. When family holdings were barely large enough to maintain one nuclear family there was little incentive to acquire additional mouths to feed.[30]

The death of the *pater familias,* however, did not bring immediate relief. In the early Renaissance, men left their estates to their male offspring as "universal heirs," who then tended to divide their inheritance equally among themselves and to become economically independent within a brief period of time.[31] This division of the family patrimony often resulted in individual shares too small to support a wife. Marriage would have to be delayed until a man could buy or lease additional land to support himself and his family. Whether living in his father's hearth or established in his own, marriage was more dream than reality in a young man's life (see Table 2–4).

The odds in favor of marriage did not improve in the sixteenth and early seventeenth century despite changes in social and economic conditions as well as marriage and inheritance patterns. Increasingly, Pesciatine families tried to maintain their property intact by imposing a *fideicommissum* upon their legacies. This arrangement was designed to prevent the alienation of property outside the family and did not necessarily limit the partibility of property among heirs although in practice more and more fami-

30. The effects of these choices on household structure can be seen below.
31. Exceptions among the Florentine patriciate have been discussed by Kent, *Household and Lineage.*

lies began to keep their property undivided. Those that did divide their property did so reluctantly and apologetically. In 1624, Giuliano di Pio Ceci, for example, records in his diary, "I came to this division by force because even though I initiated it, I did it because of the extravagant expenses incurred by my brother Andrea, and on my part there will never be a division of love, but he will always be the same brother. And may the Lord God . . . reunite us always in Paradise even if here below we will live our own ways."[32]

This inability to keep family members disciplined apparently became a less common problem in the course of the next two centuries. Living in Pescia toward the close of the eighteenth century, the noted historian Jean Simonde de Sismondi described the strength of family cohesion and the prevalence of non-partible inheritance:

> . . . at the father's death, one cannot help being astonished to see the eldest son become the head of the family, control the purse without rendering an account to his brothers, arrange their labor and dispose of its fruits without consulting them, feed and clothe them without ever giving them money; and all these brothers live always in perfect harmony, without complaint about a division that seems so bizarre and without envy of the luck of their eldest brother.[33]

The heightened sense of lineage evidenced by *fideicommissum* led some families to combine it with entail and primogeniture.[34] Wills would painstakingly and exhaustively determine the order of succession under all possible eventualities so that the oldest male heir descended from the male line should inherit the family's patrimony. Starting in the sixteenth century, the survival of the family dynasty became an obsession and testators went to great lengths to try to ensure it.[35]

32. BComPe, I.B.52, *Ricordi Ceci,* fols. 78r–v.
33. Jean Simonde de Sismondi, *Tableau de l'agriculture toscane* (Geneva, 1801), p. 100.
34. This has also been observed among the sixteenth-century patriciate of Florence: Richard Goldthwaite, *Private Wealth in Renaissance Florence* (Princeton, 1968), pp. 271–72.
35. One will went so far as to stipulate what should happen if all males descended from the male line had died and the only survivors were a widowed grand-daughter with a male child from her first marriage and

What was good for the dynastic family, however, was not always good for the young man with marriage in mind—unless he
happened to be oldest male heir. Sismondi tells us that in eighteenth-century Pescia only the oldest son married.[36] Indirect evidence suggests that this was already the pattern in the sixteenth
and seventeenth centuries as men delayed marriage even more
than they had previously in response both to changed inheritance
practices and to longer expectations of life.[37] As in the rest of the
state, the number of women entering convents rose considerably,
from about 2 percent of the female population in 1427 to about
6.8 percent in 1622.[38] The scarcity of men interested in marriage
had so driven up the size of dowries that few fathers could afford
to find husbands for their daughters.[39] Florentine officials summed
up the situation when they supported Pescia's move to establish
a convent at the Spedale di Santa Maria Nuova because "it will
benefit the poor fathers who have no means to marry their daughters nor place to put them as nuns because there are two other

---

another one from her second. At the time the will was drafted the testators' grand-daughters were not yet married. ASF, *Notarile Moderno* 4033,
Vincenzo Piero Gialdini, fols. 108r–116r.

36. Sismondi, *Tableau,* p. 101.

37. There are no precise data on age at marriage at Pescia in the sixteenth
and early seventeenth century. Scattered data for other parts of Tuscany
point in the direction of rising ages. Herlihy and Klapisch, *Les Toscans,*
pp. 206–9.

38. The latter figure was derived from the census of 1622 which lists 225
nuns at Pescia and a lay population of 6,810 people. BNF, *Magliabechi,*
II.I.240.

39. This commonly observed Tuscan phenomenon resulted in a spectacular
rise in Pesciatine dowries, from a few hundred scudi among the more
prominent families at the beginning of the sixteenth century to 3000 and
4000 florins at the end. In 1593, when Maria di Lorenzo Bonsi married
Baldassare Turini, he received a dowry of 4000 scudi. Maria was a Florentine girl but this was the price that a prominent and eligible Pesciatine
bachelor could command. Matteo Tommaso Ricci received 3000 scudi
when he married his wife Livia. Rafaello Francesco Testini's wife brought
a dowry of 1,570 scudi in 1605. These were astronomical sums compared
with those of the early Renaissance when the daughter of the richest man
in Florence married Giovanni Rucellai for a mere 1200 florins in 1431.
ASF, *Notarile Moderno,* 11398, Lorenzo Stefano Simone, fols. 43r–44r;
Notarile Moderno, 10649, Stefano Pierfrancesco Simi, fols. 186v–87v.
BComPe, *Turini,* unnumbered document dated 2 October, 1648.

monasteries at Pescia which cannot accommodate the number of young girls who are disposed to serve God in the Cloister."[40] Yet the construction of this convent in 1558, followed by the completion of another one in 1618, did not meet the rising need. In 1620 an official observed that of thirty or forty girls applying to Pescia's convents each year, only twelve to fifteen were accepted.[41] A growing number of Pescia's young adults remained unmarried either outside or within monastic walls.

The social pathology engendered by enforced celibacy among the young has already been explored by a number of scholars. Violence and juvenile delinquency were the all too frequent expressions of the sexual frustrations of a large segment of the male population.[42] At Pescia the fifteenth-century sources are too meager to throw much light on these behavior patterns but it should not be surprising that an officially licensed brothel was established at this time. When so many young men remained unmarried the social control of sexual activity became a subject of concern to the city government. Prostitution may have been regarded as a way of channeling potentially dangerous sexual drives.[43] The sixteenth-century record, however, attests to the limited success of this measure. In 1552, not obviously an atypical year for this small town of 4400 people, a young male servant knifed an eighteen-year-old girl to death; Benedetto Jacopo, a soapmaker, was sentenced to six-months' banishment at Pisa for attempted rape; and Bastiano d'Alberto Orlandi was condemned to four years in the galleys for sleeping with a married woman and then wounding her husband when he surprised them in bed. All told, twenty criminal cases involving assault with knives and swords were brought to the vicar's court in a period of twelve months. Many of these involved groups of young men who had been idling in the streets and who began to taunt one another with obscene language or practical jokes which quickly escalated into

40. ASF, *Pratica Segreta*, 4, ins. 73, September 1558.
41. ASF, *Miscellanea Medicea*, 322, ins. 7.
42. David Herlihy, "Some Social and Psychological Roots of Violence in the Tuscan Cities," in *Violence and Civil Disorder in Italian Cities, 1200–1500*, ed. Lauro Martines (Berkeley, 1972), pp. 129–54.
43. For a similar situation in southeastern France, see Jacques Rossiaud, "Prostitution, jeunesse et société dans les villes de Sud-Est au XVe siècle," *Annales E.S.C.*, 31 (1976), 289–325. The brothel served fiscal as well as social functions. See below, p. 166.

armed encounters.[44] One consequence of the family's strategy for survival was endemic violence.

HOUSEHOLD STRUCTURES

Marriage and inheritance patterns had a powerful impact on the structure of households and undoubtedly on the ties of affection and identity among family members.[45] By Tuscan standards, Pescia's households in the early Renaissance were small. According to the catasto they averaged 3.71 members compared with 4.42 in the Florentine state as a whole. Yet despite their small size, these households embraced a large variety of arrangements. The extended family was not dead, although a combination of late age at marriage, low expectation of life, and inheritance practices made it a less frequent institution than the nuclear family. In 1427, one-fourth of Pescia's households included extended and multiple families, most of them (two-thirds) involving vertical rather than horizontal extensions. At some point in their developmental cycle, most nuclear families were likely to be part of a larger kinship unit, especially because economic constraints encouraged men to stay within their family's hearth even after marriage. (Two-thirds of married men of age 18 to 32 lived in an extended or multiple family household.) Yet at the same time, these very constraints led to the postponement of marriage until such a late date that the extension of the family could only be small and short-lived. Households consisting of one married couple and their married offspring numbered only 35 (8 percent). About twice that many had married children living with a widowed parent.

The division of property after the father's death contributed

44. This count includes only the criminal cases involving Pesciatines since the court had a wider jurisdiction. Criminal Sentences Handed Out by Bastiano Chanigiani, Vicar of Pescia, ASF, *Camera Fiscale*, 2306.

45. The impact on household structures is reflected in the catasto, but the evidence must be approached with caution. The catasto was not a population census but rather a fiscal document describing patrimonies and the families living from them. Although in most cases this unit corresponds to co-resident family members, there are some exceptions, especially among single-person households. Often these are children or widows living at least partly from a separate patrimony than that of other co-residents in their household. Since they are listed separately they distort the number of households.

Table 2–5. Size distribution of households, 1427 and 1591

Persons per householda	Percent of households 1427[b]	Percent of households 1591[b]
1	17.5	3.6
2	23.8	10.7
3	14.0	16.0
4	13.0	16.1
5	10.0	14.9
6	8.4	13.3
7	5.2	9.4
8	2.9	6.6
9	2.7	3.4
10	1.0	1.1
over 10	1.5	3.2

[a] Includes servants and others residing in the household since the Census of 1591 does not distinguish family members from others.
[b] Includes only households established at Pescia whose members are listed.

Source: ASF, *Catasto,* 258; Archivio Capponi, IV.2.24.

Figure 2-4. Size distribution of households at Pescia, 1427 and 1591

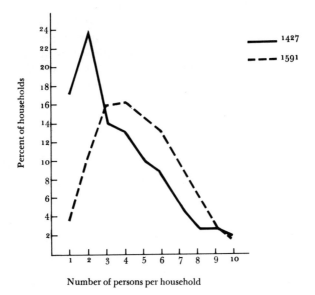

Number of persons per household

to the fragmentation of early Renaissance households. Pescia in 1427 had only 16 (3.8 percent) fraternal and 6 (1.4 percent) fraternal-joint households. Once the father died and the property was divided there was little incentive to maintain the cohesion of the household.

The size and structure of the household also varied with the age of the man heading it. Not surprisingly, as he married and had children a man's household grew, but, less expectedly, his household began to shrink after he reached his early fifties. This is an unusual pattern for a rural society in which so many young people remained in their father's house after marriage and contrasts markedly with other parts of rural Tuscany.[46]

The explanation for this pattern lies in the outmigration of young adults in search of better economic opportunities during the early decades of the fifteenth century.[47] The young found it easier to leave Pescia than the old. Hence, almost half of the men over age 62 at Pescia were living either alone or just with their wives. Some of them may have had offspring living in separate households in the town, but for many growing old at Pescia meant growing old without the comfort of close filial ties.

The structure of households changed as a function of new marriage and inheritance patterns in the sixteenth and seventeenth centuries. The average size of households increased from 3.71 to 5.1 by mid-sixteenth century and remained there for the next few decades as extended families became more common (see Table 2–5 and Figure 2–4). Reduced mortality rates in this period, as we will see, may also have contributed to larger households. A growing number of the aged probably lived to see their grandchildren grow to maturity.[48]

BIRTHS

Marriage and inheritance practices also had a strong impact on birth rates.[49] Demographers consider delayed age at first mar-

46. Herlihy and Klapisch, *Les Toscans*, pp. 470–79.
47. See below, pp. 51–53.
48. See below, pp. 69–70. A slightly larger number of servants may also have contributed to larger households. The data do not allow exact estimates but evidence for the city of Florence suggests that in the course of the fifteenth century households grew both because of more extended families and because of more servants. Herlihy and Klapisch, *Les Toscans*, p. 520.
49. Delayed marriage and high rates of celibacy were probably the most

riage among males a less effective limitation on fertility than it
is among females, but it is nonetheless a limiting factor because
it tends to shorten the life span of a marriage and also to reduce
the capacity for procreation during its duration.[50]

As we have seen, at Pescia in the early Renaissance, men generally delayed the age at first marriage until their mid-twenties
and early thirties and, furthermore, this was related to wealth.
The age at first marriage in turn affected the general fertility ratio of the population.[51] Table 2–6 shows that in three out of four
wealth categories the estimated fertility ratio increased with
wealth.[52] Some of this increase may be attributed to the practice

---

widely practiced and effective birth rate regulators. Doubtless, contraception was practiced, as it has been from time immemorial, but the absence
of data on birth intervals does not permit adequate analysis. The fulmi-
nations of Tuscan preachers against *coitus interruptus* are discussed by
John T. Noonan, Jr., *Contraception: A History of Its Treatment by the
Catholic Theologians and Canonists* (Cambridge, Mass., 1965), pp. 220–30.

50. A. Vermeulen, R. Rubens, and L. Verdonck, "Testosterone Secretion and
Metabolism in Male Senescence," and M. W. H. Bishop, "Aging and Re-
production in the Male," in Andrós Balázs *et al., Reproduction and Aging*
(New York, 1974), pp. 196–231; E. S. E. Hafez, "Reproductive Senescence,"
Aging and Reproductive Physiology (Ann Arbor, 1974), pp. 15–30.

51. The general fertility ratio is defined as the number of births per year per
1000 women of childbearing age (in this case age 15–44). The crude birth
rate is the number of total births per year per 1000 population. It should
be noted that while the catasto of 1427, the baptismal registers of Pescia,
and the population censuses provide a great deal of information about
births, none permits an exact calculation of crude birth rates or general
fertility ratios because they record, not the number of annual births, but
rather the survivors at the time of redaction. As a result, analysis must
be restricted to (1) lowerbound *estimates* of crude birth rates and general
fertility ratios, and (2) comparisons of longitudinal and cross-section
variations of these estimates—the assumption being that within any one
type of source the data are internally consistent.

52. Demographers make use of several different measures of fertility such as
the size of completed family, the child-woman ratio, age-specific birth
rates, and so on. Because of the limitations of the data only two possible
measures could be applied to the catasto, the general fertility ratio or the
child-woman ratio. I have chosen to use the former for purposes of cross-
section comparisons because infant mortality rates were less sensitive to
socio-economic variables than child mortality rates. Most infant mortality
was caused by medical problems for which no effective counter measures
were available until the late nineteenth century. See E. A. Wrigley,
Population and History (New York, 1969), p. 170. The categories of

Table 2–6. Estimated fertility ratio distributed by wealth, 1427

Assessed per capita wealth of household	Number of infants	Number of women	Fertility ratio (per 1000 women age 15–44)
<1 fl.	4	27	148
1–50	26	135	193
51–100	19	68	279
>100	6	28	214

Source: ASF, *Catasto*, 258.

of sending the children of wealthier women to wet nurses, but the decline in the estimated fertility ratio of the wealthiest group indicates that marriage patterns were also significant. The poor married later than the moderately wealthy. It is not surprising therefore that the general fertility ratio was lowest among the poor and that there is seemingly a positive relation between fertility, age at marriage, and wealth. Neither is it surprising that among the wealthiest category the general fertility ratio begins to decline, since males in this group delayed marriage more than the moderately wealthy and were also considerably older than their wives, hence presumably leaving behind a large proportion of widows of childbearing age. Yet such a group was conspicuously absent in 1427,[53] suggesting instead that the lower fertility ratio among the rich resulted from the relatively undistinguished sexual performance of men in this category. That the old among Pescia's rich chose young wives shows that they were not entirely oblivious to the carnal pleasures of matrimonial life, but the lower fertility of their wives indicates that these women were married to males whose reproductive capacities, not to say their attractiveness, must have been less than optimal.

Unfortunately, there are no records that allow us to assess the impact of marriage patterns on births in the sixteenth and seventeenth centuries. One would expect, however, that the rising age at marriage and the higher proportion of permanent celibates exerted further pressure toward lower fertility ratios.

---

assessed wealth are not based on the total assessed wealth of the household, but rather on the assessed per capita wealth.
53. Of nine widows of age 15 to 44, only two lived in households with more than 60 florins in per capita wealth.

Yet remarkably, despite the elaborate social adaptations that discouraged high fertility, crude birth rates at Pescia appear to be very high in the fifteenth and most of the sixteenth century. The catasto records 55 infants in a resident population of 1,590, from which we derive a crude birth rate of at least 35 and probably closer to 45 per 1000—a high rate even among preindustrial populations.[54] This high rate of births is particularly astonishing because the age structure of the population did not favor such high rates of reproduction. A combination of selective mortality and outmigration had decimated the ranks of those with the highest reproductive potential, i.e., adults age 15–44.[55] Indeed, the population was made up largely of the very young and the very old (Table 2–7 and Figure 2–5). On the other hand, Pescia had been hit by the plague in 1423, and as was often the case, infants and small children had been the most vulnerable (see Table 2–8).[56] The high birth rates of 1427 may reveal the population's effort to make up its losses.

54. The lower, more conservative estimate was derived by selecting only those persons actually residing at Pescia without making adjustments for under-registration of live infants or adults. The higher estimate, closer in range to crude birth rates experienced in Central America and parts of Southeast Asia in the 1960s, was derived by assuming an infant mortality rate of 250 per 1000. There is, however, considerable disagreement about the severity of infant mortality rates in preindustrial Europe. See T. H. Hollingsworth, "The Importance of the Quality of Data in Historical Demography," in Population and Social Change, D. V. Glass and R. Revelle, eds. (London, 1972), pp. 80–81; E. A. Wrigley, "Mortality in Preindustrial England," ibid., p. 268; Louis Henry, "The Population of France in the Eighteenth Century," in Population in History, D. V. Glass and D. E. C. Eversley, eds. (London, 1965), p. 447; Pierre Goubert, Beauvais et le Beauvaisis de 1600 à 1730 (Paris, 1960), 2:64–65.

55. This striking age structure has been found, but to a lesser extent, in all of Tuscany in the early fifteenth century. Cf. Herlihy and Klapisch, Les Toscans, pp. 370–80. Data from model-stable populations with any combination of crude birth and death rates ranging from 37 to 45 per 1000 lead us to expect that about 44 to 48 percent of the population will be in the 15–44 age category and that 3 to 6 percent will be over 65. In Pescia 35 percent of the population were age 15–44 and 17.9 percent were over 60. Cf. Ansley J. Coale and Paul Demeny, Regional Model Life Tables and Stable Populations (Princeton, 1966), passim.

56. The higher mortality rates among children in the plagues of the late fourteenth and early fifteenth century are analyzed by Herlihy and Klapisch, Les Toscans, pp. 370–80.

Table 2–7. Total population of Pescia distributed by age, 1427

Age	Percent of total population
0–14	33.7
15–29	19.2
30–44	15.8
45–59	13.4
60 and over	17.9

Source: ASF, *Catasto,* 258.

Figure 2-5. Age composition at Pescia, 1427

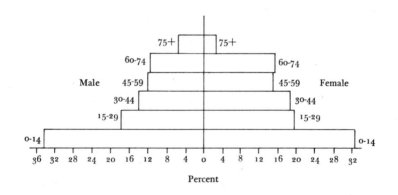

Percent

Table 2–8. Plague-related mortality among young children

Age in 1423	Age in 1427	Number of children
Unborn	1	61
Unborn	2	62
Unborn	3	62
0	4	31
1	5	19
2	6	23

Source: ASF, *Catasto,* 258.

In the sixteenth century the birth rate climbed even higher, reaching about 48 per 1000 population in the 1550s.[57] Most likely, as we will see, this rise was related to an influx of young adults who came to Pescia in search of economic opportunities. Their number was sufficient to counter the downward pressure exerted by the more restrictive marriage patterns of the time.

The first indication of a leveling off appears toward the close of the sixteenth century. Baptisms began to average 44 per 1000 population. By the 1620s a decline was clearly under way. With 287 baptisms in a population of 7,850, the birth rate had come down to around 37 per 1000 (see Appendix 2). As the economy of Pescia began to slow down so did the influx of immigrants. The probable consequence was a slightly older population, one which would not reproduce as quickly as that of the previous 150 years.

MIGRATION

It is obvious from the discussion above that migration has an important bearing on birth and fertility rates. Yet migration is the most difficult demographic variable to estimate in the medieval and early modern periods. When people married, were born, or died, they frequently left behind records of these important events in their lives. They went to church, were blessed by the priest, and the occasion was recorded in the town register or the notarial cartulary for all to see. But when they moved, they left no official record of their departure or arrival. Often the migrants sought to depart unnoticed—running from creditors and political enemies. When they arrived at their new homes they were eager to blend in, to find work, and to become members of the community. Small wonder that so little is known about these population movements.

Yet the fragmentary evidence suggests that migration if largely unnoticed was nonetheless important.[58] In the years immediately

57. Baptisms averaged 210.5 annually in a population of 4400; see Appendix 2.
58. A glimpse at the widespread geographic mobility of people can be gained from the catasto. Four percent of households filing tax declarations at Pescia were no longer residents of the community. Another 9 percent were residents who came from outside the Florentine state, and an additional 15 percent came from other parts of the Florentine district or contado, most of them from towns near Pescia such as Uzzano, Pietrabuona, or Buggiano.

following the Florentine takeover of Pescia there was considerable outmigration for political reasons. In 1339 some 47 Ghibellines were banished. Those allowed to remain were deprived of many of their legal rights. They were forbidden to marry Guelphs, and they could not carry arms. One can easily imagine the innumerable hardships they faced in their daily lives.[59] Many of them may have chosen to leave, especially during the 1340s when war between Florence and Pisa led to renewed sanctions against them because of Pesciatine fears of a fifth column. In 1342 heads of 54 Ghibelline families were banished from Pescia.[60] How many actually left and how many took their families with them is not known. Their departure, however, must have contributed significantly to the depopulation of Pescia in the pre-plague period.

As Pescia was integrated into the Florentine state and the political upheavals of the early years diminished, politics gave way to economics in promoting emigration. The movement of population away from Pescia became serious enough to be a major concern to the city's government. In order to remedy the situation the city council reversed its anti-Ghibelline stand by allowing the families of exiles to return.[61] It also asked Florence to reduce its fiscal exactions since many people allegedly left Pescia to escape the burden of taxes. These, the council claimed, were the principal cause for the town's depopulation and economic misery.[62] The demographic consequences of Florentine fiscal policies may have been exaggerated by a council bent on reducing taxes but there was more than a grain of truth in the claim. The proportion of old people at Pescia far surpassed that at Florence and even other parts of Tuscany. Whereas in the capital city those of age 60 and over made up 11.7 percent of the population, at Pescia they came to 18 percent. Young people, and young men especially, left in search of better economic

59. BComPe, Statuti 1339, Bk. 2, R. 37; BCatPe, Memorie Galeotti, pp. 91, 96, 99; Baldasseroni, Istoria di Pescia, p. 188; Torrigiani, Le castella della Valdinievole, p. 158.
60. BCatPe, Memorie Galeotti, p. 91.
61. Ibid., p. 146; ASF, Statuti dei Comuni Soggetti, 566, Bk. 4, R. 77, fol. 234r.
62. "Que res fuit et est principalis causa nostre totaliter depolationis et destructionis et calamitatis et miserie nostre"; ASPe, Del., 22, fol. 141r.

opportunities and undoubtedly Florence exercised the main attraction.[63]

Neither the burden of taxes nor the outflow of people from Pescia was alleviated until mid-fifteenth century, when the Florentine government granted tax exemptions to people settling at Pescia and large numbers of immigrants began to come in from Lombardy, Genoa, and parts of Tuscany. This change of circumstances, however, did not lead to widespread rejoicing. The city once more had grounds for complaint. The immigrants, according to a government report of the 1460s, were thieves and freeloaders who preyed on good and honest Pesciatines. To discourage them, the local government ordered that anyone living in Pescia for more than ten years be subject to the same taxes and guard duty as the natives. Furthermore, any debtors coming to Pescia from other parts of the Florentine state were to be constrained in every way possible to pay their old debts.[64]

Growing hostility and stricter tax laws did not stem the flow of people. In 1483 they were still described as an "enormous multitude of foreigners that everyday come to live in said land and territory [Pescia] with an enormous quantity of useless mouths and who every day damage Pesciatine property."[65] All foreigners seven years or older living in Pescia since 1470 were now to pay a tax of two lire every six months. Two years later all tax privileges were abolished.[66] Yet the arrival of immigrants continued. Among the 584 landowners at Pescia in 1535, 194 were foreigners (forestieri). Clearly, population losses were no longer

63. Interestingly, while the sex ratio for the total population at Pescia as in all of Tuscany favors men, partly because of the under-registration of women, in the age group 15–59, the ratio of Pesciatine men to women is 98 to 100. In Florence it is 125. For comparisons and an extended analysis of distortions in the sex ratio, see Herlihy and Klapisch, Les Toscans, ch. 12.

64. "Et veduto en decta terra et comune sono venuti ad habitare lombardi, genovesi, contadini di Pistoia, et di molti altri luoghi e di diversi conditioni i quali traghono fruto delle possessione di pesciatini taglando fructi, castagni, e boschi in grandissimo danno alla decta terra . . . e vengono ad habitare nella terra e comune di Pescia inganhando sotraendo e rubbando e buoni mercatanti. . . ." ASF, Statuti dei Comuni Soggetti, 565, fol. 120r–120v.

65. ASF, Diplomatico, Pescia, 11 August 1483.

66. Ibid., Pescia, 25 August 1485.

something to worry about. What Pescia had to offer was so desirable that people were willing to pay a fairly high price.

This large influx of people helps to explain the fast rate of population growth that occurred at Pescia compared with the rest of Tuscany. The immigrants contributed in several ways. Most obvious is the simple addition of the migrants themselves to the general population. But equally important are the ways in which they may have affected rates of birth and death. Like the people that left Pescia in the late fourteenth and early fifteenth century, those that now arrived were probably young adults. Their presence in the town undoubtedly altered the age structure of the population and helped boost the birth rate to the record numbers experienced in the late fifteenth and sixteenth century.

Because of their age, the migrants would also have influenced mortality rates. On the one hand, the proportion of mortality resulting from geriatric illnesses should have been reduced; on the other, infant related mortality should have increased. The net effect is not certain, but whatever the causes, it does appear that from the 1450s to the 1620s the death rate at Pescia, as in the rest of Europe, was lower than during the preceding period.

DEATH

Death is, of course, difficult to measure because of the paucity of burial registers until well into the seventeenth century. That it was never far from the living, however, even during the best of times need not be doubted. Take the family of Pio di Giuliano Ceci, a notary typical of the lower ranks of Pescia's patriciate in the golden years of the second half of the sixteenth century. Pio was born in 1564 to a father who did not see him pass adolescence. At age 24 he married Lucretia di Andrea Benincasa, with whom he had eleven children in twenty-five years of marriage. Five of these children died as infants, one at age three. Pio recorded all of these deaths stoically in his diary but he could not contain his grief at the death of his wife who would not have been much over forty. "I record," he writes, "how on the 3rd of September, 1614, Lucretia, my beloved wife passed to a better life, leaving me disconsolate with five children."[67] Pio himself

67. BComPe, I.B.52, *Ricordi Ceci*, fol. 69r.

died in 1622 at age 57. His son, Giuliano, continued the family diary. The litany of deaths was much longer in his generation.

Pio was fortunate. He was born at a time when death gave the living a relative respite. None of his family died in war, none were stricken by plague. Most of his children died shortly after birth and he and his wife both died after brief and apparently uneventful illnesses.

The last half of the Renaissance was, if not the best of times, at least a better time when it came to dying.[68] War-related casualties were certainly higher between 1340 and 1450, when almost one in three years either brought war to the Valdinievole or carried the men of Pescia to serve in other battlefields with the Florentine army.[69] In contrast, between 1453 and 1630 peace was interrupted only by the French invasion and the war for the reconquest of Pisa in the 1490s, by the fall of the Florentine Republic in the late 1520s, and by the conquest of Siena in the mid-1550s. In all there were only about fifteen years of war between 1453 and the early decades of the 1600s.

To the extent that war is a harbinger of famine and disease, its abatement also contributed to their decline. To be sure, there are many causes, some of them still unknown, for crop failures and outbreaks of epidemics,[70] but it is no coincidence that these occurred less frequently after mid-fifteenth century, and that when they did, more often than not, fighting was also taking place.[71]

68. An excellent discussion of sixteenth-century trends in size of population and mortality rates, as well as of problems of documentation, may be found in Karl F. Helleiner, "The Population of Europe from the Black Death to the Eve of the Vital Revolution," in *The Cambridge Economic History of Europe*, M. Postan and H. J. Habakkuk, eds., vol. 6 (Cambridge, 1967), pp. 1–95.

69. See below, pp. 132–36.

70. Improved sanitation in the sixteenth century may have contributed to a decline in mortality. In 1588 Pescia's sewers, for example, were repaired and covered for the first time. Anna Maria Gallerani and Benedetta Guidi, "Relazioni e rapporti all'Ufficio dei Capitani di Parte Guelfa," in Giorgio Spini, ed., *Architettura e politica da Cosimo I a Ferdinando I* (Florence, 1976), p. 321. In 1549 the city government also financed the building of a slaughterhouse "cosa necessaria, civile, et utile alteso che prima si macellavano le bestie nella strada pubblica con spurcitia et dishonore di quel publico." ASF, *Pratica Segreta*, 159, fol. 138r–139v.

71. Military activity coincided with grain shortages and plague epidemics in

Indeed, it was soldiers who brought to an end the period of
low mortalities enjoyed at Pescia since mid-fifteenth century.[72]
In 1629 German and French soldiers descended into Italy, bringing with them the plague epidemic that was already raging across
the Alps. By the end of summer 1630 the plague had killed
60,000 people in Milan and was spreading quickly to northern
and central Italy. Bologna, Modena, Lucca, Florence, all were
hit and experienced appalling losses. Only Pescia seemed to be
spared. Like most other Italian cities, Pescia tried to minimize
its exposure to the disease by prohibiting the movement of people and merchandise to and from infected areas.[73] The strategy
appeared to work. In May 1631, when the plague was already
on the wane, no one was yet afflicted in the town. On the 26th
of that month, however, Pescia's luck ran out. Vicar Giovanni
Carnesecchi wrote to the Florentine authorities: "As I have written in my other letters to your Illustrious Lordships many times,
this land has enjoyed perfect health without the least suspicion
of illness, but now it has come to pass that I can no longer say
so."[74] Three people had been struck by the plague. Within a
month so many were afflicted that the large Turini paper mill
which had been used as a pest-house could no longer contain
them.[75] By the time the plague epidemic ended, 2800 people,
one of every three Pesciatines had perished.[76] It was one of the
worst catastrophes in Tuscany. "The affliction," wrote Giuliano

---

1496–97, the 1520s and early 1530s, 1555–57, and 1628–31. Additional
grain shortages occurred in 1503–5, 1579, 1591, and 1619–20. Plague epidemics that were unrelated to war also struck in 1462 and 1478.

72. For an extended analysis of the plague epidemic of 1631 at Pescia, see
the forthcoming book on that subject by Carlo M. Cipolla.

73. ASPe, Sanità, 193, fols. 10r-v, 16v, 19v. For the progress of the plague
in Italy and public health measures widely adopted to meet the emergency, see Carlo M. Cipolla, Public Health and the Medical Profession
in the Renaissance (New York, 1976).

74. Letter from Giovanni Carnesecchi, 26 May 1631, ASF, Sanità: Negozi,
157, fol. 847.

75. ASPe, Sanità, 193, fols. 36r, 57r-v.

76. I am grateful to Carlo M. Cipolla for supplying this figure. Half of the
dead were town dwellers and half had lived in Pescia's contado. A more
detailed analysis of differential mortality rates will appear in C. Cipolla's
forthcoming book.

Ceci, "was sudden in this land and it did more harm in this brief period than in any other place where it had been."[77]

Giuliano tells us of the horrors of the plague and how they affected his family:

> In my house, the first to get sick with this malady in June was my brother Andrea who had a carbuncle in his kidneys, and through the mercy of God he recovered. Next, my wife Gabriella, who also recovered through the mercy of God, became sick with terrible fever and headaches and a swelling under the arm which spread to her back, and a carbuncle in her chin. Next, my eldest daughters Lucretia and Caterina got sick. Lucretia with fever and enormous headaches, but no swellings were found or anything else, except for worms, of which she vomited five large ones after ten days. And Caterina had four carbuncles and a swelling in her leg; and after suffering thirteen days the first, and eight the second, both died. May it please the Lord God to have gathered them to his most holy bosom. Lucretia was eight years old, going on nine and Caterina was seven going on eight. At this time they endured unspeakable sufferings and pain from this malady, and especially poor Caterina, on whom were found small spots and I saw that they were very black around the waist, and it was in effect the most pernicious malady which there was around. Afterwards the servant became ill with a carbuncle and swelling and she recovered. Finally, I succumbed with a swelling between the legs and the torso and I cut it out, and through the mercy of God and his most glorious Mother I have recovered, although I don't think that I am yet completely free from this malady this day 20 September 1631.[78]

Why was the plague so devastating at Pescia? How could such catastrophe occur in a town that until recently so many had sought as a land of promise and opportunity? Perhaps the answer lies precisely in this. Pescia had reached the limit of its growth potential. There were too many mouths to feed and too little to feed them with. Judging from the number of annual baptisms, population growth had already begun to peak in the 1620s. The grain scarcities that occurred at Pescia as in all of northern

77. "Il male in questa terra fù repentino, e fece più in questo poco tempo data la parità, che in altro luogho dove sia stato." BComPe, I.B.52, *Ricordi Ceci*, fol. 86r.

78. *Ibid.*, fols. 85r–86r.

Italy in 1628–29 compounded the problem. And the disruption to
the food supply caused by the plague itself was the final blow. In
April 1631 the city government asked the Florentine grain officials
for grain to aid "the poor of this commune who are dying of need
and there is no way of carrying them until the harvest on account
of the great penury and scarcity of foodstuffs."[79]

The difficulties created by the food shortage were aggravated
by the disruptions to all trade. As the towns around Pescia one
after another succumbed to the plague, trade with them was
prohibited in an effort to minimize the contagion. Trade with
Bologna had ended in June 1630, with Modena and Reggio in
August 1630, and with Lucca the following month. Pescia, which
had by this time developed a complex and specialized economy
dependent on interregional trade, was slowly being strangled. A
more backward place, one which was more self-sufficient, might
have fared better. When the plague finally came to Pescia, almost a year later, it found a town crowded with people who had
been deprived for too long to offer resistance. What happened
at Pescia was the fulfillment of Giovanni Carnesecchi's worst fears
when he wrote to his superiors in May 1631: ". . . what bad
state we would be in if the malady stuck its foot here because
this land is populated all out of proportion and the most part
are poor and most of these destitute. . . ."[80]

The plague epidemic of 1631 brought Pescia's Renaissance to a
close. The town would grow and rebuild again but would do so
with new people and on a different socioeconomic basis. Looking
back over those first three centuries under Florentine domination it is obvious that population decline was not an inevitable
consequence of Florentine rule and that an understanding of
Pescia's demographic history requires a look not only at its relations with the dominant city but also at broader demographic,
socioeconomic, and cultural patterns that affected people's choices
over those events in their lives which had a close bearing on
demographic outcomes. Decisions about marriage, place of resi-

79. ASPe., *Del.*, 75, fol. 83v.
80. ". . . in chè cattivo termine ci troviamo se il male ci fermasse il piede,
    poi che questa terra è populata fuor di modo et la maggior parte sono
    poveri, et il più di essi miserabili, che non hanno uno assegnamento al
    mondo"; ASF, *Sanità: Negozi*, 157, fol. 847.

dence, and so on were difficult decisions then as now, and they were dependent on economic status, educational values, inheritance practices, and other factors, among which people's status as subjects of the Florentine government was only one.

When Pescia was incorporated into the Florentine state it was a depopulated town suffering from the effects of war and selective migrations. These were compounded in the next century by plague epidemics that were European in scope and by the emigration of the most economically productive members of society, its young adults, in response to better economic opportunities elsewhere and to Florentine tax policies. Improved mortality rates and more favorable fiscal relations with Florence after mid-fifteenth century helped to end population losses. But these were regional phenomena and do not explain Pescia's spectacular demographic recovery compared to the situation of other towns in the Florentine state. Clearly, what made Pescia distinct was the high rate of immigration, a demographic variable which leads to more fundamental socioeconomic issues. If people came to Pescia and started families there, they must have expected better living conditions than they had experienced elsewhere; and if they continued to move to the town for one and a half centuries, the economy and society of Pescia must have been able to sustain them and accommodate their needs. The population upswing that took place must have had significant implications for the structure and growth of Pescia's economy. How this growing society and economy fit into that of Tuscany and into Florentine economic policy will be explored in the following pages.

3
The Economy

From the time of its integration into the Florentine state until the end of the Renaissance, the economy of Pescia underwent a slow but radical transformation.[1] This transformation involved first the development of a specialized agricultural economy that produced commercial crops for a Tuscan market, and second the introduction of industries that either complemented the new agricultural economy or catered to the demands of the Tuscan economy at large. A wide variety of forces brought about these changes, and among these forces were shifts in demand, in market prices, and in the political framework. Pescia's ability to accommodate itself successfully to its new position as a dependency of Florence brought with it new opportunities and a better life for most of its people. Whether such improvement was facilitated by its political role within the Florentine state or accomplished in spite of it will be one of the themes to be explored. But it remains incontrovertible that, at least at Pescia, Florentine domination was not incompatible with economic growth. The notion that Florentine imperialism inevitably brought with it economic decline in conquered areas must therefore be discarded.[2]

1. Most studies of pre-modern European economies, including this one, of necessity rely on tax records as their primary source. Since these sources have obvious limitations (see Appendix 1), they have been supplemented whenever possible with data from other sources, including notarial contracts, family diaries, account books, communal legislation, and so on.

2. Several scholars have argued that a combination of high taxes and

THE AGRICULTURAL ECONOMY
The Size of the Cultivated Area

As in most rural societies, land was Pescia's most important economic asset.[3] Our knowledge about the land comes primarily from the tax records, especially the catasto of 1427 and the Decima of 1535, which like all documents compiled for fiscal purposes contain a number of biases and omissions. Some lands escaped the eyes of tax officials, others were recorded but without reference to use or to size. More important, all of the tax records contain systematic gaps, such as the exclusion of lands owned by non-residents. These gaps, together with the procedures employed to compensate for them are outlined in Appendix 1. When used with care, however, these documents can provide a great deal of information about the agricultural economy, including reliable estimates of the amount of land under cultivation and the crops being raised.

Because of the depopulations that occurred in the last half of the fourteenth century, the supply of cultivated land at Pescia

---

mercantilist policies imposed by Florence after mid-fourteenth century over all or part of its subject territories led to their economic decline. See, for example, Becker, *Florence in Transition,* 1, pp. 3–4; Herlihy, "Santa Maria Impruneta," pp. 266–67. For Pescia in particular the thesis of economic exploitation has been stated most forcefully by Giuseppe Calamari. He states: "Non va inoltre trascurato che il comune rurale [Pescia] diventava uno strumento passivo della politica agraria della città dominante, il cui contegno verso la campagna fu essenzialmente egoistico. La città mirava unicamente ad assoggetarne e a indirizzarne le forze all'incremento della propria potenza. E il trattamento giuridico doveva essere conforme al trattamento economico"; Giuseppe Calamari, *Lo statuto di Pescia* (Florence, 1928), p. 40. Earlier views supporting theories of economic exploitation in Florentine territories during the Middle Ages were outlined by Gaetano Salvemini, *Magnati e popolani in Firenze dal 1280 al 1295* (Florence, 1899); and by Romulo Caggese, *Classi e comuni rurali nel medioevo italiano,* 2 vols. (Florence, 1907–8). An effective rebuttal was offered for the medieval period by Fiumi, "Sui rapporti economici fra città e contado." David Herlihy also emphasizes the economic advantages derived from integration into the Florentine state; see Herlihy, *Pistoia,* pp. 155–60; also Herlihy and Klapisch, *Les Toscans,* p. 300.

3. In 1427 the total taxable wealth declared in Pescia's catasto came to 84,853 florins, of which 69,225 were in land.

was fairly elastic throughout the Renaissance. Many tax declarations in the early fifteenth century testify to the abundance of land by including complaints of the difficulties encountered in trying to farm certain areas because of the shortage of labor.[4] This readily available supply of land enabled the inhabitants to extend the cultivated area as population grew after mid-fifteenth century. To what extent, however, did the growth of the arable keep pace with the rapid growth of population?

Although the amount of land under cultivation at any one time can only be approximated, the size of the cultivated area appears to have grown from 12,689 quartieri in 1427 to 22,860 quartieri with no significant change in the share held by ecclesiastical institutions. In short, while population doubled so almost did the amount of land under cultivation.

Crops

At the same time that the cultivated area increased in size, there occurred a profound transformation in land use. Before outlining this transformation, however, a few words need to be said about the system of multiple crop farming that characterized Tuscan agriculture.

Scholars have noted that Tuscan farmers until the twentieth century did not confine themselves to planting two or three crops in succession in any one parcel of land.[5] Rather, they simultaneously planted a variety of crops, from cereals to vineyards, olives, and so on. Often these crops were planted in the same fields in alternating rows. Some crops such as vines or mulberry trees could also be found along the edges of fields that were generally planted with cereals. These practices make it difficult to establish land usage with any exactitude at any one time. Com-

4. Bartolomeo di Simone Puccini, for example, listed some land that once was planted with vines and which by 1427 "è stata soda più anni che non si truova chi lla lavori." Another vineyard, listed by Leonardo Nardi, was not cultivated because "non se ne truova chi lla facia." ASF, *Catasto*, 258, fols. 388, 435. In all, 120 parcels of land out of 3,511 (3.4 percent) were described as "non lavorati."

5. For a discussion of this system of agriculture, appropriately called "agricoltura promiscua," see Carlo Pazzagli, *L'agricoltura toscana nella prima metà* del'800 (Florence, 1973), ch. 2.

menting on this problem with respect to viticulture, Carlo
Pazzagli, in a detailed study of early nineteenth-century Tuscan
agriculture states:

> We can perhaps know with a certain generic precision where
> vines were cultivated, but we cannot know the relation between
> density of cultivation and the extent of the cultivated area.
>
> This relationship varies notably, as is obvious, for example,
> in the case of intensive viticulture *a vigna* or a strictly pro-
> miscuous viticulture tied to the cultivation of other shrubs or
> grasses. In this respect we are in exactly the same situation in
> which De Baillous found himself over 150 years ago, when in a
> letter to the Prefecture of the Department of the Arno he ob-
> served: "The cultivation of vines in Tuscany is mixed with
> that of cereals and of olives and it is impossible to give figures
> of the extent of landed area devoted to this culture. . . ."[6]

The obstacles posed by multiple crop farming in determining
land usage are compounded, in the case of Pescia, because data
about ecclesiastical holdings exist only for the year 1427, and
even these are far from complete. Only 45 percent of parcels
listed by ecclesiastical institutions include information about
crops. This, of course, does not render the information meaning-
less, but simply enlarges the possibility of error. Because the
missing data appear to be distributed randomly, it was assumed
that the known crop distributions were not biased and reflected
those of all productive ecclesiastical holdings. The results, shown
in Table 3–1, are that crop distribution in ecclesiastical properties
in 1427 was basically similar to that in secular properties (see
Table 3–2).

Since comparable data for ecclesiastical properties cannot be
obtained for the sixteenth century, it was assumed that the
similarities in land use between ecclesiastical and secular holdings remained unaltered. In any case, the transformations in
secular holdings alone were so dramatic that neither the am-
biguity of crop categories stemming from multiple crop farming
nor the incomplete nature of the data can conceal them.

In the early fifteenth century cereals were the most important
crops grown at Pescia. Approximately half of the land declared

6. *Ibid.*, p. 219.

Table 3–1. Crop distribution in ecclesiastical properties, Pescia, 1427

Crop	Percentage of land
Cereals	48
Vineyards	16
Olives and vineyards	16
Woods	3
Olives	1
Other	16

Source: ASF, Catasto, 258.

Table 3–2. Crop distributions in non-ecclesiastical properties, 1427–1535 (in quartieri)

Crop	1427		1535	
Cereals	4,483	(47.1)[a]	2,577	(15.1)
Vineyards	1,617	(16.9)	1,563	(9.1)
Vineyards and olives	1,521	(15.9)	1,235	(7.2)
Woods	277	(2.9)	6,191	(36.3)
Meadows and uncultivated land	260	(2.7)	300	(1.7)
Olives	277	(2.3)	788	(4.6)
Vineyards and cereals	192	(2.0)	939	(5.5)
Vineyards and woods	132	(1.4)	—	
Orchards	41	(0.5)	19	(0.1)
Olives and woods	41	(0.5)	117	(0.6)
Mulberry trees	—		1,356	(7.9)
Mulberry trees and vines	—		327	(1.9)
Mulberry trees and olives	—		161	(0.9)
Mulberry trees and cereals	—		210	(1.2)
Other 2-crop combinations	92	(0.9)	336	(1.9)
Other 3-crop combinations	325	(3.4)	397	(2.3)
Unknown or missing	309	(3.2)	629	(3.7)
Total	9,517	(100)	17,145	(100)

[a] Numbers in parentheses are percentages of the total area declared.

Source: Catasto, 258; Decima, 1535, Pescia.

in the catasto was devoted to their cultivation.[7] Second to cereals were vineyards and olives. Planted either singly or in combination with each other they accounted for about one-third of the land. But of the two, vineyards were probably more extensive. When grown singly they accounted for 16.9 percent of the land, compared with 2.3 percent for olives. While olives and olive oil were becoming increasingly popular in Tuscany, demand did not really soar until the seventeenth and eighteenth centuries.[8]

Meadows were scarce in the early fifteenth century, barely over 3 percent of the land. This scarcity was reflected in the small quantity of cattle listed in the catasto. Only 70 declarations (16 percent) list any cattle, and none of these lists a sizable herd. Most of those who owned animals had one or two beasts of burden plus several calves, sheep, goats or pigs.[9] Still, only one-third of Pescia's households were in this category. Animals in general, even small ones, were considered a problem by the community because of their incursions into farmlands and the destruction of crops that they occasioned. Indeed, no subject is discussed as often in the communal statutes as the need to restrict the movement of animals. Time and again the government of Pescia limited the number of animals a family might own and imposed stiff penalties for the destruction of crops. Judging by their frequency, however, these measures were of no avail.[10] Not until sometime in the seventeenth or eighteenth century, with

7. Wheat was by far the most important cereal, though there is some mention of millet and rye among the crop yields in the catasto. The importance of wheat in comparison to other cereals or legumes in the diet of fifteenth-century Florentines has been observed by Giuliano Pinto, "Il personale, le balie e i salariati dell'ospedale di San Gallo di Firenze negli anni 1395–1406: Note per la storia del salariato nelle città medievali," *Ricerche storiche* (1974), pp. 146–47.

8. *Ibid.*, pp. 149–50.

9. The catasto may under-report the number of animals at Pescia because the cattle owned by people living outside the jurisdiction of Pescia and leased *in soccida* to Pesciatine residents was listed in the place of residence of their owners.

10. See, for example, ASPe, *Statuti 1339*, Bk. 2, R. 72; Bk. 5, R. 7, 13; a law of 1477 specifically prohibits anyone from putting any sheep or goats to pasture at Pescia "perchè il territorio Pesciatino e cultivato vignato domestico ed arborato ed senza pasture." ASF, *Statuti dei Comuni Soggetti,* 566, p. 321.

the development of a system of stall feeding, was a solution found for the lack of pasture.[11]

Also scarce in the fifteenth century were productive woods, which account for only 3 percent of lands declared in the catasto. Given the demographic decline of the period and the references to cultivated lands that were not being worked because of a shortage of labor, it is probable that the extent of forested land in 1427 was much larger than that recorded by the catasto but that such land escaped mention precisely because it was not used.

In the forests that were recorded one could find fruit trees, chestnuts, and a variety of other trees generally referred to as poplars.[12] Trees were of value as fuel, building material, food, and to a more limited extent as live supports for vines.[13] But surprisingly, the tree which in time became the most valuable agricultural commodity of Pescia—the mulberry—is almost completely absent from the catasto, as it is from most other records of the period.[14] It was not until after 1435, when Francesco Buonvicino introduced the white mulberry, that the tree became more widespread. Its eventual popularity, as we will see, was related to the greater suitability of this species to sericulture than the black mulberry and also to the growth of the silk-cloth

11. G. Targioni Tozzetti, *Relazioni d'alcuni viaggi fatti in diverse parti della Toscana,* 5 (Bologna, 1971; orig. ed. Florence, 1773), p. 228.

12. The word "pioppi" used for these trees does not refer to poplars per se as some Pescia scholars have thought, but to any number of trees such as maples, poplars, and others; Pazzagli, *L'agricoltura,* p. 227.

13. Chestnuts were especially valuable as food in the regions of higher altitude where they were grown; Herlihy, *Pistoia,* p. 37. The use of live trees, which became the most common method to support vines in the lowlands of Pescia and the Valdinievole in the eighteenth century was still limited in the fifteenth, as can be seen in the small amount of land combining vineyards and woods; Targioni Tozzetti, *Relazioni d'alcuni viaggi,* pp. 234–35.

14. Because mulberry trees were mentioned in the communal statutes of 1340 some scholars have claimed that they already were a great source of income as early as the thirteenth century; Cecchi and Coturri, *Pescia ed il suo territorio,* p. 70. Another argument, but one difficult to sustain in view of the dearth of land-use documents before mid-fourteenth century, is that mulberry tree cultivation was extensive before Pescia's incorporation into the Florentine state and declined thereafter; Pucinelli, "La Valdinievole," p. 29.

industry in Florence as throughout Italy in the fifteenth and sixteenth centuries.

The uses of land in the agricultural economy of Pescia by the sixteenth century contrast quite sharply with those revealed in the catasto. In the Decima of 1535 there are over 1300 quartieri (7.9 percent) of land planted with mulberry trees. An additional 4 percent of land was planted with mulberry trees in combination with other crops such as olives or vines, and undoubtedly some of the land casually described as "terra boscata" or "terra alberata," amounting to 36 percent of the land in the Decima, was also planted with them. Based on our knowledge of mid-sixteenth-century silk output at Pescia and estimates of the number of mulberry trees required to produce this amount, we can calculate that there were approximately 36,500 mulberry trees in Pesciatine territory in 1535.[15] By the end of the century the number had probably more than doubled.[16]

The area devoted to the cultivation of vineyards and olives singly or in combination with other crops also increased slightly, from approximately 4,680 quartieri to 5,753 quartieri.[17] But this

15. According to Galeotti, in 1546 Pescia produced 8,939 lbs. of silk, equivalent to 6,679 U.S. lbs. Since 1,278,320 lbs. of mulberry leaves were needed to produce this amount and an average young tree (probably only young trees were used at Pescia, see below, p. 80) yields 35 lbs. of leaves or fewer, it took about 36,523 mulberry trees to produce Pescia's silk. These figures are derived from eighteenth-century estimates of Pesciatine production made by Sismondi, who lived at Pescia; BComPe, *Fondo Sismondi*, 6:10 (see n. 65); and Giorgio Doria, *Uomini e terre di un borgo collinare dal 16 al 18 secolo* (Milan, 1968), p. 64.

16. The first water-powered silk throwing mill introduced in 1589 was allowed to process 25,000 lbs. of Pesciatine silk annually; ASF, *Pratica Segreta*, 17, fols. 77r–77v.

17. These figures were derived as follows:

1427: 1,617 q. vineyards + 1,521 q. vineyards and olives + ½ (192 q. vineyards and cereals) + ½ (132 q. vineyards and woods) + 227 q. olives + ½ (40 q. olives and woods) + 708 q. in ecclesiastical properties + 426 q. underestimation = 4,680 quartieri.

1535: 1,563 q. vineyards + 1,235 q. vineyards and olives + ½ (327 q. vineyards and mulberry) + 788 q. olives + ½ (117 q. olives and woods) + ½ (161 q. olives and mulberry) + ½ (939 q. vineyards and cereals) + 872 q. in ecclesiastical properties + 523 q. underestimation = 5,753 quartieri.

increase was not sufficient to offset their relative decline in importance. Whereas they made up over one-third of the cultivated area in 1427, they came to about one-fourth in 1535. Another significant change is the altered relation between vines and olives to the benefit of the latter. Olives were beginning to show an increase in popularity that did not abate until recent decades.

Despite the doubling of population, the area devoted to cereals declined from 6,043 quartieri to 4,304 quartieri, a one-third contraction.[18] In relative terms, the decline of cereal cultivation was even more pronounced, from about half of Pescia's farmlands to barely one-fifth in 1535. The reason for this is that some cereal lands were converted to other crops but most importantly, as population grew and new lands came under cultivation, they were planted with mulberry trees, vineyards, and olives.

The importance of this shift in output cannot be underestimated. It represents more than just a change in land use. It implies, rather, a basic transformation of Pescia's agricultural economy, involving not only changes in land use, but also changes in the relation of the factors of production throughout Pescia's market networks and in productivity.

In the early fifteenth century Pescia's agricultural economy did not produce a large variety of crops, but it did produce somewhat more than was needed for self-sufficiency, as can be readily seen from estimates of agricultural production and habits of consumption.[19] Turning first to the production side, we can

---

In estimating the totals, it was assumed that when vines or olive trees were planted together with other crops, they constituted half of the acreage. Two other assumptions were that in 1535, the crops planted in ecclesiastical properties were distributed similarly as in secular properties (as they appear to have been in 1427), and that both, in the catasto and Decima, the amount of land not reported to tax officials came to approximately 10 percent of the total (see Appendix 1 for a discussion of the sources).

18. These figures were derived as follows:

    1427: 4,483 q. cereals + ½ (192 q. vineyards and cereals) + 915 q. ecclesiastical properties + 549 q. underestimation = 6,043 quartieri.

    1535: 2,577 q. cereals + ½ (210 q. mulberry and cereals). + ½ (220 q. woods and cereals) + ½ (939 q. vineyards and cereals + 652 q. ecclesiastical properties + 391 underestimation = 4,304 quartieri.

19. The concept of self-sufficiency, as opposed to subsistence, does not make

derive the quantity of food staples produced from the catasto. Landowners who worked their own lands themselves or with the help of wage-labor were required to list the average annual yields of their lands during the three years preceding their declarations. The mean annual wheat yield per quartiere reported in these statements was 3.5 staia. Assuming that approximately 6,043 quartieri were planted with cereals and that the yields in ecclesiastical properties were roughly comparable with secular holdings, then Pescia produced 21,151 staia of wheat annually.

Similarly, it can be calculated that Pescia's vineyards, covering approximately 3,352 quartieri, produced 21,184 barrels of wine annually, and its olive orchards, covering 1,328 quartieri, produced 1,221 barrels of oil.[20] The amount of meat produced is more difficult to determine and no attempt will be made here although it was an obvious, if still infrequent, component of people's diets.[21]

Having derived average production figures for three important food staples in the years 1424–27, what may be said about consumption? It should be noted at the outset that for Tuscany as a whole, as for other Italian regions, a history of food consumption has yet to be written. We have some knowledge of consumption habits among the upper classes and aggregate figures for the consumption of food staples in a few large cities such as Florence

---

any claims regarding people's basic needs for survival. It simply compares the output of a population to its consumption habits. Despite its modest claims, however, precise measurement of self-sufficiency requires data on both production and consumption which is not readily available for preindustrial times and for Tuscany in particular. Our exploration of self-sufficiency at Pescia will perforce be based on scattered evidence which allows reasonable *estimates* until more systematic data is found.

20. The mean yields per quartiere in the catasto were 6.3 barrels of wine and 7.3 pounds of olive oil. The area covered by vines and olives was derived from ftn. 17.

21. Compared to other agricultural products, which were reported on the basis of three-year averages, the number of animals reported in the catasto were those living at the time the declarations were made and this number may have been subject to wide seasonal fluctuations. The weight and age of animals would also have been of relevance but about these we have no information.

and Prato. The diets of the lower classes and the rural population, however, remain to be examined.[22]

The evidence that does exist suggests that the bulk of people's diet, even after the massive depopulations of mid-fourteenth century, when presumably per capita meat consumption increased,[23] consisted of bread and wine. According to Villani and several other sources, in mid-fourteenth century the per capita grain consumption of Florentines reached one staio of wheat a month (18 kg.). This probably remained the average for the remainder of the Renaissance.[24]

How does this amount compare with cereal consumption at Pescia? The only observation available is for the year 1591, but it is consistent with the figures for Florence. On 10 March, Pescia's government petitioned the Florentine government for grain to stave off famine. The amount requested was based on the belief that per capita consumption between mid-March and harvest time would be $3\frac{1}{4}$ staia, or about one staio per month.[25] Assuming that this was the per capita amount also consumed in the early fifteenth century, Pescia would have needed to produce

22. Among studies concerned with diet, see C. Mazzi, "La mensa dei priori di Firenze nel secolo XIV," *Archivo storico italiano*, 20 (1897), 336–68; Enrico Fiumi, "Economia e vita privata dei fiorentini nelle rilevazione statistiche di Giovanni Villani," *Archivio storico italiano*, 91 (1953), 207–41; Pinto, "Il personale"; Charles M. de la Roncière, *Florence: Centre economique regional au XIVe siècle* (Aix-en-Provence, 1976), bk. 1, pt. 4, ch. 1.
23. Ruggiero Romano, "La storia economica dal secolo XIV al Settecento," in *Storia d'Italia*, vol. 2, ed. G. Einaudi (Turin, 1974), p. 1877; Fernand Braudel, *Capitalism and Material Life, 1400–1800* (New York, 1967), pp. 127–30.
24. Villani, *Cronica*, 11:94. During the famine of 1346, when the Florentine government distributed a slightly lower amount to the needy, its actions were met with vociferous complaints about the inadequacy of a dole amounting to three-fourths of a staio of wheat monthly; Fiumi, "Economia e vita privata," p. 217. In the fifteenth century the Florentine government imposed several taxes based on an estimated monthly per capita wheat consumption of one staio. The same estimate was reported by Varchi in 1529 (*ibid.*, p. 208). See also a similar estimate made by Lodovico Ghetti: "Inventiva d'una impositione di nuova gravezza," Appendix 11, in William Roscoe, *The Life of Lorenzo de' Medici Called the Magnificent*, 10th rev. ed. (London, 1872), pp. 427–31.
25. Archivio Capponi, IV.2.24.

21,600 staia of wheat annually for self-sufficiency. This is just about what it produced in 1427.[26]

The second most important staple in people's diet was wine. The large quantities consumed are difficult for modern men to imagine. Wine was not only a pleasant tasting beverage imbibed for its mind-altering effects. It was an important source of calories and of body heat. It was also used for medical and religious purposes. According to Villani, in the 1330s Florentines drank 550,000 barrels of wine annually.[27] This translates into 225 liters per person—a daily ration of $2/3$ liter. That wine consumption remained at these high levels during the next two centuries is illustrated by Alvise Cornaro's advice in the sixteenth century regarding the virtues of the *vita sobria*. He cites his own Spartan diet as an example worthy of imitation and tells us he drank 143 liters of wine a year.[28] With a per capita consumption of about 225 liters annually, the amount needed for self-sufficiency at Pescia would have been 405,000 liters, or 9,975 barrels annually.[29] Since the town produced over 20,000 barrels there was enough for its own needs as well as for export.

Another component of people's diet was oil. Although most of the fat consumed in the Renaissance was probably animal fat, olive oil was becoming increasingly popular as olive trees became more widespread throughout Italy. If we assume that annual per capita consumption was not more than 7.2 kg., Pescia would have been self-sufficient if it produced 449 barrels of olive oil per year.[30] Since output was about 1,220 barrels, Pescia had three times the oil it consumed.

---

26. One staio × 12 months × 1800 population = 21,600 staia.
27. Villani, *Cronica*, 11:94.
28. Fiumi, "Economia e vita privata," p. 233.
29. One barrel of wine contained 45.58 liters. Consumption is based on the following calculation:

$$\frac{1800 \text{ population} \times 225 \text{ liters}}{45.58 \text{ liters}} = 9{,}975 \text{ barrels}$$

30. According to Ghetti in mid-fifteenth century per capita oil consumption in the Florentine state was $1/4$ orcia (7.2 kg.); Ghetti, "Inventiva," pp. 427–31. On the spread of olive tree cultivation and consumption of oil, also see Federigo Melis, "Note sulle vicende storiche dell'olio d'oliva (secoli XIV–XVII)," in *Dell'olio e della sua cultura* (Florence, Cassa di

The surplus quantities of wine and oil constituted Pescia's principal exports in the early fifteenth century. Olive oil and wine from the Valdinievole were sold at Lucca as well as within the Florentine dominion.[31] Indeed, Pescia and the entire Valdinievole became famous for their wines, which were mixed with lower quality Tuscan wines to improve their quality. Pescia became the most important wine market between Pisa and Florence, exporting not only its own wines but also acting as a regional market center for the Valdinievole. Merchants such as Marco Datini would send buyers from Prato, Florence, Arezzo, and other Tuscan cities to purchase at Pescia the red wines of the Valdinievole and the white trebbiano produced at Montecatini. So sought after were they that they fetched twice the price of average Tuscan wines.[32]

To the extent, then, that Pescia's agricultural economy was linked to the rest of Tuscany in the early fifteenth century, it was primarily through the export of its own wine and oil and through its role as a marketing intermediary between the smaller towns of the Valdinievole and other parts of Tuscany. Over the next century, the variety of agricultural commodities linking Pescia with a wider regional economy grew, and just as important the commercial exchanges began to include products that linked Pescia to Florentine industry and hence indirectly to international markets.

As Pesciatines chose to produce other agricultural commodities, cereals, which had been so important in the early Renaissance, gradually lost their primacy. By 1546, a year of good harvests, Pescia seems to have produced barely enough to feed its own population only if we include the harvest of minor grains

Risparmio di Firenze, 1972), pp. 11–21. A barrel of oil contained 28.8 kg. Consumption is based on the following calculation:

$$\frac{1800 \text{ population} \times 7.2 \text{ kg.}}{28.86 \text{ kg.}} = 449 \text{ barrels}$$

31. See, for example, ASL, *Gabella Maggiore*, 41, 44, 45.
32. Federigo Melis, "Vini medievali delle colline lucchese e della Valdinievole che ritornano alla ribalta," *Vini d'Italia*, 9 (1967), 167–71. The price of average wines fluctuated between 1.7 and 2.3 lire, about half of the price of Valdinievole wines; Pinto, "Il personale," p. 149.

and chestnuts in the total.[33] The gap between production and consumption widened thereafter. In 1550 Florentine grain officials drew up a list of places from which they might regularly requisition a portion of the harvest in times of emergency, leaving out those places from which "little is harvested."[34] Pescia's name was among those left out. Half a century later the town was producing only enough grain to feed just over half of its population.[35]

The grain consumed at Pescia by the late sixteenth century was largely produced in other parts of Italy and Europe. This dependence on outside supplies of grain reflected a Tuscan-wide movement. Although parts of the Florentine state, Pescia among them, had been self-sufficient in cereals in the fifteenth century, the trend in agricultural production was in the direction of other, presumably more profitable crops. As early as the fourteenth century Florence had imported grain from other parts of Italy and the western Mediterranean. By the sixteenth century grain was occasionally coming from such distant places as Poland and Northern Europe. Like Tuscany in general, Pescia had become increasingly tied to international markets for the very staff of life.[36]

The import of cereals served to integrate the town more closely with a larger economic world, and the export of agricultural commodities served the same function. Pescia's wines continued to be sold in Tuscany, but they were no longer as important a component of the agricultural output as they had been in the fifteenth century. In part this was because the expansion of viticulture failed to keep up with the growth of Pescia's population. From 1427 to 1535 the amount of land planted with vines

33. With a population of approximately 4300 in 1546 Pescia needed 51,600 staia of wheat annually. It produced only 47,000. BCatPe, *Memorie Galeotti*, fols. 393–95.

34. ASF, *Medici del Principato*, 633, fol. 6r.

35. According to the grain officials, Pescia had 6,238 people and produced 30,764 staia of wheat, 2,419 staia of broad beans, 4,721 staia of chestnut flour, 4,407 staia of millet, and 330 staia of barley. This would feed about 60 percent of the population. The document is undated but the population cited and dates in nearby pages suggest that it belongs to the first decade of the seventeenth century. ASF, *Miscellanea Medicea*, 27, fol. 241.

36. Richard Goldthwaite, "I prezzi del grano a Firenze nei secoli XIV–XVI, *Quaderni storici*, 28 (1975), p. 25.

increased by about 10 percent, but during the same period the population doubled. Consequently, only about 6 percent of the 23,466 barrels of wine produced annually was exported.[37]

In contrast, the cultivation of olives became much more widespread, occupying approximately 2,040 quartieri. If we assume the same yield per quartiere and the same per capita consumption as in 1427, then Pescia produced 1,877 barrels of which it could export over 53 percent.[38] If, however, the near threefold increase in the amount of land planted with olives alone had been part of a gradual transition to a method of cultivation similar to that practiced at Lucca, in which olive trees were planted by themselves and very close to each other, then the amount available for export would have been much higher.[39] We do know that at Prato in the early seventeenth century most of the oil consumed came from Pescia.[40]

Yet, despite their importance, neither wine nor olive oil played as significant a role in Pescia's agriculture in the sixteenth and early seventeenth century as sericulture. The development of this activity meant the incorporation of Pescia into an international economic network, both for the importation of raw materials and for the export of the finished product. We have already seen that in mid-sixteenth century a large part of Pesciatine territory was covered with mulberry trees whose leaves provided food for the thirteen million cocoons that produced Pescia's raw silk at that time.[41] In order to assure themselves of a readily

37. The amount consumed at Pescia is based on the following calculation:

$$\frac{4000 \text{ population} \times 225 \text{ liters}}{40.6 \text{ liters}} = 22,167 \text{ barrels.}$$

38. The amount consumed at Pescia is based on the following calculation:

$$\frac{4000 \text{ population} \times 7.2 \text{ kg.}}{28.86 \text{ kg.}} = 998 \text{ barrels.}$$

39. The marked growth in the cultivation of olives by themselves, evident in the Decima, may be an indication of the adoption, already by the sixteenth century, of the Lucchese system common in the Valdinievole by the eighteenth century. On the cultivation of olives in different parts of Tuscany and the agricultural methods followed, see Pazzagli, *L'agricoltura*, pp. 253–66.

40. Carlo M. Cipolla, *Cristofano and the Plague* (Berkeley and Los Angeles, 1973), p. 34, n. 3.

41. It requires about 2000 cocoons to produce one pound of silk; William F. Leggett, *The Story of Silk* (New York, 1949), p. 9. Since the annual

available supply of cocoons, Italian silk producers reserved a portion of each year's silkworms for mating rather than for silk production. They also purchased silkworm eggs, directly or indirectly, from international merchants. To list the sources of such supplies is to conjure up remote and exotic places—Talich and Lahidjan by the Caspian Sea, Turkey, Asia Minor, and Chios—in addition to more familiar spots in southern Italy, especially Sicily.[42] In a series of purchases in March and April 1549, Bendinello di Jacopo Cheli of Pescia, for example, bought 70 ounces of silkworm eggs from Palermo. He subsequently sold most of them, keeping enough to produce only five pounds of raw silk.[43] Unfortunately, his account book does not reveal the provenance of his own suppliers. They may have been Sicilians or Tuscan merchants. Most likely there were Pisans who sold the eggs at the point of debarkation to other Tuscan middlemen such as Bendinello who were close to the centers of raw silk production.

Whatever the exact form of the linkages, it is certain that Pescia was closely tied to international markets for its supplies. The quantity of silkworm eggs purchased by Bendinello could be expected to produce 1000 pounds of raw silk, or over one-eighth of Pescia's output in the 1540s.[44] If, as seems likely, Bendinello was not the only egg buyer in town, a substantial share of Pescia's supply must have come from outside sources.

Bendinello's occupational and economic status also suggest that the type of purchase he made was not at all uncommon. He was not an international merchant, nor even a prominent businessman by local standards. He was merely a shoemaker who tried to make a little cash on the side. While at Pisa or Pistoia,

---

output at Pescia in 1546 was over 6600 pounds of silk, the estimated number of cocoons was derived as follows:

$$6600 \text{ lbs.} \times 2000 = 13,200,000.$$

42. F. Edler de Roover, "Lucchese Silks," *Ciba Review*, 80 (June 1950), 2908–9; *idem.*, "Andrea Banchi, Florentine Silk Manufacturer and Merchant in the Fifteenth Century," *Studies in Medieval and Renaissance History*, 3 (1966), 237–39.

43. ASF, *Libro di Commercio*, 305, fols. 52–55.

44. One ounce of eggs yields a potential average of 40,000 caterpillars, which in turn produce about 20 pounds of silk. Jacopo's purchase of 70 Pesciatine ounces should have produced 1000 pounds of raw silk. Leggett, *The Story of Silk*, pp. 9, 19.

buying Levantine cordovans or other leathers for his shoe business, he probably had the opportunity to buy the silkworm eggs
recorded in his account book in 1549.[45] The ease with which a
small provincial artisan could make such a purchase vividly
attests to the density of economic networks that linked Pescia to
the international economy by mid-sixteenth century.

At the other end of the production process, that is, on the
demand side, international markets were even more important.
The preparation of silk cloth in the Renaissance was a very complex process, requiring expensive raw materials, highly skilled
labor, good management abilities, and well-organized commercial
institutions to handle the import of raw materials and the export
of finished cloth to distant markets. For these reasons, the production of Italian silk cloth, at least through the seventeenth
century, took place primarily in large urban centers like Florence,
Lucca, or Venice, where trained labor, capital, and entrepreneurial skills were abundant.[46] From these production centers,
the silk cloth was shipped for sale to the Levant and to the rest
of Europe. The function of such small cities as Pescia in this
industrial process was to supply the raw materials for production. The profitability of sericulture at places like Pescia then
was intimately bound up with the international demand for silk
cloth and with the ability of neighboring cloth-producing centers
to fulfill this demand.

In the fourteenth and early fifteenth century, before Florence
became a prominent silk-cloth producer, the principal market
for Pesciatine silk was presumably Lucca, the oldest and largest
silk-cloth manufacturing city in Tuscany. As shown earlier, however, the amount of silk produced in the Valdinievole at this
early date must have been very small and would have constituted
just a fraction of Lucca's silk supply. Indeed, silk from the Valdinievole does not appear among the imports recorded in the few
surviving volumes of Lucca's *Gabella Maggiore*.[47]

45. Leathers from the Levant are mentioned throughout Bendinello's account book.
46. Jordan Goodman, "The Florentine Silk Industry in the Seventeenth Century," Ph.D. diss., University of London, 1977, pp. 63–68.
47. ASL, *Gabella Maggiore. Introito della Gabella.* Volumes for the following years were consulted: 1373–76, 1378, 1386–87, 1389, 1401, 1403–4,
1406–10, 1412, 1433.

The next largest market for Pescia silk was Florence, where in the course of the fifteenth century the manufacture of silk cloth gradually replaced that of woolen cloth as the leading industry. Florentine manufacturers like Andrea Banchi purchased Valdinievole silk directly from silk merchants of the region. In quality and price the silk compared favorably with that of other parts of Italy, but despite the spread of sericulture at Pescia and the surrounding area in the last half of the fifteenth century, silk was still not available in sufficiently large quantities to supply the growing Florentine industry.[48] In part, the reason may have been that some of Pescia's silk was sold elsewhere. In 1510, for example, the Florentine government complained that Pesciatines were selling their silk outside the Florentine state at the same price as at Florence and that this was not advantageous to Florentine industry.[49]

Both the quantity of silk sold in Florence, and the share of the silk supply used by Florentine industry, apparently grew in the course of the sixteenth and early seventeenth century. The silk-cloth firm of Giuliano di Piero Capponi alone bought 1,654 pounds of silk from Pescia and the Valdinievole between December 1566 and August of the following year.[50] Pandolfo and Vincenzo Galli, who bought large quantities of silk from the Valdinievole in the last years of the sixteenth century, purchased over 922 pounds of Pesciatine silk in October 1595.[51] The large quantities bought in single purchases like the above suggest that the total amount purchased by Florentine firms was quite substantial. In the last years of the sixteenth century Florence was buying 170,000 pounds of silk annually of which 21,200 (12.5 percent) came from Tuscany, and primarily from the Valdinievole. As sericulture spread to other parts of the state the Florentine silk industry came to depend more heavily on local silk supplies,

48. F. E. de Roover, "Andrea Banchi," p. 239. De Roover believes the scarcity resulted from the marketing of almost all Valdinievole silk at Lucca. The absence of Valdinievole silk in that city's gabelle records, however, undermines that theory and points the problem in the direction of the small size of the supply.

49. BCatPe, *Memorie Galeotti*, p. 203.

50. BNF, Archivio Capponi, 33. *Libro Debitori e Creditori di Giuliano di Piero Capponi*, fols. 68, 72, 105, 108.

51. ASF, Archivio Cerchi, Fondo Galli. *Libro Debitori e Creditori di Pandolfo e Vincenzo Galli*, fols. 46, 108, 145, 202, 229, 260.

which in 1610 accounted for one-fourth of all silk used and in 1650 for two-thirds.[52] What share came precisely from Pescia we do not know but judging from the number of basins used for reeling, which grew steadily from 94 in 1546 to 157 in 1619, the growth in Florentine demand for Tuscan silk outpaced the expansion in the supply.[53]

As Florence became an increasingly important outlet for Pescia's silks, the economies of the two cities must have become more closely integrated. Pescia's argicultural economy, as a result, became more specialized and commercially oriented. By the mid-sixteenth century only a limited share of its output was produced for local use. Hence through its agricultural products Pescia became part of the international world of commerce.

This transformation contributed to and was itself a product of fundamental changes in the relation of Pescia's labor force to the agricultural economy. The gradual replacement of cereals by vineyards, olives, and sericulture created new employment opportunities which increased the participation ratio of the population in the labor force.

Labor

In the early Renaissance, Pescia's agriculture, centering as it did on cereal cultivation, provided limited employment opportunities for women, children, and the aged. Although these sectors of the population probably performed some agricultural tasks such as winnowing or grape or olive harvesting, the major tasks associated with cereal cultivation were performed by strong, able-bodied males. Presumably women could operate the light Mediterranean plow, the *aratro*. That they did so infrequently may suggest that they were less effective with it than males. More important, however, the *aratro* was not commonly used at Pescia, or for that matter in most of Tuscany until well into the nineteenth century.[54] The cultivation of cereals depended on the

52. Goodman, "The Florentine Silk Industry," p. 87.
53. ASPe, *Archivio Vicariale*, 74, Francesco Leoni, vicar, unnumbered page; *Archivio Vicariale*, 279, Giulio Zati, vicar, fols. 1–23. The Florentine silk cloth industry expanded in the sixteenth century and remained level in the seventeenth. See Goodman, "The Florentine Silk Industry."
54. Tuscan agriculture revolved around the use of the *vanga*. See Pazzagli,

use of the spade (*vanga*)—a back-breaking, slow, and labor intensive method that only strong men could perform well for long
periods of time. As a consequence, there was a very low ceiling
on the amount of land that could be farmed and on total agricultural output. In the early nineteenth century, Biffi Tolomei
reported that a twenty-five-acre farm devoted primarily to the
cultivation of cereals required at least four or five men capable
of using a spade. This in turn meant a household of twelve to
fifteen people, most of whom were idle or underemployed during much of the agricultural cycle.[55]

No complete description of crop rotation or agricultural practices in Renaissance Pescia has survived. Our knowledge is limited to fragmentary evidence, coupled with eighteenth-century
descriptions of agricultural techniques that presumably differed
but slightly from those followed earlier. According to Sismondi,
in eighteenth-century Pescia the land was never fallow. The crops
succeeded one another in three- or four-year cycles, and the
farmer's only break from his labors came in the winter months.
In the early fall he sowed broad beans, harvested the grapes, and
pressed them to make wine. In October he turned over the earth
with his spade in order to plant wheat the following month.
Over several weeks, starting in mid-fall, he picked the olives, one
by one, using a technique unchanged since Biblical times. Before
the winter set in, bringing with it a welcome respite, he had to
gather wood from the forests to provide heat. In spring the pace
of work began to accelerate once more. No sooner did the vines
begin to bud than they had to be pruned and tied to supporting
stakes. If legumes were to be planted in a small patch near the
house, the earth had to be turned over with a spade or hoe. For
the rest of the spring and summer these had to be constantly
weeded. In May the farmers cultivated the vines and the olives
with a hoe. The former usually needed to be tied to their stakes
once more. The broad beans planted the previous fall were harvested, the earth turned over, and millet planted in their stead.
By this time it was the end of June and the wheat was ready for
harvesting. The farmers at Pescia mowed the grain with a sickle,

---

L'agricoltura, pp. 165–78. Also Carlo Poni, *Gli aratri e l'economia agraria
nel bolognese dal XVII al XIX secolo* (Bologna, 1963).

55. *Ibid.*, p. 177.

cutting the stalk at mid-point. After allowing it to dry out for several days, the grain was winnowed by flailing it with leather thongs. The stalks left in the fields were mowed with a scythe, stacked, and used as straw for the animals. In August the vines and olives were hoed once more. While the weather was still dry and warm, farmers also cleaned and dug the drainage ditches around their fields and shored up the terracing on the hillside.[56]

The picture that emerges from the agricultural work cycle is of a farming system that was dependent on labor-intensive techniques. But not all hands could be used for many of the time-consuming and important tasks. Preparing the soil before each new planting, scything the wheat, pruning the olive trees, digging ditches, and terracing were all done best by strong, healthy males. For each of them, however, there were six women, children, or old men in early Renaissance Pescia.[57]

The introduction of mulberry trees and silkworm cocoons was an ideal solution to the problem of how to make use of potentially productive labor. Silkworms require intensive care but only during a short period in the spring of each year. The labor of women, children, and old men could still be used to harvest grapes and help with farm chores from mid-summer to early spring. Sericulture could therefore be added to the agricultural economy of the region without drawing much labor away from the production of other commodities.

The *morus alba,* introduced at Pescia in 1435, is the hardiest of all varieties of mulberry trees. It can grow in almost any type of soil, without occupying much space, and its leaves contain more potential filament than any other variety of mulberry tree. Most important, in the Valdinievole it was not allowed to grow to its full height so that the leaves could be picked from the ground without the aid of a ladder. Targioni Tozzetti marveled at so curious a practice and could not account for it.[58] But there is little to be puzzled about. A small tree or bush can be readily picked by women or children, and this appears to have been the

56. The agricultural tasks at Pescia were culled from various sources, among them: ASF, *Statuti dei Comuni Soggetti,* 566, fols. 238v, 370r–372v; Ildebrando Imberciadori, *Campagna toscana nel '700* (Florence, 1953), pp. 247–49; Targioni Tozzetti, *Relazioni d'alcuni viaggi,* pp. 227–56.

57. See Ch. 2.

58. Targioni Tozzetti, *Relazioni d'alcuni viaggi,* p. 236.

normal practice at Pescia. In the surviving account books of the region the recipients of payments for mulberry leaves were mostly women.[59]

Similarly, it was mostly women, with the aid of children and the aged who raised the cocoons and later reeled the raw silk. Silkworm eggs were laid out in the sun to hatch in May or June when the mulberry trees began to bud, but if the sun was not hot enough, the women would place the eggs to hatch in their bosoms.[60] Sliced mulberry leaves, harvested daily, were then placed on a net spread over trays containing the worms. These required frequent feedings during their first month until ready to spin their cocoons.[61] At this point the required amount of care diminished but it resumed again after about two weeks when the spinning was near completion because if the silk moth were allowed to emerge from the cocoon the silk filaments would be damaged. As soon as the caterpillar finished spinning, the cocoon had to be dropped in boiling water and this brought the process to an end. Although it required large amounts of labor twenty-four hours a day, the raising of silkworms took up only a few weeks. Moreover, unlike the labor inputs for other agricultural tasks, no special skills or physical attributes were needed. The

59. See, for example, ASPe, 1188. *Repertorio dello Spedale di S. Maria Nuova*. ASPi, *Conventi soppressi*, 723. In the eighteenth cenutry, Sismondi used "women's work days" to compute the amount of labor required to gather leaves and care for the cocoons. BComPe, *Fondo Sismondi*, 6:10.

60. Robert Dallington remarked on this in his *Survey of the Great Dukes State of Tuscany* (London, 1605), p. 33.

61. Repeated harvesting of leaves is required because silkworms will eat only dry, freshly-picked leaves. The harvesting therefore takes place almost every day, after the dew has evaporated and sufficient quantities must be collected to provide a two-day supply in case of rain. In addition to harvesting leaves, raising caterpillars requires frequent cleaning of the trays and frequent feeding. During the first few days, the worms have a voracious appetite and climb through the nets to get to the leaves five or six times a day and two or three times at night. Toward the end of the first month, just prior to cocoon spinning the frequency of feeding increases to once every half hour. It has been estimated that if all the caterpillars hatched by one ounce of eggs survived to the cocoon-spinning stage, they would require 1,365 lbs. of mulberry leaves. A detailed description of sericulture may be found in Leggett, *The Story of Silk*. A similar but briefer account is provided in *Encyclopaedia Britannica*, 22 (Akron, Ohio, 1905), 64–67.

only requirement was constant vigilance. Practically all members of a household could be utilized, but those most frequently associated with this type of activity were women and children.[62]

The labor of women, assisted by children or otherwise unoccupied members of the household, was also responsible for processing cocoons into raw silk by reeling or spinning (see Figure 3–1).[63] Over one-third of the basins used for silk reeling in sixteenth-century Pescia were owned by women and most basins, regardless of ownership, were clearly worked by them.[64]

Sericulture thus constituted an important source of additional employment for the population. Just how important can be estimated from mid-sixteenth century production figures (see Table

62. Sismondi accurately assessed the importance of sericulture for the employment of women and children when he wrote, "La manufacture de soie . . . avait été pendant long-temps la soeur et l'émule de l'agriculture, à laquelle elle est intimement liée; elle l'avait excitée, elle l'avait secourue dans les temps de pénurie, et elle avait constamment fourni une occupation profitable aux femmes et aux filles des laboureurs, pendant les intervalles de désoeuvrement que laissent les travaux de la campagne . . . ," Sismondi, *Tableau*, p. 265. The expansion of employment opportunities for women and children in the late Renaissance and early modern periods was not confined to rural areas. See J. Brown and J. Goodman, "Women and Industry in Renaissance Florence," *Journal of Economic History*, 40 (1980), 73–80.

63. There were two methods for making raw silk from the killed cocoons. The first, used on perfectly formed cocoons, was reeling; the second, reserved for pierced, double, or otherwise damaged cocoons, was spinning. The purpose of reeling is to bring together the filaments of four or five cocoons in order to make a single strong thread. In order to do this the cocoons were immersed in hot water to soften the gum that held the filament together. The cocoons were stirred in the water with a small brush of twigs until the outer end of the filament became entangled in the twigs. After securing the filaments the cocoons were placed in a basin of warm water where they floated while the silk was being reeled off and wound into hanks. Usually one woman watched the cocoons to ascertain that the thickness of the strand remained constant, while a young assistant turned the crank.

64. In 1546 all persons operating silk reeling basins had to declare to the vicar how many basins they owned and how much silk they processed. Thirty-eight out of 94 declarations were made by women. Moreover, most of the declarations made by men were similar to those made by Giovanni Cinelli, who wrote: "Aportata di Giovanni di Checho Cinelli da Pescia della seta a hauto e tratta per Ma. Maria donna del decto Giovanni fatta in casa sua." ASPe, *Archivio Vicariale,* 74, Francesco Leoni, vicar, unnumbered pages.

Figure 3-1. Women silk-reelers in the sixteenth century. Giulio Campagnola, drawing no. 1786F. *Source:* Gabinetto dei Disegni, Florence.

3–3). At this time, Pescia produced 8,939 pounds of raw silk, of which 1,594 pounds were spun and the remainder reeled. To produce this amount required first the full-time efforts of 568 people in a 45-day season just to raise the silkworms. To reel the silk required the additional labor of 44 women working full-time for 100 days, and to card and spin took the efforts of another 26 women working 200 days.[65] Of course, the actual number involved in sericulture was much larger because most of the work was done by women in addition to their other chores, so they did not work full days at making silk. If we look at silk reeling, for example, which was probably one of the more concentrated activities—both because it had to be done relatively quickly and because it required a minimum investment of capital in equipment—we note that there were 94 silk-reeling basins in use in 1546. Since usually two women operated each basin, there were about 188 women, ranging from peasants to the wife of a book dealer, who were engaged part-time in this occupation alone. Employment in silk reeling as well as the other related tasks rose even higher over the next decades as sericulture spread. In 1619, silk reeling occupied over 300 women in a town of 7800 people.[66]

If cereal cultivation was male-labor intensive, sericulture, it seems, was female and child intensive. The only tasks performed by able-bodied men were probably the planting and pruning of the mulberry trees and wood-cutting for the fires required in

65. In the late eighteenth century, when the technology of sericulture remained essentially unchanged from what it had been in the sixteenth, Sismondi estimated that at Pescia, to produce 1 lb. of cocoons required 20 lbs. of mulberry leaves. It took 7.69 lbs. of cocoons to produce 1 lb. of spun silk and 10 lbs. of cocoons to produce 1 lb. of reeled silk. The labor necessary to process the silk, expressed in Pesciatine libbre (equivalent to .74 lb. avoirdupois) was as follows: to raise 1 libbra of cocoons required 0.3 workdays; to produce 1 libbra of reeled silk required 0.6 workdays; and to produce 1 libbra of spun silk required 3.3 workdays. In lbs. avoirdupois labor inputs come to 0.4 workdays, 0.8 workdays, and 4.4 workdays respectively. These are the ratios used in my calculations for the year 1546. The length of the working season was also adopted from Sismondi. Reeling was usually done in a few months after the cocoons were killed in order to prevent rotting. Spinning on the other hand was done intermittently as an agricultural by-occupation during slack periods. BComPe, *Fondo Sismondi*, 6:10.

66. There were 157 silk basins in 1619; ASPe, *Atti civili al tempo del Vicario Giulio Zati*, 279, fols. 1–23.

Table 3-3. Sericulture at Pescia, 1546

	Quantity (lbs. avdp.)	Total work days	Duration of season (in days)	No. of full-time workers
Mulberry leaves	1,278,320	—	45 May–July	
Cocoon raising	63,916	25,566	45 May–July	568
Reeled silk	5,478	4,382	100 July–Dec.	44
Spun silk	1,188	5,227	200	26

Note: the quantity of reeled and spun silk produced, based undoubtedly on the declarations made to the vicar in ASPe, *Archivio Vicariale,* 74, is reported by F. Galeotti, *Memorie,* pp. 393–94. All other figures are derived using the procedures outlined in n. 65.

Sources: F. Galeotti, *Memorie,* pp. 393–94; BComPe, *Fondo Sismondi,* 6:10.

reeling. By introducing this semi-agricultural activity to Pescia, more intensive use was made of society's labor resources. By mid-sixteenth century a significant portion of the total population found employment in sericulture. The transformation of Pescia's agricultural output between the fifteenth and the sixteenth century then enlarged not only the economic world in which Pescia operated, but also the number of productive human beings in the economy.

The Role of Prices

Presumably, the shift in production from cereals to other crops resulted from changes in the relative profitability of various crops. Profitability, however, is difficult to estimate, depending as it does on costs of production on the one hand, and market prices on the other—two variables for which there are rarely adequate data before the modern era.

Scattered price data for Pescia (see Appendix 4) indicate that long-term price movements there followed those of Florence and Pistoia, respectively 40 and 15 miles distant.[67] Since a useful price

67. The similarity of price trends among various cities in Tuscany has already been noted by Torben Damsholt, "Some Observations on Four Series of Tuscan Corn Prices, 1520–1630," *Scandinavian Economic History Review,* 12 (1964), pp. 145–64. See also Romano, "La storia economica," p. 1832.

series, except for silk, is not available for Pescia, prices for Pistoia and Florence have been used as surrogates.[68]

The movement of commodity prices in Florence and Pistoia (see Tables 3–4 and 3–5) suggests that after some initial short-term adjustment, Tuscan grain prices (in terms of money) were approximately one-third higher during the century following the Black Death than they had been in the 1330s and 1340s. Despite this increase in money prices, it appears that the price of grain relative to other commodities declined. It is not surprising, there-fore, that the amount of land planted in cereals declined in Tus-cany as it did elsewhere in Italy.[69] The explanation for these changes must be understood in terms of changes in per capita income and in the income elasticity of demand for different agri-cultural commodities. Following a period of adjustment in the middle decades of the fourteenth century, per capita income in-creased in the century that followed the Black Death.[70] Since the income elasticity of demand is generally greater for non-cereal foods than it is for cereals, demand for the former increased more than the latter, causing the relative price of grain to slip (see Table 3–4).

A slow but steady reversal of these relations began toward the end of the fifteenth century, and as with previous price move-ments, this one was also related to demographic changes. The population of Tuscany and western Europe began to grow again around mid-fifteenth century. This led, starting in the 1480s and 1490s, to a gradual increase in the price of most agricultural commodities, and especially of grain, whose price in relation to other products grew at an accelerating rate. But the rising rela-tive price of grain did not result, as might be expected, in a larger share of the land being devoted to grain, at least not in Tuscany. Rather, it led to a growing dependence on grain im-ports from other parts of Europe.

The rising price trend in agricultural commodities, beginning

---

68. The prices for Pescia silk have been presented because there are no other Tuscan silk prices available for the sixteenth century.

69. Romano, "La storia economica," pp. 1843–44.

70. Goldthwaite, "I prezzi del grano," p. 16; Fernand Braudel and F. Spooner, "Prices in Europe from 1450 to 1750," *The Cambridge Eco-nomic History of Europe,* M. Postan and H. J. Habakkuk, eds., 4 (Cambridge, 1967), 425–30.

Table 3-4. Price of wheat, oil, wine, and meat, 1326–1427
(in soldi della lira di piccioli)

	Florence wheat/staio	Pistoia wheat/staio	Pistoia wine/barrel	Pistoia oil/quaderna	Pistoia beef/lb.
1326–50	17 (100)[a]	21 (100)	12.5 (100)	32 (100)	14 (100)
1351–75	24 (141)	28 (133)	22.5 (180)	50 (156)	—
1376–1400	25 (147)	32 (152)	40 (320)	55 (172)	29 (207)
1401–25	20 (118)	30 (143)	35 (280)	62 (194)	26 (184)

[a] Numbers in parentheses are index numbers, where prices for the years 1326–1350 are the base.

Sources: R. Goldthwaite, "I prezzi del grano," pp. 32–33; D. Herlihy, Pistoia, pp. 126–28.

Table 3-5. Selected commodity prices at Florence and Pescia, 1450–1599
(in soldi della lira di piccioli)

	Florence wheat/staio	Pescia reeled silk/lb.	Pescia wine/barrel
1450–59	21 (100)[a]	250 (100)	—
1460–69	18 (86)	—	—
1470–79	23 (110)	—	28 (100)
1480–89	26 (123)	220 (88)	34 (121)
1490–99	29 (138)	200 (80)	45 (161)
1500–09	34 (162)	214 (86)	31 (111)
1510–19	27 (129)	—	—
1520–29	45 (214)	211 (84)	—
1530–39	51 (243)	—	58 (207)
1540–49	45 (214)	217 (87)	44 (157)
1550–59	74 (352)	232 (93)	58 (207)
1560–69	66 (314)	284 (114)	40 (142)
1570–79	69 (328)	234 (94)	—
1580–89	74 (352)	—	—
1590–99	125 (595)	460 (184)	50 (178)

[a] Numbers in parenthesis are index numbers. The base years are set at 100.

Sources: Goldthwaite, "I prezzi del grano," pp. 34–37; Parenti, Prezzi in Firenze, p. 27; Appendix 4.

in the late fifteenth century, did not include raw silk. In the 1450s silk from the Valdinievole seems to have sold at Florence for about 250 soldi per pound. The price dropped to a low of 200 soldi toward the end of the century and thereafter fluctuated at around 220 soldi until the last half of the sixteenth century. Although it is hazardous to speculate about the causes for these movements on the basis of the scanty information available, it is possible that in the fifteenth century any price above 200 soldi for a pound of silk was considerably above the costs of production and that the resulting high profitability of sericulture was encouraging farmers to enter this activity. This would explain the simultaneous expansion of sericulture and the downward movement of silk prices in the last half of the fifteenth century.[71]

The relationship between the supply of raw silk and demand for it from European cloth producers changed in the course of the sixteenth century, the century of silk.[72] Tuscan silk cultivation increased by three-fourths from 1440 to 1576, more than doubled in the following twenty-five years, and increased by two and a half times between 1610 and mid-seventeenth century.[73] But this rapid expansion failed to keep up with the growth in demand. This was especially true in Tuscany in the late sixteenth century, when cloth manufacturers began to experience difficulties in obtaining raw silk from their major suppliers in southern Italy.[74] Hence, despite successful efforts to expand the supply of the local product, prices rose at the same rate as that of wheat, leaving other agricultural commodities behind (see Tables 3–5 and 3–6).

What these agricultural commodity prices and land usage patterns (see Table 3–2) suggest is that, while changes in the relative

71. A Florentine law of 1440 ordering that mulberry trees be planted throughout the state apparently did not contribute significantly to the expansion of sericulture; see below p. 90. The decline in the price of silk may also be a fortuitous result of the scarcity of data. There is only one observation for the 1450s, and it comes from a Florentine source: F. E. de Roover, "Andrea Banchi," p. 239.

72. Fernand Braudel has characterized the sixteenth century as a period of the " 'boom' de la soie"; Braudel, La Mediterranée, p. 343.

73. The expansion of silk cultivation between 1440 and 1576 was noted in a report to Francesco I; ASF, Pratica Segreta, 10, ins. 16. The other figures were derived from Goodman, "The Florentine Silk Industry," p. 87.

74. Ibid., pp. 83–85.

Table 3–6. Index of commodity prices, 1540–1620 (in silver)[a]

	Wheat	Wine	Oil	Beef	Beans	Silk
1540–49	100	100	100	100	100	100
1550–59	173	90	115	122	108	107
1560–69	124	117	125	122	—	131
1570–79	159	—	129	—	92	108
1580–89	176	—	133	159	116	—
1590–99	298	—	162	174	167	211
1600–09	203	—	—	207	169	—
1610–20	181	158	152	217	164	—

[a] With the exception of silk, all commodity prices are for Florence. Silk prices are for Pescia.

Sources: T. Damsholt, "Tuscan Corn Prices," Scandinavian Economic History Review, 12 (1964), 144–64; Appendix 4.

prices of agricultural commodities—and hence in the profitability of various crops—were probably the most important force in determining the evolution of Pescia's agriculture, they were not the only ones. We have seen that the availability of already existing supplies of labor was one factor. Government policy, although often inconsistent and inefficient, was another.

Already in the Middle Ages, especially in times of crisis, governments would attempt to fix the prices of agricultural commodities and regulate their import and export. Occasionally, more long-term efforts were made. The government of Pescia, for example, ordered the planting of fig and mulberry trees on all properties as early as 1340.[75] And a century later the Florentine government ordered all landowners in the state to plant almond and mulberry trees until they had fifty of each on their holdings.[76]

Legislation to influence the agricultural economy of the state gained momentum after the 1530s when the Medici rulers of Tuscany began to adopt proto-mercantilist measures to encourage economic development and the economic unification of the state.[77] Tariffs were placed on the export of cocoons and raw

75. BComPe, Statuti 1340, Bk. 4, R. 86.
76. ASF, Pratica Segreta, 10, ins. 16.
77. The political economy of the Medici grand dukes has not yet been explored. The author, however, is currently working on a book on the political economy of Cosimo I.

silk, some agricultural commodities such as mulberry leaves were
not allowed to leave the state, and a concerted effort began in
1576 to introduce sericulture in various parts of Tuscany, starting
with the Valdelsa.[78]

The aim of all of these laws was to increase the supply and
lower the price of certain commodities. But the gap between
theory and reality, as government officials well knew, was enormous. In their 1576 proposal to extend sericulture throughout
the state, for example, the grand duke's councillors proposed that
only a small area, well suited to mulberry cultivation, be selected
first because:

> seeing that [the program] is profitable, each neighbor by him-
> self will begin to plant similar trees, as seems to have happened
> in the past, when their own utility induced men to plant mul-
> berries in suitable lands more than the fear of the law, since
> the provision of 1440, which constrained all agricultural work-
> ers of the Contado and District of Florence to plant up to 50
> mulberry and 50 almond trees fell into disuse.[79]

Similar lessons in the economics of the marketplace were
learned during times of food shortages. Efforts to control the
price of grain, olive oil, and wine usually ended in failure.[80] In
October 1560, for example, the government ordered that olive
oil not be exported from the state because of a shortage and
fixed the maximum price at 14 lire per barrel. The result was
that by December of that year oil had disappeared from the market and the government ordered a return to the market price.[81]

In a pre-modern society the role of the government in bringing
about economic change was perforce very limited. It could provide a framework within which individuals could act. It could

---

78. A more detailed discussion of specific legislation may be found in Ch. 4,
    "Gabelles" (see p. 140). Taxes and trade regulations in effect at Pescia
    between 1545 and 1566 were summarized in a report by grand ducal offi-
    cials; ASF, *Pratica Segreta*, 7, ins. 84. For subsequent legislation see
    Lorenzo Cantini, *Legislazione toscana, 1532–1775* (Florence, 1800–1808),
    7, pp. 91–92; 10, pp. 7–34; ASF, *Miscellanea Medicea*, fol. 994 (Vecchio).
79. ASF, *Pratica Segreta*, 10, ins. 16.
80. Giuseppe Parenti, *Prime ricerche sulla rivoluzione dei prezzi a Firenze*
    (Florence, 1939), pp. 87–88, App., pp. 77–79; Goldthwaite, "I prezzi del
    grano," pp. 25–26.
81. ASF, *Pratica Segreta*, 5, ins. 85, 89.

favor some activities and hinder others as in 1423 when farmers engaged in sericulture were encouraged to sell their silk and mulberry leaves at Florence by exempting these items from the city's gabelles.[82] But ultimately the government could not force the production or sale of commodities that people did not find profitable. The agricultural transformation that took place at Pescia, then, occurred for a large variety of reasons including changing relative prices, suitability of the soil, supplies of labor, and government encouragement. The comparative advantage of the agricultural economy of Tuscany in general, and of Pescia in particular, lay in the production of such high quality foods as wine and olive oil, or industrial crops such as mulberry trees which supplied the raw materials for the luxury industries of the Italian cities.

Land Values

Since price changes by themselves are not fully adequate to explain shifts in crop distributions, they can be supplemented by information on changes in land values found in the catasto of 1427 and the Decima of 1535. Both of these documents provide data on the area planted in different crops and the assessed value of landed property. In order to use them, however, a few simplifying but plausible assumptions are necessary. First, we shall assume that a farmer's main concern was to make as profitable a use of land as was possible. Since profitability per acre of land is the difference between the revenues it yields and the costs of production, we would ideally like to have data on the prices of agricultural commodities produced, their yields per acre, and the costs of producing those yields. Such data, as we have seen earlier, do not exist. But since there is no reason to believe that production costs changed significantly in the fifteenth or sixteenth century, it is reasonable to assume that per acre valuation and the total value of land planted to different crops reflect the profitability of producing different crops. From data on valuation, then, we can observe the transformation of Pescia's agricultural economy as it adapted to changing economic opportunities.

The changes in valuation per quartiere of land planted in dif-

---

82. Repetti, *Dizionario*, 4:120.

ferent crops are given in Table 3–7. Because the methods by which the valuations were reached may have differed in the catasto and the Decima, the mean valuations cannot be compared longitudinally. What we can compare, however, are the relative valuations in each of the two sources, and these very clearly agree with the shifts in land usage shown in Table 3–2.

In both 1427 and 1535 orchards were among the most highly valued land, perhaps because they were frequently adjacent to houses and urban properties. If so, their valuations are as much a function of this as of agricultural values. For this reason, they have been omitted from our analysis of agricultural change.

With the exception of orchards, then, the most highly valued land in the sixteenth century was that planted with mulberry trees. Since these were not listed separately in the catasto we cannot make a direct comparison with the fifteenth century, but if they were included with woods, as seems likely, their inclusion would have increased the average valuation of forest land. This may help to explain the relative decline in the value of woods in 1535, when mulberry trees were mostly listed separately. Be that

Table 3–7. Land valuations at Pescia, 1427–1535

	Cereal	Woods	Olive	Vine	Orchard	Mulberry
Mean value per quartiere, 1427[a]	3.49	1.62	10.03	19.05	17.30	—
Mean value per quartiere, 1535[b]	.72	.22	1.99	2.08	3.40	2.4
Index 1427	100	46	287	546	496	—
Index 1535	100	30	276	288	472	333
Standard deviation, 1427	3.69	4.39	7.16	18.92	25.54	—
Standard deviation, 1535	0.62	0.31	1.87	0.96	1.27	2.4
No. of observations, 1427	1,042	178	123	631	83	—
No. of observations, 1535	567	670	258	362	32	531

[a] In florins.
[b] In lire.

Sources: ASF, Catasto, 258; Decima 1535, Pescia.

as it may, in the sixteenth century the high valuation placed on land planted with mulberry trees was undoubtedly a reflection of its high relative profitability, and was the primary cause for its expansion in the course of the Renaissance.

The third most highly valued lands were vineyards. Their relative valuation, however, had slipped considerably in comparison with olive groves and cereal lands since the early Renaissance. The relative decline, I believe, was related to rising relative prices of cereals and olives beginning in the last decades of the fifteenth century. This relative decline in prices affected the profitability of such lands and resulted in a smaller share of the cultivated area being planted with vines (see Table 3–2).

In contrast, the value of olive groves, compared with cereals, remained basically unchanged. Why then did the acreage devoted to olives increase so dramatically? The answer may lie in the adoption of the Lucchese-style olive groves that produced higher yields per acre. The increased yields may have more than offset a 23 percent decline in the price of olives compared to that of cereals and to account for the expanded area planted with this crop.

This then is the basic structure of Pescia's agricultural landscape as it developed by 1535: a much larger cultivated area than in 1427 and a shift toward the production of commercial crops. This new structure suggests that Pescia's agricultural economy became more closely integrated into a wider regional economy— an economy in which Florence and the demands of the international market played a much larger role than ever before.

Tenurial Relations

The transformation from a self-sufficient to a predominantly commercial agriculture can be influenced by land tenure systems. Agrarian reform and agricultural development often have been frustrated because of obstacles posed by property rights and tenurial relations.[83] To what extent did these influence or were they themselves influenced by the changed orientation in Pescia's agricultural economy?

83. Theodore W. Schultz, *Transforming Traditional Agriculture* (New Haven, 1964), pp. 119–20; Jan De Vries, *The Dutch Rural Economy in the Golden Age, 1500–1700* (New Haven, 1974), pp. 15, 167–68, 196–97.

According to a recent interpretation of changes in tenurial relations during the Renaissance, the large depopulations of mid-fourteenth century constitute a sharp dividing line in the history of the Tuscan countryside. The new availability of land and capital and the scarcity of labor allegedly led to the abandonment of the fixed rent contract and the adoption of sharecropping (*mezzadria*). The new tenurial system was "fairer to the land and people." It not only brought more favorable conditions of tenancy for the peasant because it spread risks between landlords and peasants, but also contributed to an improvement in agricultural techniques and output by encouraging capital investment on the part of the landlords.[84]

A contrary view, and one that is closer to Pescia's experience, has been elaborated by Philip Jones, who argues that in the spread of *mezzadria* "the post-plague period represents no landmark nor any lasting amelioration of tenurial conditions . . . *mezzadria* was already for many a 'miserable system' (A. Young), yielding a bare subsistence and breeding discontent. It represented a 'proletarization' of the peasantry. And so equally did tenancy 'afitto.' "[85]

At Pescia, the progress of *mezzadria* was slow. Only a handful of notarial contracts in the last half of the fourteenth century mention it, and the catasto reveals that it was not a widespread arrangement in the early fifteenth century. The tax declarations of 1427 include 2,330 plots of land with known tenure systems. Of these, only 148 (6.35 percent) were sharecropped and almost all were scattered rather than concentrated in the compact holdings (*poderi*) associated with *mezzadria classica*. Despite the altered land/man ratio, the fixed rent contract continued to be a more common form of land tenure. It was found in 505 plots (21.67 percent) listed in the catasto. Most of the land, however, was neither sharecropped nor leased, but was worked by the owner himself or by wage labor. This arrangement appears in

84. David Herlihy, "Population, Plague, and Social Change in Rural Pistoia, 1201–1430," *Economic History Review*, 18 (1965), 243. Also Herlihy, "Santa Maria Impruneta," pp. 275–76.

85. P. Jones, "From Manor to Mezzadria: A Tuscan Case-Study in the Medieval Origins of Modern Agrarian Society," in *Florentine Studies: Politics and Society in Renaissance Florence*, ed., Nicolai Rubinstein (London, 1968), pp. 227, 225. Also, P. Jones, "Review of D. Herlihy, *Medieval and Renaissance Pistoia*," in *Economic History Review*, 24 (1971), 512–17.

1,548 land parcels (66.43 percent). Only 126 out of 353 landowners leased any portion of their holdings, and 25 of these were elderly women without families, who were in no position to do agricultural work. Unfortunately, no other tax records of the Renaissance include data about land tenure systems. Examination of notarial contracts for the fifteenth, the sixteenth, and the early seventeenth century, however, suggests the continued importance of direct holdings and of fixed rents. These were still commonly found in the Valdinievole as late as the nineteenth century, when *mezzadria* was the almost exclusive tenure system found in the central part of Tuscany.[86]

What are the implications of these tenure systems for the improvement of agricultural techniques and for capital investment at Pescia? An examination of the terms of the *mezzadria* contracts themselves quickly dispels any notion that at Pescia *mezzadria* encouraged improvements by providing incentives for the landlords. The duties of the *mezzadro* were usually spelled out in great detail. He was to work the land well and diligently, plant beans, grain, and other crops, tie the vines, hoe, weed, prune, fertilize, and so on, all at the proper time and with the appropriate techniques. What did the landlord promise to do in return? Nothing. The unrelenting silence of the contracts on this point leads to only one conclusion—the burdens and responsibilities of capital investments and labor inputs rested on the tenant. As if to confirm this, the list of duties imposed on the tenant usually ended with the stipulation that all were to be done at his own expense.[87]

To be sure, *mezzadria* contracts sometimes included loans to

86. Pazzagli, *L'agricoltura*, p. 393. As late as 1767, at the nearby Medici estate of Altopascio, where one would expect *mezzadria* to be well entrenched, only 18 percent of the population were sharecroppers. Frank McArdle, *Altopascio: A Study in Rural Society, 1587–1784* (Cambridge, 1978), p. 31. The limited extension of *mezzadria* in Tuscany as a whole is discussed by Giovanni Cherubini, "La mezzadria toscana delle origini," in *Contadini e proprietari nella Toscana moderna: atti del Convegno di studi in onore di Giorgio Giorgetti*, vol. 1, ed. Mario Mirri *et al.* (Florence, 1979), pp. 131–52.

87. ASF, *Notarile*, Baldo Gherardi, G. 135, I, fol. 54v; G. 135, III, fols. 39v, 97v, 98r, 99v, 112v; *Notarile*, Venanzio Orlandi, O. 48, II, fol. 33r. An excellent discussion of the stipulations of agricultural contracts may be found in Giorgio Giorgetti, "Contrati agrari e rapporti sociali nelle campagne," in *Storia d'Italia*, 6:1 (Turin, Giulio Enaudi, 1973), 701–58.

the tenant, but these loans, found also in fixed rent contracts, were to be repaid at the end of the tenure period. Legally, they differed from direct capital investments on the part of the landlord because the responsibility for repayment was shouldered by the tenant. Undoubtedly, many tenants were unable to repay and fled upon termination of the contract. In this, however, *mezzadria* did not differ from a fixed rent system. At Pescia there is no evidence that *mezzadria* was accompanied by a growth in the landlord's interest or capital investment in his property.[88]

Neither is there evidence that the wealthier and presumably more progressive landlords, those allegedly imbued with a "capitalist spirit," adopted *mezzadria* much more quickly than others. In 1427, only 9.3 percent of the parcels owned by the wealthiest 10 percent of Pescia's landowners were farmed under *mezzadria*. More than half of the parcels (52 percent) were farmed under fixed rent contracts, and 38.5 percent were farmed by wage labor.

Underlying the theory that *mezzadria* was adopted by "capitalist" landowners and that it involved larger capital investments by the landowner is the belief that *mezzadria* was also a more profitable system for the landlord. This hypothesis can be tested with data from the catasto. Given any one crop, differences in profitability among tenure systems can be expected to have resulted in differences in the valuations per quartiere of land. For example, if *mezzadria* were more profitable than fixed rent, the valuation of one acre of vineyards under *mezzadria* should have been higher than one acre of vineyards using a fixed rent system.[89]

Was this so at Pescia? The results, presented in the following table (3–8), indicate that the relation between tenure systems and returns to the landlord was very weak. This is not surprising. Theoretically, there is no reason to believe one tenure was in all cases more profitable than another. Since everyone was free to enter tenure agreements and these presumably were fulfilled at

88. There have been lengthy polemics on the merits and shortcomings of *mezzadria*, including the problem of landlord intervention in the operation of his farms. See Pazzagli, *L'agricoltura*, pp. 385–458. The findings of P. Jones on the detailed conditions of cultivation imposed on sharecroppers as well as his findings on landlord investment and peasant indebtedness are in accord with my own. Jones, "From Manor to Mezzadria," pp. 223–25.

89. The reason for this is that the catasto valuations were directly dependent on the return to the landlord.

Table 3–8. Relation between tenure system and land valuations, 1427 (in florins)

Cereals, value per quartiere	Number of parcels		
	Fixed rent	Owner cultivation	Sharecropping
≤2.6	137 (41.8)[a]	110 (27.1)	5 (25)
>2.6 to <3.8	148 (45.1)	92 (22.7)	9 (45)
≥3.8	43 (13.1)	203 (50.1)	6 (30)

Cramer's V = 0.27

Mean value per quartiere: fixed rent   = 2.94
                          owner cult.   = 5.10
                          sharecropping = 3.84

Vines, value per quartiere	Number of parcels		
	Fixed rent	Owner cultivation	Sharecropping
<12	16 (44.4)	111 (31.8)	15 (25.9)
≥12 to ≤23	11 (30.6)	117 (33.5)	19 (32.8)
>23	9 (25.0)	121 (34.7)	24 (41.4)

Cramer's V = 0.07

Mean value per quartiere: fixed rent   = 18.36
                          owner cult.   = 20.74
                          sharecropping = 21.77

Vines and olives, value per quartiere	Number of parcels		
	Fixed rent	Owner cultivation	Sharecropping
<10	13 (59.1)	90 (33)	7 (20.6)
≥10 to <17	3 (13.6)	90 (33)	13 (38.2)
≥17	6 (27.3)	93 (34)	14 (41.2)

Cramer's V = 0.12

Mean value per quartiere: fixed rent   = 12.12
                          owner cult.   = 15.21
                          sharecropping = 16.45

[a] Numbers in parentheses are percentages for the column.

Source: ASF, *Catasto,* 258.

the same cost, competition for land among workers and for labor among landowners insured that the returns on land and labor would not be affected by tenure.[90] Moreover, to argue that *mezzadria* was inherently more profitable even while observing that farmers at Pescia, as in many other parts of Tuscany, did not adopt *mezzadria* very frequently is to argue that these farmers were not interested in profits—a notion that defies most observations of agricultural life in Renaissance Tuscany. If the returns on *mezzadria* were much larger than on fixed rents, why would farmers not have switched almost exclusively to such a system? There were, after all, no institutional barriers to change. Tenure contracts under both systems lasted only three to five years and could be easily altered. They were not, however, because returns to the landlords were basically the same regardless of the tenure system.

But the question remains, if the two systems were equally profitable to the landlord, why were both to be found at Pescia? Why not just one? The answer, I believe, lies not with profitability, but with risk. Much has been written with respect to risk aversion and sharecropping, especially in relation to the effects of bad harvests due to weather or other natural calamities.[91] The desire to avert risk of damage to long-term investments as a result of improper farming techniques, however, has not been broached. It is this type of risk aversion that probably determined tenure choices at Pescia.

If we observe the distribution of tenure systems by crop we can distinguish a well-defined pattern (see Table 3–9). For all crops in 1427 direct owner cultivation was the most frequent way to work the land, but it was least prevalent in cereal lands and most common in olive groves and vineyards. By way of contrast, the next most popular tenure system, fixed rent, was most commonly found among cultivated crops in cereal lands and most infrequently in olive groves and vineyards, where *mezzadria* was most prevalent. The reason for this pattern was the desire on the part of landlords to avoid risks. Both vineyards and olives represented many years of investment in the land. It could take a long time

90. S. N. Cheung, *The Theory of Share Tenancy* (Chicago, 1969); Joseph D. Reid, Jr., "Sharecropping in History and Theory," *Agricultural History*, 49 (1975), 426–40.

91. Reid, "Sharecropping," pp. 430–39.

Table 3–9. Relation between crops and tenure systems

Crop	Owner[a] cultivation	Sharecropping	Fixed rent	Other[b]
Olives	94 (82.5)[c]	8 (7.0)	11 (9.6)	1 (0.8)
Olives and vines	326 (81.7)	43 (10.8)	26 (6.5)	4 (1.0)
Vines	440 (80.0)	65 (11.8)	41 (7.4)	5 (0.9)
Orchards	47 (77.0)	1 (1.6)	10 (16.3)	3 (4.9)
Woods	48 (68.6)	0 (0.0)	2 (2.9)	20 (28.5)
Cereals	456 (51.8)	21 (2.4)	374 (42.5)	30 (3.4)

a Includes land worked by the owner himself and with the help of wage labor.
b Includes unworked parcels and parcels worked by some mixture of the other tenure categories.
c Numbers in parentheses are percentages for the row.

Source: ASF, Catasto, 258.

for a vine to yield significant quantities of grapes, and decades for an olive tree to bear its maximum output. One careless pruning could wipe out the investment of many years. To protect these investments landlords preferred, whenever possible, to work such lands themselves with the aid of wage labor, if necessary. It was the best way to guarantee proper farming practices and maintenance of the plants. Sharecropping was the next best method to direct cultivation while keeping an eye on one's property.[92] Hence its prevalence among olives and vineyards. The least protection from permanent damage to the trees and vines was to be found in fixed rents and these were therefore associated with cereal agriculture. If a tenant paid his rent but did not farm the cereals properly, no permanent damage was done. The landlord did not have to worry about close supervision.

As the share of land devoted to vines, olives, and mulberry trees increased the fixed rent system may have lost some ground to *mezzadria*. But the scarcity of *mezzadria* contracts in sixteenth- and early seventeenth-century notarial contracts suggests that most of the land remained under direct owner cultivation or was leased at a fixed rent.

92. Greater landlord control under *mezzadria* has also been noted by Pinto, "Ordinamento colturale."

Distribution of Land and Agricultural Wealth

The typical unit of agricultural production throughout the Renaissance was the small farm. Out of 353 tax declarations by non-ecclesiastical landowners in 1427, half reported less than 13.57 quartieri (3.35 acres). The largest holding came to 247 quartieri (61 acres). A century later, the median size of holdings remained the same, but the mean had increased from 23 quartieri (6.62 acres) to 29 quartieri (8.35 acres).

Although small holdings remained the rule, their distribution did undergo some significant changes. The most important was that a smaller percentage of Pescia's population owned land in the sixteenth century than in earlier times. Whereas the population more than doubled between 1427 and 1535, the number of landowners grew by only 65 percent. In addition, as may be inferred from the above data on size of holdings, the distribution of land among landowners became more unequal. Table 3–10 makes evident the changed pattern of land distribution. The median size of holdings among the smallest 10 percent of farmers decreased from 1.45 to 1.16 quartieri. On the other hand, that of the largest 10 percent of farmers increased from 82.1 to 126 quartieri. Paralleling this concentration of land into the hands of the few was a concentration of landed wealth (see Table 3–11).

Table 3–10. Distribution of land among non-ecclesiastical landowners

Percent of landowners	Percent of land 1427	Percent of land 1535
10	0.63	0.40
20	2.41	1.32
30	4.95	3.07
40	8.54	5.82
50	13.46	9.94
60	20.09	15.32
70	29.40	22.95
80	41.91	34.54
90	60.51	52.97
100	100.00	100.00

Gini Index, 1427 = 0.57; Gini Index, 1535 = 0.64.

Sources: ASF, Catasto, 258; Decima 1535, Pescia.

Table 3–11. Distribution of landed wealth among non-ecclesiastical landowners

Percent of landowners	Percent of landed wealth, 1427	Percent of landed wealth, 1535
10	0.44	0.42
20	1.82	1.54
30	4.33	3.42
40	8.23	6.22
50	13.24	10.53
60	20.03	16.37
70	29.45	24.51
80	42.41	35.99
90	61.11	53.39
100	100.00	100.00

Gini Index, 1427 = 0.57; Gini Index, 1535 = 0.63.

Sources: ASF, Catasto, 258; Decima 1535, Pescia.

In 1427, the bottom 10 percent of landowners owned 0.63 percent of the landed wealth of Pescia and the top 10 percent owned 40 percent. A century later the two groups owned 0.40 percent and 47 percent respectively.

The growth of farm size and of inequality in the distribution of land is not a prerequisite for the transformation of an agricultural economy, but it is frequently a consequence of such change.[93] At Pescia, as in many developing countries today, agricultural innovation was spearheaded by the largest landowners. Their reward for their efforts was a larger share of the land and its wealth.

As Pescia's agricultural economy became more commercialized, the largest shift away from cereals and toward market-oriented crops took place among the large landholders. In 1427, when the cultivation of cereals took up close to half of the arable, the upper 10 percent of landholders devoted almost two-thirds of their land to them. A century later, they grew cereals on only 13 percent of their land compared to 24 percent among the remainder of the population. The rich were better able to innovate both, because they could afford the risks of innovation and because the new crops required, at least initially, a greater outlay of capital

93. Schultz, Transforming Agriculture, pp. 110–28.

Figure 3-2. Distribution of land at Pescia, 1427 and 1535

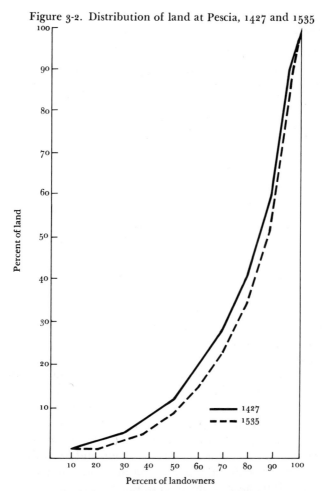

Note: The distribution of landed wealth produces a virtually identical curve.

and a longer wait for a return on one's investment than was the case with cereals.

In addition to replacing cereals with mulberry trees, vineyards, and olives, large landowners began to consolidate their holdings into more compact farms. Although the cultivated area increased, the fragmentation of holdings into scattered parcels decreased. The upper 10 percent of landowners in 1427 owned an average of 27.6 parcels of land with a mean size of 3.33 quartieri per parcel. In 1535 they owned an average of 23.6 parcels of land with a mean size of 7.94 quartieri per parcel. The integration of land into larger units probably allowed for a better use of labor inputs. Less time was spent in reaching scattered parcels, allowing them closer supervision of workers and tenants, and more efficient use of workers' time.[94]

By transforming their farms into more compact and market-oriented units, the largest landowners at Pescia were probably able to increase their profits faster than others. These profits could then be used to purchase additional land for cultivation. The process of agricultural development thus contributed to the growing inequality of landed wealth.

Many people who had been small farmers were bought out by their larger neighbors and driven either into tenancy or away from agriculture. The number of such people was probably much larger in 1535 than appears at first glance from the number of landowners mentioned in the tax records. Frequently, the small "landowner" mentioned in the Decima owned just an orchard or a few vines, less than one quarter of an acre, attached to his house or inherited from his parents or grandparents. Such people could not derive their income from their landed property. They worked for other landowners or found employment in activities which were most often directly related to the agricultural sector. The agricultural economy that developed by the sixteenth century, as we have already seen, provided new employment opportunities in sericulture. These opportunities were not confined to the actual production of raw silk but also to its sale. Some Pesciatines, like Giorgio d'Alessandro Benucci, in the 1590s, made a living by purchasing and delivering raw silk on commission for Florentine silk firms.[95] Similar opportunities could be found by selling some of the other agricultural products of the Valdinievole. In general, the growth of agricultural exports meant a greater need for middlemen to act as intermediaries between the farmers and the urban markets where Pescia's agricultural output was sold.

The development of a more specialized agricultural economy

94. The movement toward more compact holdings among the wealthiest landowners was common in Tuscany at this time. Its effects on agriculture are discussed in Cherubini, "La proprietà fondiaria," pp. 29–30.
95. ASF, Archivio Cerchi, Fondo Galli. *Giornale di Pandolfo and Vincenzo Galli,* fols. 21, 116, 234.

also meant growing opportunities in non-agricultural activities. Goods and services that once had been supplied by each individual household now often were purchased. The result was the emergence of a more complex urban economy.

THE NON-AGRICULTURAL ECONOMY

Perhaps every society needs a myth about a golden age. Pescia's golden age is generally set in the thirteenth century, when political autonomy allegedly coincided with an economic prosperity based on a complex urban economy and a system of commercial agriculture.[96] According to the myth, Pescia was one of the earliest paper producing centers in Tuscany and an early producer of silk threads.[97] These were the twin pillars of the urban economy whose prosperity was broken only by the descent from freedom into political captivity, first at the hands of Lucca, and then of Florence.

If such an economy existed, the evidence for it is hard to find. The scarcity of mulberry trees at Pescia until the last half of the fifteenth century is hard to reconcile with the purported existence of silk filatures prior to that time. Similarly, there is little evidence, as we shall see, for believing that Pescia manufactured paper until much later.

The urban economy of Pescia in the late Middle Ages and the early Renaissance was just beginning to develop. This is not surprising when we consider that most inhabitants were locked into a largely self-sufficient agricultural economy. Crafts, industry, and commerce were to be found, but on a much smaller scale than local historians have imagined. Perhaps because of their vulnerability and small scale, the town government enacted a number of measures to encourage their growth. The statutes of 1339, for example, stipulate that the books of merchants and woolen cloth manufacturers are to be trusted as evidence in any disputes involving less than 100 denari.[98] A year later the authorities ruled that cloth merchants could build a tenting shed

---

96. Cecchi and Coturri, *Pescia ed il suo territorio*, p. 70; Nori A. Galli, *La grande Valdinievole* (Florence, 1970), p. 33.

97. *Ibid.*

98. ASPe, *Statuti 1339*, Bk. 1, R. 52.

on the public meadow without charge,[99] and that foreigners want-
ing to come to Pescia to exercise the wool trade were welcome to do
so upon payment of 100 soldi to the *Arte della Lana* of Pescia.[100]
Adding to these incentives, in 1413 the authorities ruled that the
wool cloth merchants could build, free of charge, facilities for
dyeing cloth in the public meadow.[101] These attempts to facilitate
manufacturing, coupled with the obvious preponderance of agricultural matters in the statutes, all suggest that what we are dealing with here is a basically agricultural economy struggling to
develop other sectors.

Still, there were sufficient artisan industries and people engaged in service and trade to justify the creation of guilds. By the
last half of the fourteenth century the following ten guilds included some twenty-one occupations in their jurisdiction:

1. judges, doctors, and notaries
2. woolen cloth and retail merchants
3. dealers in spices and haberdashers
4. tailors, furriers, and doublet-makers
5. butchers
6. iron workers and blacksmiths
7. wood workers and saddle-makers
8. vintners
9. millers and bakers
10. shoemakers, leathermakers, and shoe repairmen.[102]

How extensive were these occupations and what share of the
goods and services produced at Pescia could be attributed to
them? A clear answer cannot be derived from the sources, but a
rough estimate can be made for the early fifteenth century when
the catasto provides us with the only overall picture of Pescia's
economy that we have. The number of persons known to have
engaged in various non-agricultural occupations in 1427 is shown
in the following table (3–12).

Undoubtedly this list underrepresents the number of people in

99. ASPe, *Statuti 1340*, Bk. 4, R. 27.
100. ASPe, *Statuti 1340*, Bk. 4, R. 90.
101. ASF, *Statuti dei Comuni Soggetti*, 566, fol. 223r.
102. ASPe, *Deliberazioni*, 9, fol. 10r.

Table 3–12. Occupations in 1427

Occupation	Number employed
judges, doctors, and notaries	10
woolen cloth and retail merchants, wool workers	7
dealers in spices and haberdashers	6
tailors, furriers	6
butchers	3
iron workers, blacksmiths, swordsmiths	7
millers, bakers	7
stoneworkers, brickmakers	4
barbers	2
soldiers	2
teachers	1
shoemakers, leatherworkers, leather saddlers	10
carpenters	2
Total	67

Source: ASF, *Catasto,* 258.

non-agricultural activities. The occupations of almost one-third of the population went unrecorded in Pescia's catasto declarations. Some of these can be guessed from other information provided by taxpayers, but others, especially those of small artisans, are hopelessly out of reach to us. Despite this limitation, a number of reasonable statements can be made about the urban economy.

The most numerous workers appear to be those producing leather goods. In 1427 Pescia had five shoemakers, five furriers, two leather craftsmen, and one leather saddler. The size of leather crafts was partly related to the proximity of large, cheap supplies of sheep skins. Pescia was located near the transhumance routes between the Apennines and the Tuscan Maremma. In addition, leather artisans purchased higher quality pelts from Genoa, Spain, and the Levant at the nearby port of Pisa, or more indirectly through Lucca.[103] Another reason for the apparent popularity of leather working, given proximity to the raw materials, was that good profits could be made without resorting to large capital investments. In 1381, for example, Antonio di Giovanni Iuntorini formed a one-year partnership with Giovanni di Piero Dini. The

103. ASF, *Notarile,* Baldo Gherardi, G. 135, III, fol. 115r; ASF, *Libro di Commercio,* 19:6, 19, 31.

amount of capital invested in their partnership came to 140 florins.[104] Another partnership, formed in 1396 by Jacopo di Nucchi Nardi, Niccolò di Giovanni, and Antonio di Matteo Stefani, operated with an investment of only 200 florins. Two of the partners supplied 100 florins each, while the third supplied his labor. The working partner was to get one-half of the profits. The other two partners were to get one-quarter each.

What the profits were in this particular instance the records do not tell us, but the possibilities can be seen in the records of a third partnership. In 1417, the notary Ser Stefano di Martini Gini, his son, and Leonardo di Niccolai Nucchi, invested 1,928 lire (480 florins) in a leather company. The enterprise lasted nineteen months and made a gross profit of 967 lire, or 50 percent on the total amount invested. Net profits came to 880 lire, which when split among the partners gave Ser Stefano and Leonardi Nucchi each 27 percent on their investment. Antonio, who had supplied the labor, received 360 lire for 19 months of work. All in all, this was not a bad return.[105]

Another industry that was well represented at Pescia was the iron and metal products industry, which included three iron-workers, three blacksmiths, and one sword maker. Legend has it that Pescia developed as a Roman center around a place called Ferraia, where iron deposits gave rise to a well-developed iron industry. But the only suggestion of such deposits is the name Ferraia for one of the town's quarters. The iron worked at Pescia probably came from Elba and the presence of metal workers in the town can be explained as part of a general spread of the iron industry in the northwest part of the Florentine state where prox-imity to plentiful supplies of wood and running water allowed a more efficient operation of forges.[106]

More important than either leather or metal for Pescia's future economic development was the production of textiles. In 1427 there were at least five woolen cloth merchants and probably two to three times that many workers residing in the town. Their enterprises were very modest in size. The capital of the largest woolen cloth company amounted to 628 florins, which included the value of a tenting shed, a loom, dyeing vats, and supplies of

104. ASF, Notarile, Neri Belloni, B. 1046, I, fol. 73r.
105. ASF, Notarile, Baldo Gherardi, G. 135, III, fol. 4v.
106. Herlihy, Pistoia, 173–75; Herlihy and Klapisch, Les Toscans, p. 284.

wool and cloth.[107] The significance of the industry consequently lay not so much in its size as in the availability of its equipment and of its output for the use of other industries in the future, and perhaps also on the familiarity that it gave entrepreneurs with the problems of investment, production, and marketing.

Conspicuous for its absence from the catasto is the manufacture of paper, thought to have existed at Pescia from the late Middle Ages. This omission from the tax records as well as from other sources suggests that paper making at Pescia did not originate until a later period.[108] The capital equipment it required

107. ASF, *Catasto,* 258:359, 562.
108. The widespread belief that paper making at Pescia dates from the late Middle Ages rests on very little data. For the thirteenth century, it has been argued that the terms *calthoria* and *cartiala,* used in several Lucchese parchments as reference to place names within the vicarage of Pescia, are proof that paper was manufactured in that area. While there is a similarity in the terms to the word *carta,* this, in and of itself, is not a very compelling argument for the existence of paper manufacturing.

As further evidence reference has also been made to an agreement, notarized at Montevettolini, between the procurator of Pistoia and the abbott of Fucecchio, and written on "carta di bambacia." Presumably the geographic proximity to Pescia has been taken as an indication of paper manufacturing at Pescia itself but since the provenance of the paper is not cited this is hardly sufficient proof. E. Magnani, *Cartiere toscane* (Pescia, 1960).

For the fourteenth century, the argument that Pescia, as well as Colle di Valdelsa and Prato, were the most important paper manufacturers in Tuscany rests on the identification of watermarks by Charles Briquet. In his monumental catalogue of medieval and Renaissance watermarks, he identified two as originating in Pescia. One, in the shape of a flower, was found in a document of 1340 at the Archivio di Stato of Bologna. Another, in the shape of pliers, was found in a document of 1355 at the Archivio di Stato of Florence. The attributions are not very satisfactory. The first case involved a design adopted by several paper manufacturers in different towns, and Briquet gave no reason for selecting Pescia as one of them. The second involved some correspondence of the Florentine *signoria,* and again no particular reason was given by Briquet for the attribution. Equally puzzling is his inclusion of Pescia among the most important paper manufacturing centers at this time, when he found only two watermarks that he could attribute to the town, compared with more than half a dozen for such places as Colle di Valdelsa. Charles M. Briquet, *Les Filigranes: Dictionnaire historique des marques du papier dès leurs apparitions vers 1280 jusqu'en 1600* (New York, 1966; orig. ed. 1923), 4:781; 2:364; 4:715. The watermarks of Colle are

was greater than for most other industries in the Renaissance. Large water-powered stamping mills had to be constructed to macerate the raw materials that went into the final product. Heavy presses were used to squeeze the moisture out of the sheets of paper once they were formed and partially dried and the buildings where paper was made were of necessity very large in order to accommodate the spacious, well-ventilated lofts where the sheets were hung to dry.[109] How could such facilities exist and not be included in the catasto of 1427?

These, then, are the major activities found in Pescia's urban economy during the early Renaissance. The major features that emerge from the catasto, the notarial records, and the legislation of Pescia's government suggest a very simple non-agricultural sector. While there were some artisan industries in the town, they were not very large or varied. Most of the urban sector was engaged in service and petty trade that provided the iron ware, foodstuffs, leather products, clothing, and other modest consumer articles that were in occasional demand by the local population.

Clearly, the urban economy of Pescia did not provide many opportunities for those seeking to make their fortunes. Indeed, the evidence suggests that in the early Renaissance the people of Pescia were poor. Indebtedness was rampant. Many complained that they could not collect the money owed them. "I don't expect to recover the debt," wrote Agnolo da Cristofano in his tax return "because . . . Stefano is very poor and sick and has no means of livelihood."[110] Fully one-sixth of households owed money to Ventura di Sabatino, a Jewish moneylender. The sums were small, mostly less than 30 lire. These were obviously consumption loans for which the demand—and the risk—were so great that interest charges reached 2.5 percent monthly.[111]

---

also described and analyzed in A. Lisini, "I segni delle cartiere di Colle," *Miscellanea storica della Valdelsa*, 5 (1897), pp. 247–50.

In my own search for evidence of paper manufacturing, I did not find either of these watermarks in any of the surviving documents at Pescia's archives. Neither did I find any reference to paper making in any sources for the early Renaissance.

109. André Blum, *On the Origins of Paper* (New York, 1934); Francesco Dini, *Le cartiere in Colle di Valdelsa* (Castelfiorentino, 1902); Warren Chappell, *A Short History of the Printed Word* (New York, 1970).

110. ASF, *Catasto*, 258, fol. 155v.

111. *Ibid.*, fol. 969v.

The extent of poverty can be gauged from data on the level of wealth supplied in the catasto (see Table 3–13). This, of course, is a different measure of prosperity than income, but the relatively low level of wealth at Pescia is a good indication of low income as well since most of the wealth listed in the catasto was in the form of land, and this was assessed on the basis of the gross income it generated. Moreover, as we have seen, there was little opportunity to derive one's income outside of the agricultural sector since there was still very little industry in the town.

According to the catasto, 10 percent of households did not have any taxable wealth, a figure that should be raised considerably if we take into account that many of the poor were able to escape the notice of tax officials. Another quarter of all households had a taxable wealth of less than 50 florins. What does this mean in terms of contemporary standards of wealth?

The catasto can provide us with only a rough estimate of comparative well-being because the wealth of large urban centers, such as Florence, Pistoia, and Prato, was undervalued compared to rural areas. The reason for this is that the income of wage-earners, who made up a large proportion of the urban population, was not subject to the tax. Consequently, the inhabitants of Pistoia, the nearest large city, appear to be only slightly better off than Pesciatines, with a mean per capita wealth of 60 florins com-

Table 3–13. Distribution of wealth at Pescia, 1427

Percent of households	Taxable wealth[a]	Percent of wealth
10	0	0.00
20	1– 20	0.53
30	21– 43	2.08
40	44– 73	4.86
50	74–108	9.47
60	109–141	15.78
70	142–203	24.49
80	204–303	36.82
90	304–467	55.84
100	468–2,080	100.00

[a] In florins.

Source: ASF, *Catasto,* 258.

pared to 54 florins at Pescia. In fact, however, both the level of prosperity and the employment opportunities were much higher in the large cities and nowhere more so than in Florence, which was so rich in relation to other places that even the leveling effect of the catasto rules cannot mask its prosperity. Mean per capita wealth at Florence reached 205 florins—eight times that of Pescia. Wealth was clearly concentrated in the largest cities and in Florence in particular.[112] Little wonder that so many Pesciatines, like their neighbors in the *contado* and district, complained of poverty and fled to Florence hoping to get a share of that city's riches. Florence, and to a lesser extent the large secondary cities of Tuscany—Pistoia, Prato, Volterra, among others—offered a larger variety of employment possibilities. This more than anything else contributed to the exodus of young people from the town in the late fourteenth and early fifteenth century.

How then did Pescia overcome these difficulties? The most important stimulus for change in the urban economy and in levels of prosperity was the transformation of the agricultural economy beginning in mid-fifteenth century. The growth of sericulture provided an incentive for the establishment of further silk processing at Pescia itself. Silk reeling has already been mentioned as a semi-agricultural occupation that small households could easily undertake. After the silk was reeled, however, it needed further twisting before it could be dyed and woven into cloth. In a few cities, and especially in Lucca and Bologna, this process, called throwing, was performed by water-powered throwing mills (*filatoio*) as early as the fourteenth century. But with the spread of sericulture throughout northern and central Italy in the late sixteenth and the early seventeenth century, these machines were quickly adopted in many regions.[113] Pescia, not surprisingly, was one of the earliest places in Tuscany to have one. The town was in the heart of the silk growing areas of Tuscany, it had a swift-moving river to power the mills, and the townspeople had already

---

112. Differences in wealth distribution in various parts of the Florentine state are discussed by Herlihy and Klapisch, *Les Toscans*, pp. 241–49, 644.

113. F. E. de Roover, "Lucchese Silks," pp. 2916–18; Carlo Poni, "Archaeologie de la fabrique; la diffusion des moulins de soie 'alla bolognese' dans les Etats venetians du XVIᵉ au XVIIIᵉ siècles," *Annales: E.S.C.*, 27 (1972), 1475–96.

constructed two mill-races to channel its power for the various oil presses, grain mills, and cloth fulling mills that had proliferated in the sixteenth century.[114]

The first *filatoio* was introduced in 1589 by Cristofano di Simone Cappelletti, whose family was among those "unwanted" immigrants who settled in Pescia in the 1520s. The Cappelletti came from a small village in the territory of Modena, near Bologna, where perhaps they had already seen water-powered throwing mills in operation. In any event, Cristofano Cappelletti perceived their profit-making potential and he asked Ferdinand I for permission to build one. He had no difficulties obtaining his request because, as a grand-ducal official with the title of *provveditore di fiumi e strade della Valdinievole,* he was well known to Ferdinand I and because the latter was interested in promoting the silk industry. Cristofano was allowed to process up to 25,000 pounds of Pesciatine silk and an unlimited amount from the grand-ducal lands in the Valdinievole on condition that the silk not be exported outside the state. The *filatoio* must have been a great success for in the next few years other entrepreneurs developed five more and by 1603 the number of Pesciatine silk throwing mills came to 23. The rapid introduction of this technology created an unprecedented demand for labor. According to the mill owners, they provided work for 700 to 800 persons.[115] The town became a silk processing center of such magnitude that silk growers and merchants from other parts of the state sent their silk to Pescia's mills. The Florentine silk merchant Agostino Parenti alone sent over 5000 pounds of silk annually in the early years of the seventeenth century.[116] Delicate silken threads thus bound the economy of Pescia to that of Florence and the rest of the state in an economic network of ever increasing strength.

But the ties between Pescia and the larger world outside it were not confined to silk. Papermaking was introduced in 1481 by the Turini family. Already established at nearby Villa Basilica in the territory of Lucca, the manufacture of paper was brought to Pescia for some of the same reasons as the silk throwing mills— the availability of water-power and of raw materials necessary for

114. Salvagnini, *Pescia*, pp. 37, 41, 178.
115. ASF, *Pratica Segreta,* 17, fols. 76r–77v. The 23 mills of Pescia had 2 *valichi* (rows of reels and spindles) each.
116. ASF, *Pratica Segreta,* 16, fols. 306–10.

production. The paper mills, like all others, benefited from the fast moving current for operating the stamping machines that made pulp. Moreover, unlike its modern counterpart, the Pescia river in the Renaissance had clean and soft water, the kind that paper makers preferred because it did not leave unwanted residue on the paper itself or on the machinery. Raw materials such as hemp, linen, and wool rags that went into paper were also plentiful as was the animal glue, obtained from Pescia's leather tanners, and used for sizing paper to make it less absorbent.[117] In this way the economic activities already present in the town—cloth and leather manufacturing—facilitated the introduction of yet another industry. This more than the sixteenth-century export prohibitions on raw materials used in paper making contributed to the success of the industry.[118]

The Turini mill, located south of town, was a medium-sized operation with five stamping machines and probably employing about sixteen workers.[119] Through much of the sixteenth and the early seventeenth century it was leased to firms of experienced paper makers who came from Colle di Valdelsa where the industry went back several hundred years. Unfortunately, we do not know how much paper it produced, but apparently business was good enough in mid-sixteenth century to induce the operators of the mill to renew their five-year lease through several decades so that the Turini became interested in building one more mill, a considerable investment on their part.[120] Sometime before 1594

---

117. The raw materials used for paper manufacturing in preindustrial times are discussed in Dini, *Le cartiere*, p. 9; Chappell, *A Short History of the Printed Word*, p. 13.

118. In 1544 Cosimo I forbade the export of rags used in paper making and scraps of animal skin used for glue. The prohibition was renewed in 1574. Cantini, *Legislazione toscana*, 8:124–25.

119. ASF, *Notarile*, S-714, Tommaso Simi, fols. 26or–262r. By way of comparison, the eighteen paper mills of Colle Valdelsa averaged 4.28 stamping mills each. Dini, *Le cartiere*, pp. 3–4. None of the documents pertaining to Pescia's paper mills gives the number of employees. The figure cited is an estimate derived from the late eighteenth century, when, according to Sismondi, the 20 paper mills of Pescia employed approximately 325 people. BComPe, *Fondo Sismondi*, 6:10. Sismondi, *Tableau*, p. 260.

120. Among the lessees were Niccolò di Piero Nofri of Colle di Valdelsa and his son Filippo, who went into partnership in 1558 with Bartolommeo di Stefanino Bartolomei of Pescia. ASF, *Notarile*, S-714, Tommaso Simi,

the Turini built a second mill not far from the first one.[121]

As before, the operators came from outside of Pescia, but as they renewed their leases repeatedly, they effectively became residents in the town. The paper they produced, according to Domenico Antonio Felice, a one-time worker in one of them, found a market not only in Pescia, but also in Florence, Pisa, Pistoia, Lucca, and elsewhere.[122]

Just as certain industries helped bring paper making to Pescia, it too attracted other activities in its turn. Printing was first introduced by Ser Bastiano di Ser Jacopo Orlandi, who financed the efforts of the Florentine printer, Francesco Cenni, to set up shop at Pescia.[123] Presumably, Cenni and his financial backer expected that the proximity to a source of paper would confer certain advantages on the operation. Paper was the principal expense in the printing industry in the fifteenth and sixteenth centuries, accounting for about two-thirds of the cost of producing a book.[124] The ready supply of paper at Pescia and the probability that Orlandi knew Turini personally, so that a good un-

fols. 260r–262r. In 1570 Bartolommeo was no longer a partner and the lease, now for ten years, included Giovanni Maria Nofri of Colle. Despite some argument or misunderstanding about the terms of the lease, which led Giulio di Andrea Turini to seek backpayments before a court of law that same year, the dispute appears to have been settled because in 1573 we find Piero Niccolò de Nofrini "cartholarii piscie" marrying a local girl, Maria di Luca Jacopo Pucinelli, and his sister marrying a man from the nearby town of Stignano. ASF, *Notarile Moderno*, 2883, Francesco Filippo Bonagrazia, fols. 18v–19r. Other papermakers from outside of Pescia were Andrea Scotti who came from Colle di Valdelsa and Antonio di Michele Fabrica, a Genoese. ASPe, *Del.*, 75, fols. 76v–81v.

121. A second paper mill is shown in a map of Pescia's mills in 1594. Salvagnini, *Pescia*, p. 42. Reference to both of these buildings is also made in a statement by Antonio di Michele Fabrica, in which he tells the city council "da venti anni in quà ha esercitato il mestiero del cartolaio alle cartiere del S. Turini fuori della Terra di Pescia, e così tanto al edificio di sopra quanto all'edificio di sotto, facendo questo mestiero con realtà." ASPe, *Del.*, 75, fols. 76v–81v.

122. *Ibid.*

123. C. Stiavelli, *La storia di Pescia nella vita privata del secolo XIV al XVII* (Florence, 1903), p. 43.

124. F. Edler de Roover, "Cost Accounting in the Sixteenth Century: The Books of Christopher Plantin, Antwerp Printer and Publisher," *Accounting Review*, 12 (1937), 228; R. Hirsch, *Printing, Selling, and Reading, 1450–1550* (Weisbaden, 1967), pp. 36, 40.

derstanding might be reached about its price, meant that a major problem in trying to make a profit in printing was solved. Cenni and Orlandi therefore proceeded to print an edition of the *Confessions of S. Bernardino of Siena* in 1485, which was quickly followed by a treatise by Antonio di Canaro. This book apparently was not a best seller for we find that over the next decade Ser Bastiano and Raffaello Orlandi were subsidizing another printer, a German by the name of Sigismund Rodt of Bitsfeld.[125] This time the books printed ranged from jurisprudence and military affairs to Savonarola's *Compendium Logicae* but the outcome of these efforts, twenty-five different works in all, was not financial success.[126]

The problems facing a would-be printer were not just confined to obtaining an adequate supply of paper. Training the labor force, selecting suitable texts, estimating the size of editions, and finally marketing them, were also of importance. It is in these areas that the Orlandi probably ran into difficulties. While the proximity of paper mills aided in establishing printing, it was not a guarantee of success. The rapid proliferation of the paper industry throughout Italy made proximity to one source of supply less important than before. Moreover, a printing establishment at Pescia would have a difficult time overcoming the problems of marketing. The public for Pescia's books was not at Pescia but in Florence, Pisa, and other large urban centers where there was a large, educated, and well-to-do public. To find this public and to obtain familiarity with its tastes was a near impossible task for an entrepreneur in a small rural commune. The Orlandi gave up in 1495.

The lesson was not entirely forgotten, and when printing was

125. Anon., *La Tipografia Benedetti e Niccolai con un breve cenno intorno all'arte della stampa a Pescia* (Pescia, no date); Stiavelli, *La storia di Pescia*, p. 43.

126. Among the works published at Pescia at this time are *Commentaria super Tit. VIII Accusat. Inquisit. et Denuntiat. in V. libro Decretalium; Tractatus de oblationibus* by Mariano Soccini; *De bannitis* by Nello di San Gimignano; *Epitoma rei militaris* by Vegezio; *Repetitiones et disputationes Laurentii de Rodulphis; De exceptionibus, praescriptionibus et sententiis* by Felino Sandeo; *De regulis juris* by Dino di Mugello; and Savonarola's *Compendium logicae:* see Giuseppe Fumagalli, *Dictionnaire géographique d'Italie pour servir à l'histoire de l'imprimerie dans ce pays* (Florence, 1905).

introduced once more sixty years later it was done rather differ-
ently. This time the people who subsidized the venture were
Pompeo della Barba, physician to Pope Pius IV, and his brother
Simone who had well-established links in Florentine literary
circles. They managed to get Lorenzo Torrentino to bring part
of his famous printing establishment from Florence to Pescia,
knowing that for political reasons Torrentino was probably eager
to get away from Florence or at least to keep a low profile.[127] The
books published also differed from those selected earlier. The
first was an exposition by Simone della Barba on one of Petrarch's
sonnets. Della Barba's work had originally been recited at a meeting of the Accademia Fiorentina in 1552. The other two books
were Italian translations of Pico della Mirandola's *Heptalo* and
La Strega, the one translated by Antonio Buonagrazia and the
other by Turino Turini.[128] Clearly an appeal was made to a
broader audience than ever before. On the one hand, the reading
public of Florence and other cultural centers would be interested in works like Pico's, on the other, that of Pescia would be
drawn to the literary efforts of the local boys who had done the
translating. To curry further favor, all works were dedicated to
various members of the Medici family—Giulio de' Medici, Giovanni de' Medici, and Eleanor of Toledo—with lengthy words in
their praise and reminders of the special ties of service that bound
the authors to the ruling family.

Torrentino's Pesciatine press remained in operation for only
three years. After that the printer returned to Florence and resumed his work there. We do not know how profitable his years
at Pescia really were, but surely, for a printer interested in keeping in close touch with the reading public, the small town had
little to offer. The della Barba could not keep him from leaving
once he realized it was safe to return to the bigger city. No more
attempts were made to introduce printing until the late eighteenth century.

A glance at the non-agricultural economy of Pescia reveals that
the artisan industries that succeeded were generally those that
either catered to local demand, such as low quality woolens, or

127. Domenico Moreni, *Annali della tipografia fiorentina di Lorenzo Torrentino,* 2d ed. (Florence, 1819), lii–lxi.
128. Carlo Stiavelli, *Saggio di una bibliografia pesciatina* (Pescia, 1900), pp.
25–27.

that supplied the industries of more complex urban economies. Both silk production and paper manufacturing succeeded because they developed out of established local resources and because they did not require the creation of sophisticated sales organizations in far away markets. Both products were used in luxury industries that operated best in the large cities of Europe. Pescia did not have the labor or entrepreneurial skills that were found in places like Florence and it did not have the same ready access to networks of information for marketing. The urban economy of Pescia, therefore, could not hope to duplicate in small scale that of Florence or Lucca. When it tried to do so, as was the case with the printing industry, it failed.

If, consequently, the economic development of the town appears less dazzling than that of other small towns such as San Gimignano or Colle di Valdelsa flourishing in medieval times, it was nonetheless made of sterner stuff and would prove a better foundation for continued development in the modern period. Pescia's economy, built around a solid agricultural sector, and providing manufactured goods that found ready markets in Florence and other Tuscan cities, became truly integrated into a regional economy.[129] Its commercial ties with the outside world were not based on competitive relations with its neighbors, but rather on mutual needs and services provided by complementary economies.

Within this limited framework the urban economy of the town experienced a remarkable transformation. We see, first of all, the proliferation of middlemen such as Michele Fredianelli and Ottavio Bastiano Galeotti who purchased silk for Florentine firms.[130] These men marketed the commodities of Pescia's increasingly specialized agricultural sector. Second, as agriculture itself became more specialized the demand for manufactured goods and services rose. Metal workers, for example, did a lively trade in supplying basins for silk reelers and machinery for the silk throwing and paper mills of the town. Other craftsmen made the

---

129. A pattern of development similar to Pescia's in many respects was found by J. de Vries in *The Dutch Rural Economy*.

130. ASF, *Notarile Moderno*, 11398. Lorenzo Stefano Simoni, fols. 41v–42r; BComPe, I.B.19., *Libro di ricordanze di Ottavio del Capitano Bastiano Galeotti*. On the role of middlemen in silk marketing, see J. Goodman, "The Florentine Silk Industry," pp. 103–5.

furniture, household goods, and textiles that had heretofore not
been produced at all or in some cases had been crudely produced
in the home. In contrast to the household inventories of the early
Renaissance, those of the sixteenth and early seventeenth century
reveal a profusion of chests, tables and chairs, beds, mattresses,
lamps, ceramics, linens, books, silverware, and art objects, all of
which reflect the greater economic prosperity of this period and
give some indication of the growing demand for such products in
the local economy.[131]

Not surprisingly, Pescia became a lively manufacturing and
commercial town, attracting buyers from all of the nearby communities as well as from the state of Lucca.[132] In the last half of

131. The demand for these items among Pescia's patriciate will be examined
in Chapter 5. But even people who were not among the wealthiest in
town seem to have lived in more richly appointed houses. The household inventory of Cesare Agostino Bianconi, who died in 1612, illustrates the new standard of living attained by the middle sectors of
Pescia's society. Cesare was a small silk merchant who in addition to
his house owned five or six parcels of land. His household inventory
includes his account books and equipment for producing raw silk.
Among his living room furnishings are mentioned a walnut table with
6 walnut chairs, a chest, 3 other chairs, another chest, a lamp, and 3
picture frames. Next to the living room there was a small room containing a small table, a pair of andirons, a chain with a rotisserie, a
clothes hanger, a three-legged stool, 3 lamps, and 10 framed pictures on
paper. In the large bedroom was a metal bed with a mattress, blankets,
and linen, several chests, 7 paintings of saints on canvas and one small
painting of the Madonna, one sphere, an archebus, a sword and dagger,
a pair of tailor's scissors, 2 allegedly beautiful chest locks, a felt hat,
a calendar of the saints, 4 small printed books, and a small chest. The
kitchen contained an assortment of ceramic plates and metal pots and
pans. Upstairs, in a room containing primarily silk making equipment,
was a hat rack. Another upstairs room contained a bed with posts.
A second upstairs bedroom had a bed with a mattress and blanket, 2
tables, and several framed pictures on paper. ASF, *Notarile Moderno*,
10651, Stefano Pierfrancesco Simi, fols. 86v–88r.
132. The importance of trade with Lucca was illustrated in the aftermath
of a ducal law promulgated on September 5, 1549, prohibiting the use
and circulation of foreign coins throughout the Florentine state. Mint
officials informed Cosimo I that when they tried to enforce the law the
following Saturday during Pescia's market, "ne fu fatto disturbo grandissimo." The Pesciatine government requested immediately that Lucchese
coins be allowed to circulate at Pescia, "per nutrirsi quella comunità
per la maggior parte delli danari e con commercio delli circumvicini li
quali giornalmente ne venghono alle botteghe e mercato di Pescia." Its
request was granted. ASF, *Zecca*, 86, unnumbered page.

the sixteenth century it had so many shops and artisans that they could no longer fit in the large central piazza during market day. The city council was forced to extend the market's privileges to the whole town because:

> . . . the businesses and crafts and merchants in this community of Pescia have grown and multiplied and because the site of the said piazza where the market is held is not capable of holding all the shops where people can practice their trade, and many have opened shops scattered throughout this community and have in them various sorts of merchandise. . . .[133]

Among the sellers and craftsmen mentioned are drapers, woolen and linen cloth manufacturers, shoemakers, potters, iron and metal workers, bakers, and an assorted variety of food and other vendors.

As a marketing center Pescia was also aided by several measures adopted by the Florentine government at Pescia's request. The first involved moving the road linking Pistoia and Lucca from the plain of Pescia to the town of Pescia itself. As early as 1429 the town had asked that this be done so that by forcing travelers to go through Pescia they could increase trade. It was not, however, until 1501 that construction of the new road was started and not until 1564 that it was completed and the "obsolete" portion of the old road destroyed.[134]

The second measure to benefit the town was the granting of fair privileges by Cosimo I in 1562. Anxious to lure foreign and Tuscan buyers who attended the recently instituted annual fair at Pisa, Pescia requested permission to hold its own fair immediately following the close of Pisa's at the end of September. The fair was a quick success both because of the tax exemption granted to foreign goods brought to it and because of the promotion efforts of the Pesciatine government, which was eager to notify foreign merchants that if they went to Pisa they could drum up additional business by returning home via Pescia.[135]

133. Law of 1571; ASF, *Statuti dei Comuni Soggetti*, 568, Pescia, fol. 171r.
134. Salvagnini, *Pescia*, pp. 49–50.
135. In addition to being exempt from the toll collected at Buggiano, the foreign goods brought to Pescia's fair were taxed only if sold. Unsold merchandise could leave the state untaxed. ASF, *Pratica Segreta*, 6, ins. 19. Florentine officials noted the Pesciatines' anxiety to receive permission for the fair as quickly as possible so that they could notify foreign merchants (*ibid.*). Apparently their efforts paid off because ten years

Figure 3-3. Main piazza in Pescia, site of weekly markets; most façades
are late sixteenth, early seventeenth century.

As if to prove that God helps those who help themselves, the
Virgin Mary made two appearances in the town in 1572. Pescia
now became a pilgrimage center as well, and this too was good
for trade. Throngs of worshippers came to the tabernacle built
in the Virgin's honor at the site where the miraculous appearances took place, creating monumental traffic jams and a serious
shortage of sleeping and eating accommodations for visitors.
Crowding was particularly accute during Saturday's market and
on fair days, when visitors combined religion and business. But
this was hardly viewed with great alarm. Trade was booming,
new inns and taverns were opened, and clearly the benefits of
divine grace were more than simply spiritual.[136]

later the fair was so successful that it was cited as one of the causes for
the shortage of inns and taverns. ASF, *Statuti dei Comuni Soggetti*, 568,
Pescia, fol. 183.

136. ". . . havendo considerato la frequentia e concorrenzia del populo che
giornalmente concorre in detta terra di Pescia tanto per le devotioni
delle chiese e luoghi pii, e maxime per la nuova apparitione della
gloriosa Madre di Nostro signiore Iesucristo, sempre vergine Maria
Nostra advocata, sul ponte della pieve, sotto dì sei di maggio 1572 e di
poi del Crocifiso del monasterio di Sancta Maria Nuova di Pescia sotto

The growing influx of people and the rapid economic development that took place in the sixteenth and early seventeenth century were both reflected in, and encouraged by, the physical expansion of the town. The early Renaissance at Pescia had not been a time for building. Demand for private construction was slow because population losses had left a plentiful supply of houses and because the remaining inhabitants were not eager to spend their meager funds in building projects except to build several small *spedali* to house the growing sick and needy population of the town.[137] In the last decades of the fifteenth century, however, building activity was resumed, slowly at first, and with an increasing rapidity after the 1550s that was not to let up until 1630. A town that could house 1800 inhabitants in 1427 was inadequate for a population four times that size in the 1620s. Pescia literally burst through its walls. The list of people who asked for permission to cut through the town walls to make additions or changes on their houses is practically endless.[138] A report of 1674 when Pescia once more had a population equal to that of

---

dì nove di decto mese et anno, dove e concorso assi populo e del continuo concorrere e concorrera giornalmente, quando ancora essendoci ogni otto giorni il mercato dove concorre assai populo, il simile facendosi la fiera, si ancora per essere stato concesso più fa alla detta terra di Pescia dal serenissimo Gran Duca . . . di levare il passo della strada et alberghi di decta terra, nella quale li forestieri e viandanti e convincini, per la poca commodità delle hosterie che in detta terra si trovano e la mala satisfactione di detti forestieri . . . ," the city council provided that anyone may open an inn or tavern by paying a tax of 14 or 7 lire a month respectively. ASF, *Statuti dei Comuni Soggetti*, 568, fol. 183.

137. Salvagnini, *Pescia*, pp. 78–79. The lack of building activity is reflected in the absence of occupations such as brickmakers, stonecarvers, and builders from the catasto. Only two *muratori* appear in that document. The most noteworthy departures from this trend are the Church of Saint Peter and Paul, later called the Madonna di Piè di Piazza, and the Cardini chapel in the Church of San Francesco, both attributed to Andrea Cavalcanti, the adoptive son of Brunelleschi. These architectural achievements, however, date to the end of the 1440s when Pescia was already beginning to come out of its economic difficulties, and they were not followed up by similar efforts until the sixteenth century (*ibid.*, p. 83); A. Gambutti, "L'architettura del primo Rinascimento nella Toscana nord-occidentale: influssi fiorentini e caratteristiche locali," in *Egemonia fiorentina ed autonomie locali* (Bologna, 1978), pp. 463–64.

138. *Ibid.*, pp. 71–72, 81–85, 91–101.

the 1620s throws light on the building activity that had taken place in the sixteenth and early seventeenth century:

> . . . on the walls of Pescia many houses, and monasteries have been constructed, the fortified towers having even been dismantled, and the walls pierced with doors, and in particular at present there are built on these walls and towers, the monastery of S. Maria la Nuova near the Lucchese gate, the monastery of Santa Chiara, the monastery of the Carmine, and the monastery of the Madre di Dio called Colle and a street along the river full of houses, built on the wall and most of them have the entrance and windows outside the walls, and many others on the wall. . . .[139]

Almost all the monasteries mentioned in the report were built or enlarged in the last half of the sixteenth and early seventeenth century.[140] The houses, too, date to this period judging from the requests for building permits as well as from the architectural evidence that survives to this day. For Pescia, even to the casual visitor, appears to be a sixteenth- and early seventeenth-century town.[141] Building was a response not only to the housing needs of a growing population and large numbers of visiting merchants and pilgrims but also to the consumption patterns of a wealthier group of people. As many Pesciatines accumulated unprecedented wealth through the new economic activities available to them they spent part of it on building more luxurious houses—palaces that were commensurate to their recently acquired economic status. The cultural significance of these structures will be explored later on but their economic significance was also great. As the Cardini, Cecchi, della Barba, Forti, Ricci, Turini, and others

139. *Ibid.*, p. 72.
140. The monastery of Santa Chiara was built in 1492, Santa Maria Nuova in 1559 and enlarged several times in the next half century, the Carmine went up in 1625, and the Madre di Dio between 1613 and 1618. Spurred not only by the growing numbers of unmarriageable girls but also by the religious zeal of the counter-reformation, other religious buildings were built at this time as well, among them the church of the Santissima Annunziata and the monastery of the Carmelites. Still other buildings such as the Church of San Francesco were enlarged.
141. The late sixteenth-century appearance of Pescia has been noted by other scholars as well, most recently Giorgio Spini, "Architettura e politica nel principato mediceo del Cinquecento," *Rivista storica italiana,* 83 (1971), 795.

built palaces to display their wealth, they created new jobs and economic opportunities for others.[142] It is no coincidence that the Decima of 1535, though not a census, lists many more people with the appellation brickmaker or stonecutter than does the catasto of 1427. Skilled building-trades artisans—woodworkers, metalworkers, and stone masons—must have found their talents in high demand, not to mention the artisans who would be called on to make the furniture and decorative objects to put inside the new buildings.[143]

The excellent quality of Pescia's housing and the prosperous appearance of the town were the object of much local pride. Both the love for their community and the pride in the genuine economic strides that had been made became focused in the sixteenth and seventeenth centuries on the drive by local citizens to raise Pescia to the administrative status of a "city" and to make it the seat of a bishopric.[144] In their efforts to accomplish this Pesciatine officials sang the praises of their homeland to grand-ducal and papal officials. One such document, written in 1617, captures the transformation that had taken place in the town:

> The said [Pescia] from descriptions made repeatedly in recent times has approximately 5,000 people, and the rest of its Vicarate around 26,000 people, so that in all they are 31,000 people.
> And the entire city wall is fortified with many towers and a castle for its defense located in the most sublime place.
> The river that divides it is straddled by two bridges, it is full of water and at all times it is useful to many buildings such as mills, olive presses, paper mills, leather tanneries and silk throwing mills, with much utility and comfort not only to the people who live there but also to the dominant city. . . .

142. The importance of palace building for Renaissance economies has been explored by Richard Goldthwaite in "The Florentine Palace as Domestic Architecture," *The American Historical Review,* 77 (1972), pp. 977–1012.

143. See Ch. 5.

144. At the behest of Baldassare Turini, the papal Datary, Leo X withdrew the parish of Pescia from the diocese of Lucca and raised it to a *prepositura* immediately subject to Rome. Despite repeated efforts by townspeople to make it a bishopric, this did not happen until 1728. The town was granted the status of "city" by Cosimo III in 1699. Cecchi and Coturri, *Pescia ed il suo territorio,* pp. 171, 178–79.

In Pescia one lives civilly, there is an infinite number of old families and six honored by having Knights of Santo Stefano; there are 50 doctors who exercise public functions in law, judgeships, and chancellorships in the states of Your Highness, and others in the government of the Church; there are many captains, three families with wealth of perhaps 50,000 scudi, more than ten with over 20,000 scudi, and many others who are well to do so that one can absolutely say that the inhabitants are comfortable.

The houses of Pescia are very good, the town is ornamented by a noteworthy Piazza, streets, gardens, and orchards, and the produce of this town as of this Vicarate consists of wheat, other grains, red and white wines and perfect Trebbiano wines, oil, chestnuts, vegetables and exquisite fruits of all kinds, and mulberry leaves, from which great quantities of silk are derived, which are so useful and necessary to the city of Florence; reckoning that from one year to the next the income comes to 100,000 scudi, and most of it comes from foreign states through the abundance of vegetables and oil which are continually sent there.[145]

The report was perhaps exaggerated in its praise, but Pescia did have a great deal to be proud of. From a small and backward agricultural center it had become an attractive, populated, and well-to-do town with a complex urban and agricultural economy. The authors could not foresee the levelling off that would occur in the 1620s or the catastrophe of 1631—a catastrophe that took place precisely because Pescia had become attractive to so many people and because its economy, now irrevocably linked to a larger network of trade, was more vulnerable than ever to outside pressures.[146] Specialization and commerce which were fundamental to

145. The description forms part of an undated request to make the town a bishopric, but on the basis of internal evidence, it is clear the document was written in 1617. The author refers to a synod "celebrato e stabilito sotto li 2 di giugno 1617 prossimo passato." ASF, *Miscellanea Medicea*, 322, ins. 9, "Informazione della Terra di Pescia e sua giurisdizione."

146. The economic crisis of 1619–22 that affected most of Europe ushered in Pescia's difficulties at this time. The disruption of European trade led to a temporary setback for the Florentine silk industry and this, in turn, had obvious repurcussions for Pescia's agricultural sector and population. See. R. Romano, "Tra xvi e xvii secolo una crisi economica: 1619–22," *Rivista storica italiana*, 74 (1964), 31–37.

the economic development of Pescia were also its Achilles' heel. While it lasted, however, Pescia's prosperity was brilliant, and the capital, both material and human, that was accumulated during the late Renaissance provided the basis for further development in the modern period.

4

Public Finances

Along with the benefits derived from new economic opportunities, there also came added responsibilities, particularly in the form of fiscal exactions by Florence, the city that had provided much of the stimulus for Pescia's economic growth. To what extent did these mitigate the rewards of economic development?

Two months after its submission to Florence, Pescia received a set of privileges defining its status within the Florentine dominion. The document referred to the town as a "commune" and to its inhabitants as *"vere populares"* of the district and *contado* of Florence.[1] This was more than legal rhetoric designed to conceal the de facto demise of medieval political institutions and freedoms. While becoming a Florentine dependent, Pescia as we have seen retained many of its self-governing functions. Nowhere is this more evident than in the realm of public finance where the local government had the right to collect taxes and dispose of public funds as it saw fit, subject always to the legal procedures prescribed by its own statutes and subject also to the payment of certain taxes imposed by the city of Florence. In other words, as long as it adhered to its own laws and paid Florence the prescribed taxes, Pescia was free to administer its own fisc.[2] If on the one hand this freedom was not total, on the other it was much broader than complete fiscal integration into the Florentine gov-

1. ASF, *Diplomatico*, Pescia, 14 April 1339.
2. A different interpretation of local autonomy with respect to public finances in rural Tuscany has been offered by Marvin Becker, *Florence in Transition*, 2:73–74.

ernment bureaucracy. To consider this realm of action, to seek to explain the sources of public revenue and the objects of public expenditure, is also to understand many of the factors that influenced the development of Pescia's economy and its relation with Florence.[3]

EXPENDITURES

Essentially the commune of Pescia had two kinds of expenditures—local payments for normal administration and transfer payments to Florence.[4] The latter took the form of labor services, payments in kind, gabelles, and direct taxes. During the course of the Renaissance both the relation between local and transfer payments and the size of total expenditures underwent considerable transformation. To interpret these changes it is necessary to examine Pescia's public finances in terms of regional and international perspectives, since the expenditures of Pescia, like those of other Italian communes in the Renaissance, were profoundly influenced by two phenomena. The first was the endemic warfare in early Renaissance Italy, which contributed to the rapid increase in Pescia's expenditures during the first century under Florentine domination, and whose abatement after the 1430s contributed to their decrease in the last half of the Quattrocento. The second was the general European inflation of the sixteenth century, which at Pescia, as elsewhere, contributed to the rise in governmental expenditures in the late Renaissance (see Appendices 6–8).[5]

3. The sources on which this fiscal analysis is based are discussed in Appendix 5.
4. In the parlance of modern public finance, transfers to Florence are not, strictly speaking, *expenditures* of Pescia but rather *revenues* of Florence. Since the sources for the transfers to Florence, however, cannot be identified separately (they were taken out of general revenues) and since they were entered as *uscite* in Pescia's budget, they are best treated as expenditures—which is what they were to the commune of Pescia.
5. Although a very precise measurement of the aggregate price level cannot be obtained for the Renaissance, studies by Giuseppe Parenti and several other scholars indicate that, after remaining unchanged throughout most of the fifteenth century, prices began to rise slowly at the end of the century and then doubled between 1500 and 1600. Giuseppe Parenti, *Prime ricerche sulla rivoluzione dei prezzi a Firenze* (Florence, 1939); Damsholt, "Some Observations on Tuscan Corn Prices, 1520–1630," 145–64.

Local Administration

During the first years under Florentine domination, payments for governmental salaries and routine administration accounted for most communal expenditures, since the privileges granted to Pescia exempted it from most transfer obligations to Florence. The statutes of 1339 and 1340 list seventeen categories of public office which were staffed by over one hundred fifty people, most of whom, such as the one hundred members of the city council, served without pay.[6] The *podestà*, a Florentine official whose salary was determined but not paid for by Florence, received by far the largest payment in town, amounting to 1600 lire annually.[7] The total of the other forty known salaries, including those of the priors, the captains and the council of the Parte Guelfa, the treasurer, the notary, and several messengers, came to barely one quarter that amount, 372 lire annually, and the expenditures for the remaining dozen or so minor officials together with routine expenses for the chancery and the maintenance of public property probably did not bring the total annual expenditures for local administration to over 2500 lire.[8]

Over the next seventy years annual expenditures for administration increased to approximately 4000 lire and remained at that level until the end of the fifteenth century, when they con-

6. BComPe, *Statuti 1339,* Bk. 1, R. 8, 10, 11, 12; Bk. 3, R. 6, 7, 8; *Statuti 1340,* Bk. 1.

7. The salary of the *podestà* was prescribed by Florence in the privileges accorded Pescia in 1339. The money was to pay not only for the *podestà*'s salary but for the salaries of his sizable staff, which was also prescribed accorded Pescia in 1339. The money was to pay not only for the *podestà*'s by Florence: "Et quod ipsi potestas et quilibet eorum habere et tenere secum debeant in dictis eorum offitiis infrascriptas familias . . . videlicet: potestas Piscie habeat et secum ducat unum bonum judicem, unum expertum notarium, unum sotium, duos damicellos, octo familiares, duos equos, et habeat pro suo et dicte sue familie et equorum, remuneratione et salario a dicto communi Piscie, per sex menses et de ipsius communis Piscie denariis et pecunia, libras octingentas florinorum . . ." ASF, *Diplomatico,* Pescia, 14 April 1339.

8. The six priors received 4 lire each for a two-month term of office, the six captains of the Parte Guelfa received 3 lire each for three months, the twenty members of the council of the Parte Guelfa 1 lire each for six months, the treasurer 6 lire for six months, the notary 40 lire for six months, and six messengers 2 lire each for six months. This amounts to an annual expenditure of 372 lire.

stituted two-thirds of total expenditures.[9] Since the only significant additions to the staff were the appointments of a doctor and a teacher of grammar, and since local salaries did not increase, the increased cost of local administration can be attributed primarily to increased contributions to the salaries of magistrates appointed by Florence. In the last half of the Trecento, Florence ordered Pescia to pay 1400 lire toward the salary of the vicar of the Valdinievole. By the second decade of the Quattrocento, the combined salaries of the vicar and the *podestà*, amounting to 2,750 lire, constituted approximately 70 percent of total administrative expenditures.[10] The total expenses for Florentine officials did not decrease even when the office of the *podestà* was abolished and his duties taken over by the vicar in 1424.[11] It appears, therefore, that during the first century and a half of Florentine domination the costs of local government remained relatively stable with the exception of an initial rise in costs due to expenditures for Florentine officials. This stability suggests that

9. Two kinds of sources have been used for estimating expenditures at this time, the first are the *Deliberazioni* of Pescia, and the second is volume 103 of the *Miscellanea Repubblicana*, ASF. This volume contains a register of the *Regolatori delle opere del contado e distretto*, dated 1419, in which these Florentine officials attempted to regulate the expenditures of all the towns in the Florentine dominion. The document is of particular interest both because it provides information on some of the administrative expenses of rural communes and because its very existence indicates the growing desire on the part of the Florentine government to centralize and regulate fiscal matters that had heretofore been left to the discretion of local officials. At the same time, when compared to actual expenditures recorded in the *Deliberazioni* during preceding years, the expenditures permitted by Florence reveal that above all else Florence went along with local practice in these matters. The *Deliberazioni* for the years before and after 1419 show that local salaries were determined without consulting Florence.

10. Total administrative expenditures as well as expenditures for the salaries of the vicar and the *podestà* are derived as follows: salary of vicar—1400 lire; *podestà*—1,350 lire; prior—144 lire; captains of the Parte Guelfa—56 lire; council of the Parte Guelfa—40 lire; chancellor—200 lire; treasurer—40 lire; messengers—150 lire. These recorded annual expenditures amount to 3,670 lire. Since there were other expenditures for which no accurate information is available, the actual total was probably closer to 4000 lire. ASPe, *Del.*, 11, fol. 171v; *Del.*, 18, fols. 108v, 258r, 281r; ASF, *Miscellanea Repubblicana*, 102.

11. ASPe, *Del.*, 20, fol. 79v. As compensation for his new duties the vicar now received 2,266 lire annually.

Table 4-1. Annual expenditures for local administration (in lire)

Year	Amount
1339–1350	2,500[a]
1400–1479	4,000[a]
1480–1489	4,263
1580–1590	10,927

[a] Estimate.

Sources: see text and Appendices 6–8.

the functions and scope of local government remained unchanged throughout the early Renaissance.

During the course of the sixteenth century, however, major transformations took place in local administration. Although administrative expenditures represented a smaller fraction of average annual expenditures than in the late fifteenth century, by the 1580s they averaged 10,927 lire annually, more than two and a half times the amount of the 1480s (see Table 4–1).[12] In part the larger cost of local administration may reflect the general inflation of the sixteenth century, which in Tuscany resulted in a doubling of prices.[13] Paper and ink for the chancery, wax for candles, building materials for the repair of public roads and buildings, all cost more by the end of the century. Yet, albeit limited, the information provided by the budgets of Pescia suggests that factors other than inflation were at work as well.

The first of these was the increased size of staff. Although our knowledge about the services, personnel, and clientele of this staff do not go beyond the information provided in the budgets, the expenditures recorded indicate a wider range of interests in the general welfare of the people and a broader conception of governmental functions. From the cradle to the grave the inhabitants of Pescia seem to have lived under the watchful eye of their government. Shortly after birth their names were entered in baptismal registers, which by the sixteenth century were kept at the expense of the city government. As children they received public instruction in grammar and mathematics from a staff that now included a teacher of abacus and two paid assistants as well

12. See Appendices 6–8 for more detailed information.
13. See n. 5.

as a teacher of grammar.[14] As adults their time was regulated by the keeper of the clock, and their food supply in times of emergency by the administrators of the grain supply. If they needed money they could borrow from the Monte di Pietà that was established in 1509.[15] If they fell ill they could avail themselves of the public doctor or the surgeon. And if the services of these public officials failed, they could find comfort in the knowledge that their mortal remains would be properly disposed of by the commune's grave digger.[16]

Undoubtedly less comfort was derived from public knowledge of the salaries received by some of these officials. For if the size of communal staff was a major factor in the rising costs of administration, another was the increased level of salaries. That of the chancellor, for example, rose from 200 lire in the late Quattrocento to 840 lire a century later; that of the teacher of grammar from 200 to 750 lire in the same time period.

In part these increases were related to inflation, but since the rise in the level of salaries was much greater than the rise in the general level of prices, the size of salaries in the late sixteenth cen-

14. We do not know the composition of the student body or the details of the educational curriculum, but in 1560 Giuliano di Lorenzo Ceci, the teacher, voiced the perennial teacher's complaint. He wrote in his diary, "prego Dio mi conceda gratia di poter far frutto et havere honore di questi scholari che vanno tutta via rincattivendo et peggiorando et manco rispetto si trova hoggi in loro che mai." BComPe, I.B.52, *Libbro di ricordi di Giuliano di Lorenzo Ceci*. Florentine evidence suggests that in that city the student body of schools ranged from the sons of small shopkeepers to patricians. Probably the same was true at Pescia, where the number of instructors was remarkably large for a population that ranged from 4000 to 6000 in the last half of the Cinquecento. For further information about education in the Renaissance see Christian Bec, *Les marchands ecrivains à Florence, 1375–1434* (Paris, 1967); A. Fanfani, "La preparation intellectuelle et professionelle à l'activité economique en Italie du XVe au XVIe siècle," *Le Moyen Age*, 57 (1951), 327–46; Richard Goldthwaite, "Schools and Teachers of Commercial Arithmetic in Renaissance Florence," *The Journal of European Economic History*, 1 (1972), 418–33.

15. Baldasseroni, *Istoria di Pescia*, p. 270.

16. The grave digger first appears in communal budgets in 1525, the teacher of mathematics in 1538, one assistant to the teacher of grammar is recorded in 1547, and by 1569 two assistants as well as a man in charge of recording baptisms are recorded as salaried staff. The doctor and the surgeon do not appear in the budgets until the 1570s.

tury can also be attributed to a growing professionalization of government services. As governmental activity grew in the sixteenth century, there must have been an increased need for full-time, competent, and highly literate officials to coordinate activities, maintain correspondence, keep track of growing expenditures, and engage in the general paperwork that accompanies bureaucratic activity. The budgets of Pescia show that, in contrast to the Quattrocento, the government as staffed by a larger number of permanent employees whose work, if the preparation and organization of the budget is any indication, was of a much higher quality than ever before. Probably because of their skills these trained officials commanded higher salaries than their predecessors. Then, as now, a skilled staff also meant a better paid staff.

To explain the level of expenditures for local administration in the Cinquecento therefore requires an awareness of the effects of inflation as well as an awareness of the growing professionalization of government services and the new importance attached to the role of government in local society. The last two developments were, moreover, inextricably related. The changed character of communal government helped to produce and was itself a product of an educated professional class. Although not much is known about the student enrollment in Pescia's schools, there can be little doubt that in providing for public instruction the government helped supply itself with an able and competent staff. Consequently, the development of a new type of administration was inseparable from the emergence of a more educated and literate public.

Transfer Payments to Florence

1. *Labor Services.* In his *History of Florence,* Niccolò Machiavelli attributed the ruin of Florence to reliance on mercenary armies. For centuries this view influenced the outlook of historians, who saw in the abolition of the citizen militia the decline of republican virtues and institutions. In recent decades scholars have developed new interpretations of the character and foundations of republican liberties in the Renaissance. But the belief still persists that after the third decade of the fourteenth century mercenary troops had come to replace the traditional militia

armies.[17] Certainly the growing territorial ambitions of Florence and other powerful Italian states resulted in changed methods of warfare. Having conquered its own *contado*, Florence turned to the conquest of more powerful and distant rivals, engaging in protracted campaigns that were ill suited to the abilities and expectations of a citizen army. This new warfare, however, did not render the militia obsolete. Rather, it altered its functions, and diminished its relative numerical importance. But in an age of ever expanding armies, this was hardly a consolation to the inhabitants of the Florentine district and *contado*, who were called upon to supply a growing number of soldiers for the Florentine army. To the towns of the Valdinievole the new warfare meant growing cash subsidies for the activities of mercenaries, the destruction of their houses and crops by marauding bands of *condottieri*, the requisition of their grain to feed Florentine troops, and the conscription of their male population into the Florentine army.

The introduction of mercenary soldiers did not abolish the medieval obligation of castle-guard. One form of communal expenditure for labor services exacted by Florence consisted of maintaining and staffing some of the fortifications in the Valdinievole. Despite vigorous protests from Pescia, in 1390 the town was ordered to select from among its inhabitants four men to guard the nearby fortress of Altopascio. Their salaries, determined by Florence, cost Pescia 696 lire each year. By 1437 Florence added the obligation of castle-guard over the newly acquired fortress of Montecarlo, which cost Pescia an additional 720 lire annually. Hence, by the late 1430s annual expenditures for castle-guard obligations had reached approximately 1400 lire.[18]

17. Becker, *Florence in Transition*, 2:73, 105. Daniel Waley's investigation into the composition of the Florentine army before mid-Trecento shows that earlier notions about the purely non-mercenary composition of the Florentine army were misleading. Yet Waley, like Renaissance humanists, claims that after mid-century the militia quickly becomes obsolete. Daniel Waley, "The Army of the Florentine Republic from the Twelfth to the Fourteenth Century," in *Florentine Studies*, Nicolai Rubinstein, ed. (London, 1968), pp. 70–108. A much needed revision of this notion has appeared in Michael Mallett's *Mercenaries and Their Masters: Warfare in Renaissance Italy* (Totowa, N.J., 1974).

18. BCatPe, *Memorie Galeotti*, pp. 131, 169; ASPe, *Del.*, 23, f. 260v. Payments for military labor services provided by Pesciatines have been dis-

It was not until the later part of the fifteenth century that this obligation was converted to a cash payment that was presumably included in the transfer of direct money taxes to Florence. Most likely the soldiers guarding the fortresses of the Valdinievole continued to be recruited from the area, but communal responsibility for providing the personnel had come to an end.

In addition to castle-guard, after mid-fourteenth century a new function developed for the militia—that of providing protection against the growing number of mercenaries employed by Florence and other Italian states. After the peace of Lombardy in 1387, for instance, Pescia was ordered to send twenty-five men into the Florentine army to help protect Florentine territory from dispersing mercenaries who had the bad habit of looting and plundering their way home. A similar request was made after signing a peace treaty with the Visconti in 1392.[19] Rather than replace the militia, mercenary armies thus created a new and important role for it.

A second function for the militia, in part also a reaction to the use of mercenary armies, was the prevention and suppression of uprisings in areas recently brought under Florentine domination. Mercenary armies had enabled Florence to conquer new territories but they were not suitable as long-term occupying forces. Both the expense they represented and the violence they engendered were worse than any problems of insurrection. As a result, troops from the *contado* and from older parts of the district were used to keep Florence in power in newly conquered areas. Pesciatine soldiers, for example, were stationed in Arezzo after its conquest, as well as at Pisa, Livorno, and other parts of the Florentine dominion.[20]

---

cussed as transfer payments rather than expenditures for local administration such as the *podestà*'s or vicar's salaries for two reasons. First, labor services were seldom performed at Pescia itself, and, second, it is doubtful these payments would have been made if Florence had not ordered them.

19. The Florentine government sent a letter to the vicar, stating: "Per cagione della pace che ssi ragiona in Lombardia potrebbe esse che quelle genti d'arme che sono di là passerebbono di qua e però vogliamo che tu faccia una scelta nel tuo vicariato di buoni fanti e balestrieri siche se bisogno fosse gli possiamo avere al tempo per riparo della decta gente." ASPe, *Del.*, 10, fols. 43r, 54r; BCatPe, *Memorie Galeotti*, p. 136.

20. The number of men and the length of their service is not usually known,

Campaigns for new territorial conquests as well as defensive wars against the imperialist ambitions of other Italian states provided a third function for the militia. Although mercenaries were of much greater importance, all the major Florentine campaigns in or near Tuscany during the Renaissance included troops from Pescia and from other parts of the Florentine state. These troops, captained by one or two constables from the town, served alongside mercenary troops but remained in separate units and were paid by their own local government according to rates prescribed by Florence.[21]

It is not possible to establish the exact number of men drafted each year nor the expense incurred for their salaries. The frequency with which troops were called and the dolorous pleas for relief suggest that in the closing decades of the fourteenth century Florence began to impose unprecedented demands upon the subject city. In April 1384, for example, Pescia was forced to supply sixty-three men in a contingent of three hundred from the Valdinievole. With an eligible male population of less than four hundred men, the exaction was a very heavy one. Despite requests that the obligation be reduced "because it would be excessively onerous to send such a large number," in the following months Florence was issuing orders for additional contingents.[22]

Whereas in the middle decades of the fourteenth century subject areas had to provide four to five men per 100 lire of their tax obligation to Florence, by 1387 they were asked for ten men per 100 lire. Moreover, these men were to be trained in the use of crossbows, and equipped in such a way as to "bring fame and fortune" to the city of Florence.[23] Such ambitious plans never

---

but ten were stationed, for example, in Arezzo in 1386, twenty-seven were sent to Pisa in 1418, and numerous other contingents can be found at other times and places. ASPe, *Del.*, 28, fol. 35v; *Memorie Galeotti*, p. 127 and *in passim*.

21. One such contingent served with the soldiers of the famous *condottiere* John Hawkwood. They were paid the customary salary of 8 soldi each per day. ASPe, *Del.*, 10, fols. 105v–106r.

22. ASPe, *Del.*, 9, fols. 26r–v, 64v, 95r.

23. Charles C. Bayley, *War and Society in Renaissance Florence* (Toronto, 1961), p. 35. In a letter to the vicar, dated February 1387, Florentine officials wrote: ". . . dobbiate avere scripti et perscripti per lo vostro rectore . . . al nostro uficio . . . de vostri huomeni che sieno buoni acti e sofficienti a operare il balestro; quello numero de balestrieri che

quite materialized. Of the fifty men sent to the battlefield by
Pescia in 1387, only ten were crossbowmen. Still, the cost of such
armies must have been staggering for so small a town, especially
because of the frequency with which they were called. The wars
against the Visconti and later against Pisa and Lucca continued
the heavy demands for military service past the last decade of
the fourteenth century and into the first forty years of the fifteenth. Almost every year except those immediately following
the peace with Naples in 1413 witnessed further requests for
troops. By 1436, when the Valdinievole had been thoroughly
plundered by Florentine mercenaries and the Lucchese troops
they were supposed to be fighting, Pescia was responsible for supplying sixty-four soldiers and two constables to the Florentine
army.[24]

Transfer payments to Florence in the form of labor services
would never again reach these levels for such prolonged periods
of time. The relative peace of the last half of the Quattrocento
reduced the demand for troops. Only the foreign invasions after
1494 and the war for the reconquest of Pisa in the late 1490s and
early 1500s produced a heavy demand for troops. Nevertheless,
at the height of such requests in the decade of the 1490s the cost
of supplying soldiers for the Florentine army amounted to 1,450
lire over a two-year period. This was less than one-tenth of the
town's total expenditures during those two years.[25]

Military service in the Florentine army did not constitute a
significant portion of Pescia's expenditures again until the closing
days of the republic. The final struggle in 1530 saw Pescia's war
expenditures rise to 7,240 lire, an amount equal to the annual

toccherà a ciascheduno di vuoi a ragione di dieci balestrieri per ciaschuno
centinaio di livre di vostro extimo." ASPe, *Del.*, 10, fol. 36v. Having
received the list of soldiers from the vicar, the officials again wrote to
him on August 7, 1387, stating: ". . . si debbano tucti essere forniti
d'uno balestro, una corrazina, una cerugliera e uno coltello accio che
quando gli volessimo vedere in persona tucti sieno per modo che a voi
n'eseguiti e al nostro magnifico comune fame e acrescimento sappiendo
che di subito e nostri signori ne vorranno vedere mostra." ASPe, *Del.*,
10, fols. 76v–77r.

24. ASPe, *Del.*, 10, fols. 44v–45r; *Del.*, 12, fol. 14r; *Del.*, 23, fols. 203v–204r.
25. See Appendix 7 for the years 1494 and 1495.

expenditures of Pescia's government in a normal year.[26] More important, however, is that such military expenditures ended after the establishment of the Medici principate.

The reorganization of the armed forces in Tuscany under Cosimo I represented a marked break with the past. Wishing to create a system that would no longer be dependent on unruly mercenaries or reluctant conscripted subjects, Cosimo and his descendants relied on volunteers from the Florentine dominion.[27] To induce men to serve, the grand dukes offered them tax exemptions in times of peace as well as good stipends on those rare occasions when they actually had to serve on active duty.[28] The vicarate of Pescia thus supplied the Florentine army with 862 men in 1547, 1,121 men in 1571, and 2,265 men in 1606.[29] The revenues for maintaining this growing number came from the direct taxes that the vicarate paid to Florence rather than from additional taxes collected for labor services as such. In this

26. Based on a comparison of annual expenditures for the years 1525–31; ASPe, *Saldi*, 684.
27. In a letter of 1548 regarding the new military regulations, Cosimo I wrote to the captains of the military companies: ". . . nelle bande non vogliamo nè intendiamo che da qui in avanti si descrivino se non quelle persone che ci vorrano voluntariamente entrare . . . ," cited in Jolanda Ferretti, "L'organizzazione militare in Toscana durante il governo di Alessandro e Cosimo I de' Medici," *Rivisita storica degli archivi toscani*, 2 (1930), 61. The cities of Florence and Pistoia, as well as a few other places of questionable loyalty, however, were excluded from any military service (*ibid.*).
28. Recruits enrolled in the military companies continued to live at home and served actively only in case of need. Training took place every few weeks when the recruits of a local area would meet for a day to practice various drills. Tax privileges for this service ranged from two-thirds' to total exemption for themselves and their fathers from all taxes imposed on their communities, except for gabelles and the salt tax. Recruits were generally eighteen to thirty years of age (*ibid.*, pp. 63, 70–75).
29. The men were divided into pikesmen and arquebuseers until 1606 when musketeers were added to the list. The rapid growth in the number of soldiers in the vicarate of Pescia, as in the rest of the state, is entirely related to the growth of these last two groups since the number of pikesmen actually declined. To help defray the cost of arming themselves Cosimo I provided a subsidy of 4 scudi to those who needed it to buy proper equipment. (An arquebus cost approximately 7 scudi in mid-sixteenth century.) *Ibid.*, p. 70.

way separate labor services were eliminated while the state provided itself at no extra cost to Florence with the best military protection it had had in centuries.

It appears then that transfer payments in the form of labor services grew rapidly during the first years under Florentine domination, reaching their peak in the closing decades of the fourteenth century and probably remaining at that level through the first four ·decades of the fifteenth century. During the next one hundred years both a more permanent peace and the conversion of some of these services into cash payments resulted in the almost complete disappearance of labor services as transfer payments to Florence. Their final demise came with the reorganization of military services under the Medici grand dukes in mid-sixteenth century.

2. *Payments in Kind.* A second type of payment, payments in kind, underwent similar changes—they were heaviest under the Florentine republic, especially in the late fourteenth and early fifteenth century, and all but disappeared with the establishment of the duchy. Payments in kind were of two sorts: lodging and food which subject areas had to provide to soldiers in the Florentine army who might be passing through; and grain shipments to Florence during times of widespread famine and scarcity.

The quartering of soldiers at local expense was a particularly odious obligation. It often involved not only the expenses for food consumed by the troops and their horses but the unofficial redistribution of property, through theft, in favor of the unwelcome visitors. In 1448 a mob of Pesciatines became so incensed at the behavior of one group of mercenaries who were quartered in the town that it murdered several of them before its fury was spent. When in 1503 two contingents of French horsemen, numbering 1,450 men, requested lodging and food, only the Florentine government's threat to execute Pescia's emissaries persuaded the town to comply.[30]

The strong hostility exhibited by subject areas to this obligation led to a search for a more equitable arrangement during the reign of Cosimo I. In 1545, the duke declared that henceforth the quartering of troops traveling through Tuscany be the responsi-

30. BCatPe, *Memorie Galeotti*, pp. 170, 194, 197-98.

bility of the state and that the money needed to pay for this be raised by the officials known as the Five of the Contado through assessments, proportional to ability to pay, levied on all the communities of the Florentine dominion.[31] No one town needed to bear the brunt of expenses any longer. The wider distribution of costs coupled with the infrequency with which troops of any sort passed through Tuscany after mid-sixteenth century made these payments both less visible and less onerous for the subject areas.

Grain shipments to Florence also ceased to be a problem. Under the Florentine republic, such requests often coincided with times of war and political instability, so that the size and frequency of these payments were largely related to the course of Florentine military entanglements. Consequently, like labor services and a number of other transfer payments, they were largest during the last decade of the Trecento and the early decades of the Quattrocento, and again temporarily during the French invasions and the last days of the republic. The grain scarcity of the winter of 1374–1375, compounded by the outbreak of war against the papacy the following spring, resulted in grain requisitions in the fall of 1375.[32] Similarly, the war against the Visconti in the early 1390s coincided with grain requisitions to feed the army in the summers of 1392 and 1393.[33]

The establishment of the duchy ended these requirements. In part this had to do with the ability of the Medici to resort to other procurement methods and also with the Florentine acquisition of Siena in 1557, which thereafter became the breadbasket of Tuscany.[34] Even during the famine crisis of the 1590s Pescia

31. ASF, *Senato de' 48*, 14, item 14, 10 October 1545.
32. ASPe, *Del.*, 7, fol. 196r.
33. ASPe, *Del.*, 12, fols. 52v–53r, 130r, 137r. Frequently payments in kind were made directly to the soldiers in the Florentine army. The war for the reconquest of Pisa at the end of the fifteenth century led to repeated demands that provisions be sent to the battlefield. A century and a half earlier, Pescia was sending six pack animals loaded with wine, bread, and grain to the troops fighting for the conquest of San Miniato. Expenditures for these payments, according to Galeotti, may have reached as much as 900 florins in 1396. BCatPe, *Memorie Galeotti*, pp. 112–13.
34. Already prior to its incorporation into the Florentine state, Siena was a major grain supplier. During the grain shortages of 1555–57, while the war for the conquest of Siena was taking place, Cosimo I increased the supply by means of massive imports from Sicily. Baldassare Licata, "Il problema del grano e delle carestie," in *Architettura e politica da*

was not forced to give up part of its harvest, but on the contrary was the recipient of grain sold by grand-ducal officials from the state warehouses.[35]

Thus despite the intensity of feeling aroused by payments in kind, they occurred only in the republican period and infrequently even then.[36] To be sure, inasmuch as Tuscany was not self-sufficient in grain, requisitions by Florence in times of scarcity, when local needs were also great, must have been a particularly severe burden. But in the course of almost three centuries they amounted to a very small share of total expenditures. The experience of Pescia thus supports the thesis, advanced by Enrico Fiumi, that the provisions policy of Florence was aimed at filling the needs created by emergency situations and was not part of a permanent policy to fleece the inhabitants of rural Tuscany out of the fruits of their labor.[37]

3. *Gabelles.* For most Italian cities in the Renaissance, indirect taxation was one of the principal sources of revenue. Pescia and Florence were no exceptions. The two cities classed a large number of impositions as gabelles: stamp taxes on contracts, taxes on the processing and sale of foodstuffs, import and export tariffs, and monopolies on the sale of certain commodities. Following its annexation of Pescia, Florence did not abolish the gabelles that had been established previously by local authorities. Neither did it interfere with the right of these authorities to continue regulating them. Florence did, however, incorporate Pescia into the

---

Cosimo I a Ferdinando I, Giorgio Spini, ed. (Florence, 1976), pp. 335–36; see also pp. 208–9 for a discussion of state grain policies in the last half of the sixteenth and early seventeenth century.

35. Archivio Capponi, IV.2.24. There are no systematic studies comparing grain prices when bought or sold by the Medici grand dukes or state officials as opposed to private individuals. It appears, however, that at Pisa and Siena state grain officials sold grain at less than the market price during times of scarcity and during years of plenty they sold off old stock at market prices and replaced it with new stock as needed. This suggests that the aim of these transactions was to stabilize prices rather than to squeeze consumers. Licata, "Il problema del grano," p. 406; Parenti, *Prezzi e mercato del grano a Siena (1546–1765)* (Florence, 1942), p. 54.

36. Between 1375 and 1400 approximately seven payments in kind are mentioned in the deliberations of the city council of Pescia.

37. Fiumi, "Sui rapporti economici fra città e contado," pp. 38–62.

gabelle system of the Florentine state, subjecting the town's inhabitants to a variety of indirect taxes imposed by the dominant city. Consequently, while Pescia's gabelles continued to be a source of communal revenues, Florentine gabelles collected at Pescia became a source of communal expenditure.

Without doubt the most onerous gabelle imposed by Florence, and the one which aroused the most opposition, was the gabelle on salt. It forced the community to buy a given quantity of salt at a given price from Florentine tax farmers.[38] To the great displeasure of these tax farmers, Pescia was exempt from the salt gabelle as from most others during the first years under Florentine rule.[39] But by the 1370s the salt tax was already being levied and the amount probably grew over the next half century. In 1404, Pescia was purchasing 400 staia of salt annually at 1400 lire.[40] Although this was less than one-tenth of the average an-

38. Since both the quantity and the price were established by Florence, the salt gabelle, despite its name, was really a form of direct tax.

    The officials of Pescia paid the farmer of the Florentine salt gabelle the required amount and then hired a local contractor to transport the salt from Empoli, where Florentine salt was mined. Once the salt was procured, the government of Pescia appointed an official to sell it to all the "mouths" of the city in quantities and at prices established by the city council. A *bocca*, or mouth, was any inhabitant at least seven years old. Realizing the futility of attempting to collect revenues from an area that had been so devastated by decades of war, Florentine officials granted a three-year exemption from all direct taxes and gabelles with the exception of the gate gabelle of Florence: "set considerantes quod predicta communia et quodlibet eorum fuerunt jam diu in maxima guerra et pessimo statu, dederunt dictis tribus communibus . . . privilegium et immunitatem, quod hinc ad tre annos proxime venturos non teneantur nec cogi possint per commune Florentie . . . a dicto communi, solvere aliquam gabellam impositam vel imponendam, excepta gabella portarum civitatis Florentie." Guasti and Gherardi, *Capitoli*, 65, pp. 128–31, 14 April 1339.

39. The treaty of 1344, extending the original immunity from taxes, was prompted by complaints from the Valdinievole towns about the behavior of the Florentine tax farmers: "Quod ipsa comunia [Pescia, Buggiano, Uzzano] et homines et persone ipsorum comunium molestantur et gravantur pro solutione gabelle salis civitatis Florentie ab emptoribus ipsius gabelle . . ." BComPe, *Statuti 1340*, unnumbered folio.

40. ASPe, *Statuti*, 4, unnumbered folio. In other parts of the Florentine *contado* and district both the prescribed quantity and the price more than doubled in the last quarter of the fourteenth century. De la Roncière, "Indirect Taxes," pp. 158–61.

nual communal expenditures during these years, it was a considerable sum, amounting to approximately 14.7 soldi per capita.[41] Despite frequent pleas for relief, both the amount of salt and its price increased further in 1428. The town was now purchasing 446 staia at a cost of 1600 lire.[42] While delegations continued to be sent to Florence to protest and payments were constantly in arrears, complaints at the local level reached such a pitch that the city council asked the priors to consider petitions for individual exemptions and to reduce or abolish payments in extreme hardship cases.[43] The total annual expenditure for salt, however, appears to have remained relatively unchanged until 1442, when the obligation was reduced to 260 staia, thereby silencing further complaints about the onerous nature of the tax.[44]

Not much is known about the salt tax in the course of the next century, an indication that perhaps it was no longer a formidable burden. Indeed, when it comes to our attention again, in 1538, the complaints come from Florentine officials who claimed that the inhabitants of the Florentine dominion were buying salt outside the Florentine state instead of from Florentine officials, thereby causing great injury to the treasury.[45] The matter was

41. With this amount one could buy enough grain to feed one person for 22 days.

42. Pescia purchased its quota of salt in two installments, one in March and one in September. The annual quantity and the price is based on the purchase made in March 1428. The annual assessment per mouth, based on the assessment made by the officials of Pescia in March, was between 30 and 35 soldi. In addition, a number of catasto declarations show that each mouth was assessed between 33 and 35 soldi annually. ASPe, *Del.*, 21, fols. 176r–176v; ASF, *Catasto*, 258, fols. 43, 69, 89.

43. ASPe, *Del.*, 12, fol. 81v; *Del.*, 17, fol. 109r; *Del.*, 21, fol. 37r.

44. In 1432 Pescia's salt obligation was reduced to 350 staia, but the prescribed purchase price per pound established by local officials in order to pay the Florentine tax farmer suggests that the annual cost to the town was 1500 lire. Although the cost of salt in 1442 is not known, the absence of pleas for more relief suggests that it constituted a genuine reduction. ASPe, *Del.*, 22, fols. 214r–214v, 267r; *Del.*, 23, fol. 70r; Repetti, *Dizionario*, 4:119.

45. ". . . Essendo venuto a notitia del magistrato loro [Otto di Pratica] come li sudditi del dominio fiorentino non solo non levano il sale che sono tenuti levare della città ma vanno a comprarlo fuora del dominio fiorentino, et considerando il danno che reccha et recherebbe al principe et alle sue entrate . . ." 16 November 1538; ASF, *Pratica Segreta*, 156, fol. 158v.

Table 4-2. Annual salt tax

Year	Population	Amount of salt (in staia)	Salt payment (in lire)	Per capita salt payment (in soldi)
1404	1,900	400	1,400	14.7
1428	1,800	446	1,600	17.7
1550	4,742	580	6,042	25.5
1556	4,428	530	5,521	24.9

Source: see text.

straightened out in due course and by 1550 Pescia was assessed at 580 staia costing 6,042 lire. Both the amount and the price were reduced in 1556 to 530 staia and 5,521 lire because of a slight decline in population caused by the war with Siena.[46] On a per capita basis, the tax was reduced from 25.5 to just under 25 lire. In short, in nominal prices the inhabitants of Pescia were paying about 40 percent more in mid-sixteenth century than they were one hundred years earlier. This relatively small increase in the tax contrasts markedly with the growing prosperity and consequent ability of townspeople to pay, as well as with the much larger rise in the general level of prices, which saw the price of wheat go up from about 20 to 70 soldi in the same period.

Most of the other gabelles imposed by Florence on the inhabitants of Pescia were light. Unlike the salt tax, they were levied by Florentine tax farmers directly on individual transac-

46. According to a report made to the Pratica Segreta, the population of Pescia in 1550 was 4,742. At that time the town was assessed at 580 staia priced 10 l. 8 s. 4 d. per staio. In 1556, however, the population was down to 4,428 and Pesciatine officials attributed the decline both to war-related deaths and the absence of foreign residents due to trade disruptions. They consequently asked for and received a reduction in the salt tax. It is interesting to note that in considering the request, the Pratica took into account that one of the reasons for which Pescia had fallen into arrears in its salt purchases was that the poor were buying their salt in Lucchese territory where the price was lower. To remedy this in the future the Pratica ordered that henceforth Pescia distribute the salt to each bocca rather than sell it to whoever should want it, as had been recent practice. The Pratica was aware that this measure was regressive and would be hated by the poor. ASF, Pratica Segreta, 3, ins. 3, 29, 42.

tions and commodities. They therefore constitute involuntary transfer payments to Florence by the townspeople even though they do not figure in the communal finances. The amount of these payments is not known, but they were probably very small inasmuch as Florentine legislation exempted Pescia from many gabelles and those that were imposed must have been difficult to collect.

The system of gabelles imposed by Florence can best be understood in terms of Florentine commercial policy toward its subject cities. For more than two centuries Florence strove to liberalize trade within the Florentine state and to create an integrated regional economy within the Valdinievole. Although it did not choose to abrogate most restrictions on trade imposed by its dependent cities, it certainly encouraged them to do so and it set an example in this direction by lowering or abolishing many of its own gabelles.[47]

Because of the economic plight of the Valdinievole, the treaty of 1339 stipulated that for three years, Pescia, Buggiano, and Uzzano were subject only to the gate gabelle, an exemption that was extended for several more years in 1344. By 1353 all Florentine prohibitions on the trade of food commodities between the Valdinievole and the rest of the Florentine state were abolished.[48] Eighteen years later all Florentine gabelles were removed from products entering the Valdinievole regardless of origin and from all exports of local commodities irrespective of their destination. This arrangement was confirmed several times in the

47. Florentine attempts to establish a free trade policy in Tuscany actually preceded the incorporation of the Valdinievole into the Florentine state. Clauses regarding the protection of merchants and exemption from taxes, especially in the Valdinievole, were included in a treaty between Florence, Lucca, Pistoia, Prato, and Volterra, signed in February 1282; see Arias, *I trattati commerciali della repubblica fiorentina*, pp. 409–10. In 1333, restrictions on agricultural trade between Pistoia and parts of the Valdinievole were removed; see Herlihy, *Pistoia*, p. 160. In addition, in 1422, all Florentine gabelles on products originating in the Valdinievole were abolished; see n. 49. Finally, in 1475, Florence encouraged the officials at Pisa to abolish indirect taxes on wine, oil, and other agricultural commodities of the Valdinievole. The rest of the dominion was urged to follow suit shortly thereafter. ASF, *Diplomatico*, Pescia, 1 April 1475; 1 June 1475. Florentine efforts to revitalize rural trade and markets are also discussed in de la Roncière, *Florence*, bk. 3, pt. 3, ch. 1.

48. Guasti, *Capitoli*, 2:33.

course of the next two centuries, remaining the legal basis of trade relations between Pescia and the ruling city.[49] Both the Florentine and the Pesciatine government might intervene on occasion to prohibit the transport of certain agricultural products from Pescia to other parts of the Florentine state or to areas outside of Florentine control, but these were only temporary measures passed in times of crisis, especially during years of famine or crop failure. Both governments recognized that these were in violation of joint treaties and resorted to them with great reluctance.[50]

In mid-sixteenth century this free trade policy came under review for the first time as part of a Tuscan-wide fiscal reorganization program initiated by Cosimo de' Medici. On November 26, 1545, Cosimo temporarily lifted all trade privileges and gabelle exemptions granted to subject areas. This measure was to remain in effect for three years while ducal officials studied and modified the previous agreements. In the meantime, inhabitants of communities like Pescia were required to keep records of all their trading activities, on which gabelles would be levied at the end of the study period.[51] At Pescia this occurred in 1547, when most

49. ASF, *Pratica Segreta*, 168:357–58. Hearing complaints of abuses by local officials, in 1423 the Florentine government ordered that "per le cose che nascono in dette provincie [provincie di Valdarno di sotto et di Valdinievole] a lloro fu lecito et possino quelle conducere a qualunche parte et luoghi dove vorranno senza quello che al comune di Firenze o vero ad alcuno suo officiale ghabellieri o pasiaggieri dovessino paghare alcuna ghabella, passaggio o diritto." ASF, *Diplomatico*, Pescia, 21 January 1422. A confirmation of these privileges made in 1484, adds: "Item, che la facultà del condurre et mettere nelle loro terre mercantie et cose per loro exercitio et uso senza alcuna gabella sia ferma et sia loro observata." *Pratica Segreta*, 158:360–71.

50. In 1374, for example, the Pesciatine government forbade the export of all grain and foodstuffs except wine from Pesciatine territory for one year. The prohibition noted that this was contrary to previous agreements with Florence but justified the action on grounds that it was an emergency. ASPe, *Del.*, 7, fol. 24v.

51. "Che per virtù della presente Provisione . . . tutte le exentioni dalle gabelle di robe et mercantie di quelle Comunità che l'hanno pe tempi obtenuti . . . s'intendino essere e sieno casse e annullate . . . talchè l'effetto sia che tanto esse Comunità, quanto li suoi Huomini, e persone sieno obligate al pagamento delle gabelle come li non esentionati in tutto e per tutto . . . per anni tre proximi futuri da hoggi: e talmentechè l'effetto sia, che durante il tempo di detti tre anni le prenarrate Com-

of the old privileges were restored with one major change. Henceforth, the duke could impose tariffs and prohibit the import or export of whatever commodities he wished.

What effect did this measure have on Pesciatine trade? Local officials in 1566 complained that from the time the new order was put into effect ". . . diverse prohibitions and innovations, and diverse annoyances, orders, and exactions have been pursued by Your Excellency [Cosimo] and your Magistrates, with much expense and inconvenience."[52]

Yet the record suggests that in actual practice the restrictions on trade were less drastic than local officials claimed. Between 1547 and 1566 Pesciatines received permission to sell their wine and oil freely each year without gabelle payments or export prohibitions.[53] After 1566 the policy remained basically unaltered except that records were to be kept on the size of the olive harvest so that the duke might limit the quantity of exports in years of scarcity.[54] Again, however, the general practice from 1566 through the 1620s was free trade.

Somewhat more restrictive was the policy toward grain. Whereas fruits and vegetables were allowed to be exported without any gabelles or restrictions of any sort, the grain trade was more frequently regulated because it was the basic component of people's diet and shortages might have serious political repercussions. During Cosimo I's reign the years of dearth were few both because the population of Tuscany was just beginning to recover from the losses incurred in the 1520s and because the conquest of Siena in 1557 brought to the Florentine state a regular and plentiful supply of grain. Hence there were few years in which the state intervened in the market to ensure supplies of grain

---

munità, li loro Huomini, e persone non le possino godere ne anche ne sieno prive, ma sieno . . . posti debitori di quello che l'harebbe a pagare di gabelle ne libri che di sotto si diranno . . . ," Provvisione, 26 November 1545, Cantini, *Legislatione Toscana*, 1, pp. 332–36.

52. ASF, *Pratica Segreta*, 7, ins. 84.

53. "Et quanto alla tratta del vino et olio fu prohibita loro, con questo che ogni anno venissero a supplicarne alle E.V.I., la quale atteso, che'l vino et olio di Pescia non vene qua et non serve la città, ogni anno l'ha concessa loro per decreto de' suoi Magnifici Consiglieri" (*ibid.*). This statement suggests that the 1560 export prohibition on oil did not apply to Pescia. See p. 90.

54. *Ibid.*

and to legislate prices. Such intervention became more frequent in the 1590s when a series of disastrous harvests acting on a population that had been growing for more than half a century, produced a famine crisis of very large magnitude in most of Italy. Grand Duke Ferdinand I resorted to a variety of mechanisms to ameliorate the situation, among them export prohibitions, limits on the amount of individual grain purchases, restrictions on sales to certain market places, and fixing of prices. These measures, however, were lifted as soon as the grain situation improved because they were too difficult and expensive to maintain and simply unneeded in normal years.[55]

Without doubt the most important change in Pesciatine gabelle payments occurred in the area of sericulture. Beginning in mid-sixteenth century a series of gabelles and export prohibitions, clearly designed to favor the Florentine silk cloth industry vis-à-vis foreign competition, were placed on silk-related commodities. The Florentine government forbade the export of silk worms and unbroken cocoons. It also imposed tariffs on the export of broken cocoons, silk floss, and raw silk. In 1545 the tariffs on raw silk amounted to approximately 8 percent of the price of high quality raw silk (seta leale) and 16 percent of the price of lower quality silk (seta doppia). By 1600 they had increased to 10 percent and 22 percent respectively. One final measure, enacted in 1580, forbade the export of all thrown silk.[56]

These measures probably enriched the grand-ducal treasury and had a negative impact on the expansion of Pesciatine sericulture, but obviously not enough to keep this area of the economy from growing. In 1566 Pescia complained that the gabelles on raw silk exports dampened foreign demand, creating a local glut in supplies which in turn reduced the price Pesciatines could

55. Licata, "Il problema del grano," pp. 335–419. The contraband grain trade flourished despite repeated government threats to lawbreakers. It often led to the creation of complex organizations, involving complicity by grand-ducal officials. Ibid., pp. 368–69.

56. In 1545 the tax on seta leale was 18 soldi per libbra. The tax on seta doppia was 13 soldi per libbra. By 1580 the tax on seta leale was 2 lire per libbra, and the tax on seta doppia was 30 soldi per libbra. ASF, Miscellanea Medicea, fol. 994 vecchio. For a discussion of the price of silk in the sixteenth century, see Chapter 3. Only in 1560, a year of extreme scarcity, was the export of raw silk prohibited. The export of silk cocoons and floss was prohibited only in 1577.

obtain from Florentine buyers. Grand-ducal officials countered
that all silk producers, both foreign and domestic, faced lower
prices that year, an argument that may have been correct but did
not invalidate the basic charge that any export tariff reduced the
competitive advantage of Pesciatine silk abroad.[57]

We would expect that the export prohibitions on thrown silk
also had undesirable results for the Pesciatine economy. Yet the
introduction of silk throwing mills occurred after the prohibition was put into effect, suggesting either that demand was so
high that it was still profitable to go into this activity despite restrictions or that the law was not enforced effectively.

There is some evidence that the latter was indeed the case. A
law of 1652 states that the gabelles and export prohibitions of
1580 were still in effect "but it being well known that the said
ordinance was being ignored for a long time," it was necessary
to publish it again.[58] The rugged mountains of the Valdinievole,
the distance from Florence, and the proximity to the border with
Lucca made smuggling an attractive alternative among the en-
terprising merchants of the valley. To the extent that gabelles
posed a serious threat to Pescia's economy and the prosperity of
its people they could not be enforced effectively. Florentine gabelles then were not a major source of expenditure for the government or a burden on the inhabitants of Pescia.

4. *Direct Taxes.* A final form of transfer payments to Florence,
and by far the most important, was direct taxes. These took a
variety of forms but followed mostly the same pattern in the
course of the Renaissance; namely, they increased rapidly during
the war-torn century that followed Pescia's annexation to the
Florentine dominion and either decreased or disappeared entirely thereafter until the effects of the price revolution reversed
the trend once more.

The threat of war with the Visconti in 1353, and the consequent need for new sources of revenue to finance its military activities led Florence to impose the first direct tax on the towns
of the Valdinievole. Calling them to rally behind it as behooved
prosperous children whose parents were in need, Florence ordered them to pay 5,588 lire each year, of which Pescia's share

57. ASF, *Pratica Segreta*, 7, ins. 84.
58. ASF, *Miscellanea Medicea*, fol. 994 vecchio.

Table 4–3. Annual ordinary tax obligation to Florence, 1353–1600

Years	Amount
1353	f.380
1376–1405	f.649[a]
1406–1415	f.756[a]
1416–1434	f.652[a]
1435–1472	f.300 di suggello
1473–1541	f.300 larghi
1542–1630	f.332 di moneta

[a] 1 florin = 3 *l.* 13 *s.* 4 *d.*

Sources: ASPe, *Del.,* 8, fol. 1771; ASF, *CC,* 1–21; ASF, *Monte,* 1090–94.

was 1,294 lire, approximately 380 florins.[59] Once established, this tax, known as the ordinary tax, became a permanent feature of the fiscal relations between Pescia and Florence. By 1376 it was increased to 649 florins annually, and it remained at that level until November 1405 when it was increased to 755 florins (see Table 4–3).[60] Both of these increases, like the initial imposition of the tax, were related to the rising expenditures and debts occasioned by war.[61]

The curtailment of military involvements and expenditures by Florence between 1414 and 1424 resulted in a slight reduction of Pescia's ordinary tax, but no significant reductions occurred until 1435, when it was fixed at 300 florins. It was more than coincidence that this reduction took place shortly after Cosimo de' Medici's accession to power. Rising discontent with Florentine taxes among the towns of the district had already led to re-

59. ". . . dignum est quod filius in prosperitate existens parenti in necessitatibus suis iuxta posse auxilium prestet. . . ." Guasti, *Capitoli,* 2:30.

60. ASPe, *Del.,* 8, fol. 90v; ASF, *CC,* 20, fol. 290r.

61. The first increase was part of a movement to obtain a larger share of revenues from the Florentine countryside to finance the war against the papacy, a war that cost Florence 2,500,000 florins; Becker, *Florence in Transition,* 2:188–89. The second increase, occurring at a time when other forms of direct taxation were also growing rapidly, was related to the rising expenditures caused by two wars against the Visconti and a costly campaign to bring Pisa under Florentine domination. For some of the war related expenditures of Florence in the early fifteenth century see Molho, *Public Finances,* pp. 10, 61.

volts in Volterra and Arezzo. Many towns, including Pescia, had
not paid their taxes in years. Between 1428 and 1435 Pescia's
payments to Florence for the ordinary tax averaged 187 florins
annually rather than the stipulated 652. Trying to collect these
taxes could only aggravate discontent and lead to revolts that
would damage Cosimo's efforts to consolidate his power and
popularity within the Florentine state. Hence, Pescia's debt of
3,530 florins for the ordinary tax was reduced to 812 florins pay-
able over a period of ten years.[62]

With few exceptions, after 1435 the size of Pescia's ordinary
tax payments remained virtually unchanged. The first modification occurred in 1473 when Florence demanded that the 300
florin tax be paid in fiorini larghi rather than fiorini di suggello,
thereby effecting a 20 percent annual increase in the tax obligation. The second occurred between 1494 and 1510 when Pescia,
burdened with increased war expenditures and perhaps taking
advantage of the weakened position of Florence after the French
invasion, began to default on its payments. By 1510 its debt to
Florence reached 1,422 florins, which meant that in effect average annual expenditures for the ordinary tax between 1494 and
1510 had amounted to only 211 florins as compared to the 300
florins obligation. Two-thirds of the debt, however, was repaid
by 1512, and the rest was cancelled.[63] The final modification in
ordinary tax payments occurred in 1542 when the obligation was
raised to 332 fiorini di moneta, the level at which it remained
through the 1630s.[64]

To recapitulate, ordinary tax payments increased rapidly in
the late fourteenth and early fifteenth century, doubling between
1353 and 1405. During the next twenty years payments were
somewhat lower, but the most significant reduction took place in
1435 when as a result of Cosimo's accession to power and the resumption of peace they returned to their mid-fourteenth century
level. With few adjustments they remained at that level until the
end of the sixteenth century. The pattern underscores the importance of the effects of war upon the fiscal relations between the
two cities during the first hundred years of Florentine domination and the importance of inertia in the period that followed.

62. ASF, *Monte*, 1096, fol. 305; 1098, fol. 24.
63. ASF, *Monte*, 1101, fol. 90.
64. ASF, *Monte*, 1106, fols. 91, 302.

A 20 percent increase in 1473 and an 11 percent increase in 1542 make a remarkably stable record for such a long period of time.[65]

A similar pattern was followed by the lance tax, a payment made for the support of the Florentine army, and first imposed at Pescia in 1386, when the costs of war against Arezzo led Florence to seek new sources of revenue.[66] Initially, Pescia's lance payments were 251 florins annually, but by 1406 they had increased to 457 florins.[67] After a brief interruption between 1409 and 1412 they were reintroduced but never again at the high rates of the first years of the Quattrocento. The annual obligation was fixed at 200 florins between 1413 and June 1417, and thereafter was reduced to 150 florins until 1434.[68] As with ordinary tax payments, however, Pescia's lance payments between 1428 and 1435 were considerably in arrears, averaging 103 florins annually rather than the stipulated 150 florins. In this case also, two-thirds of the debt was cancelled and the lance obligation was reduced to 60 florins, the level at which it remained until 1473 when it was phased out.[69]

Another kind of military payment, also phased out by the last quarter of the fifteenth century, was the payment for the salaries of soldiers sent by Florence to guard Pescia's fortifications. In 1432 when Pescia's officials were trying to reduce their tax obligations, they claimed that since 1353 the salaries of these soldiers cost the town 3400 lire annually.[70] By the 1470s the budgets of

65. This is true even if we take into account the higher value of the florin with respect to silver-based currency (lire) in the sixteenth century. When expressed in lire the size of the ordinary tax payment increased steadily after 1435. The reason was that the lira was gradually devalued with respect to the florin. In 1435 one florin was worth 4 lire. By the 1590s it was worth 10 lire. The exchange rates used by the Florentine government to compute Pescia's ordinary tax payments were actually below this market rate, so that Pescia's annual obligation in 1435 was 1,512 lire and by the 1590s it had reached 2400 lire. ASPe, *Saldi,* 7.
66. ASPe, *Del.,* 9, fols. 75r, 77v, 169r; ASF, *CC,* 3, fol. 411v.
67. ASF, *CC,* 13, fol. 302v; ASF, *Monte,* 1090, fol. 91.
68. ASF, *Monte,* 1092, fol. 169; 1093, fol. 92; 1098, fol. 24.
69. ASF, *Monte,* 1103, fol. 273; 1096, fol. 322; 1098, fol. 24.
70. BCatPe, *Memorie Galeotti,* p. 161. My own estimate comes to 3100 lire and is derived as follows: (1) the annual salaries of the two castellans in 1416 totaled 400 lire; (2) in 1426 one of the fortresses was manned by six soldiers (in addition to the castellan) who were paid 9 *s.* each per day. Assuming that the two fortresses at Pescia were guarded by six sol-

Table 4–4. Annual lance tax obligation, 1386–1472

Years	Amount
1386–1392	f.251[a]
1393–1396	f.376
1397–1405	f.400
1406–1408	f.457
1413–1417	f.200
1417–1434	f.150
1435–1472	f.60 di suggello

[a] Before 1435 1 florin = 3 *l.* 13 *s.* 4 *d.*

Sources: ASF, *CC,* 4–28; ASF, *Monte,* 1090–101.

Pescia make no mention of these kinds of payments. Since soldiers under Florentine command still guarded the town as well as the other fortifications in the Valdinievole, their salaries were paid presumably by Florentine officials from the general revenues of the Florentine state.

By mid-sixteenth century, the system of funding local defense operations became more decentralized. The motives behind this action were related to greater administrative efficiency and to the belief that subject populations would consider taxes fairer if the revenues collected were used in the region. Accordingly, each town of the Valdinievole contributed a stipulated amount directly to the vicar. He in turn used the funds to pay for the maintenance of local fortifications, the salaries of the soldiers guarding them, the maintenance of roads, and the general upkeep of the province.[71] To be sure only some of these expenditures were for strictly military purposes. The maintenance of roads and bridges served a useful non-military function as well. By the 1580s expenditures for local fortifications and their personnel came to over 3000 lire annually. This represented half of all

---

diers each, that the belltower was guarded by three, and that all the soldiers were paid for 365 days per year, the total annual pay of fifteen soldiers is 2700 lire. To this is added the 400 lire paid to the castellans, totaling 3100 lire. ASPe, *Del.,* 17, fol. 108v; 20, fol. 110r.

71. As opposed to the companies of soldiers that constituted the Florentine army, the soldiers that guarded the fortifications were paid salaries rather than compensated by tax exemptions; Ferretti, "L'organizzazione militare," 2:70.

transfer payments made for provincial expenditures and almost one-third of the average annual expenditures of Pescia (see Appendix 8). But most importantly, the amount was about the same as that paid for garrisons in the 1430s so that in real terms the expenditures for Pescia's fortifications were half of what they had been in the fifteenth century.

A final form of direct taxation was special taxes, called *straordinarie,* imposed with a frequency that belies their name during the first century of Florentine rule. Although the sources allow for only a crude estimate it seems that expenditures for this purpose were at their highest between the late 1380s and 1430, when other forms of taxation were also at their peak.[72] Of twenty special taxes recorded in over two centuries, only three were imposed before 1389 and only one after 1430. The imposition of these taxes generally coincides with years of heavy military expenditures by Florence as it fought wars against Milan, Pisa, and Lucca.

If Pescia's obligations and actual payments reflect the trend of the entire district, and there is no reason to suppose that they did not, special taxes must have been unprecedented in frequency and size especially in the 1390s when eight of them were levied. Between 1396 and 1401 alone, the district paid over 93,000 florins in five special taxes.[73] This accounted for approximately one-fifth of the total transfer payments to Florence made by both the entire district and *contado* in that period.[74]

During the first years of the fifteenth century Pescia's special

---

72. The first reference to a special tax at Pescia occurs in 1375 when the town contributed 2400 lire to the tribute money with which Florence hoped to persuade John Hawkwood not to lay waste to the countryside; ASPe, *Del.,* 8, 9 December 1375. The following year a tax of 1000 florins was levied on the Valdinievole. Although Pescia's share of this obligation is not known, the burden was probably distributed among the towns of the vicarate in the same proportion as the ordinary tax, making Pescia's share 21 percent of the total, or 210 florins; ASPe, *Del.,* 8, 18 May 1376. A third special tax, amounting to 1100 lire was levied in 1384. Thus, compared to later years such impositions are rare before mid-1380s; ASPe, *Del.,* 9, fol. 77v.

73. A total of 12,841 florins was collected in 1396 (ASF, *CC,* 13, fol. 368v); 9,368 florins in 1397 (ASF, *CC,* 13, fol. 372r); 25,738 florins in 1399 (ASF, *CC,* 14, fols. 103v–207v, 368r); 38,211 florins in 1400 (ASF, *CC,* fols. 201r–205r, 368v); 7,145 florins in 1401 (ASF, *CC,* 16, fol. 368v).

74. Molho, *Public Finance,* p. 29.

tax payments to Florence probably averaged 252 florins annually.[75] This increased to 468 florins annually between 1407 and
1410 and after a brief respite from all special taxes settled back
to 268 florins between 1413 and 1416.[76] The need to finance renewed military efforts against Milan and Lucca in the 1420s also
resulted in the imposition of special taxes. In 1427, despite pleas
for relief, Pescia was ordered to pay 282 florins annually for a
period of five years.[77] The tax was paid almost in full, but as we
have seen, this was done at the expense of the ordinary and the
lance taxes, which went mostly unpaid during this period. The
last special tax expenditures took place in the 1440s when a tax
of 380 florins annually was levied for five years.[78] Thereafter, the
expenditures for special taxes like a number of other transfer
payments to Florence ceased to be of great significance.

To sum up, after a brief moratorium on all direct tax obligations following the conquest by Florence, Pescia's expenditures
for the payment of direct taxes rose rapidly until the second
decade of the Quattrocento and remained at that level until
1434. In little more than fifty years direct taxes increased more
than five-fold. Depending on the size of special taxes imposed,
direct payments fluctuated between 5,971 lire and 9,260 lire annually.[79] This trend began to be reversed in the 1430s when the

75. In June 1402 the vicar of the Valdinievole was ordered to collect 3000
    florins from the towns in his jurisdiction; *Memorie Galeotti,* p. 142. In
    1404 the Valdinievole was taxed 1500 florins (ASPe, *Statuti,* 4, unnum-
    bered folio). In 1406 a third tax was levied on the Valdinievole for 1500
    florins (*Memorie Galeotti,* p. 145). The estimate of Pescia's tax is based
    on the assumption that the town's obligation was 21 percent of the total.
76. ASF, *CC,* 22, fol. 311r; 25, fols. 30v, 41v; 26, fols. 23v, 29v.
77. ASF, *Monte,* 1093, fol. 337. In September 1428, a delegation from Pescia
    was sent to the officials of the Monte to ask for a tax reduction, "quod
    homines comunes Piscie sint in maximis angustiis et quod in dicta terra
    non est prestande fenerator et non possit remanere ad mutuandum."
    ASPe, *Del.,* 21, fol. 166r.
78. ASPe, *Del.,* 24, fols. 250r, 255r.
79. These sums are based on the lowest and the highest transfer payments
    made between 1407 and 1430, years when accurate information about
    special taxes was available. The sums include payment of soldiers
    guarding Pescia's fortifications, and are derived as follows: (1) in 1411
    Pescia paid 3100 lire as payment for soldiers and 756 florins for the
    ordinary tax; using an exchange rate of 3 *l.* 13 *s.* 4 *d.* per florin the total

ordinary and the lance taxes were reduced by half, and payments were no longer required for the local garrison sent by Florence. By the 1480s expenditures for direct tax payments were down to an average of 1,930 lire annually and stayed at that level through the first decades of the sixteenth century,[80] when provincial expenditures began to grow once more, reaching an average of 9000 lire annually in the 1580s.[81] This increase over the amounts paid at the end of the previous century is very large, even if we consider that the level of prices doubled between 1500 and 1600. Yet, in real terms, Pescia's direct tax payments to Florence at the end of the sixteenth century were smaller than the amounts paid in the first half of the Quattrocento.[82]

Notwithstanding their growth in the last half of the sixteenth century, direct tax payments to Florence, in real terms, followed a pattern similar to that of other forms of transfer payments. Like labor services, payments in kind, and gabelles, they grew rapidly in the late Trecento and early Quattrocento, declined thereafter, and despite occasional temporary increases and the more persistent increase in the last half of the Cinquecento they never again reached the large amounts paid one and a half centuries earlier.

Not unexpectedly, these fluctuations were reflected in the level of total transfer payments. These had grown from approximately 1300 lire in 1353 to over 10,000 lire by the first decades of the Quattrocento, becoming by far the most important items of communal expenditures. After the 1430s the size of transfer payments declined as did their relative share of total expenditures. By the 1480s they accounted for 2,106 lire out of average annual expenditures of 6,204 lire. The eruption of war in the 1490s and

payment amounts to 5,871 lire; (2) in 1407 Pescia paid 3100 lire as payment for soldiers, 756 lire for the ordinary tax, 457 florins for the lance tax, and 468 florins for the extraordinary tax; using the above exchange rate, the total payment amounts to 9,260 lire.

80. The average is based on figures presented in Appendix 7.
81. The average is based on figures presented in Appendix 8. It represents the average provincial expenditures plus direct taxes.
82. Since the general price level increased approximately 2.5 times between 1400 and 1580, expressed in early fifteenth-century lire, Pescia's average direct tax payments in the 1580s were 3600 lire annually, considerably less than the smallest recorded direct tax payment of the early Quattrocento.

again in 1529 briefly increased their size, but the downward trend continued until mid-sixteenth century, when inflation combined with a real increase in obligations brought transfer payments to 9200 lire out of average annual expenditures of 20,328 lire. Expressed in 1430s lire, however, the size of transfer payments at the end of the sixteenth century was approximately 3,680 lire, about one-third of the amounts paid during the first decades of the Quattrocento.[83]

The implications of this trend for the fiscal relations between Pescia and Florence will be analyzed later in this chapter. At present, only two features of the trend should be noted. The first is that, in real terms, the period of the largest transfer payments to Florence corresponds to the period when Florentine military needs were at their greatest. The persistent and expanded costs of warfare in the early Renaissance had created unprecedented fiscal demands on the Florentine treasury, and these were met in part by increasing the fiscal obligations of Pescia and the other towns of the Florentine dominion. The second feature is that in money terms the period in which the size of transfer payments begins to approach the levels of the early Quattrocento corresponds to the period when inflation resulted in more than a doubling of the general price level in Tuscany and many other parts of Europe.

To understand the size and fluctuation of government expenditures at Pescia therefore requires an awareness of the European inflation of the sixteenth century and an awareness of the endemic warfare in the Italian peninsula during the early Renaissance. But also important were the administrative policies of Florence. The weight of inertia, the Florentine desire to create a more efficient and seemingly equitable administration, and the desire to promote the growth of integrated regional economies help to explain some of Pescia's expenditures. The size of the ordinary tax, fixed at 300 florins for a century and barely increasing thereafter, can best be explained by the effects of inertia.[84]

83. Based on an estimated increase of 2.5 times in the general price level, and on estimated transfer payments of over 10,000 lire annually in the early Quattrocento.

84. The weight of inertia is wonderfully illustrated in the case of the town of Chiusi in the Casentino. The town was incorporated into the Florentine state in 1385 and received a set of privileges governing its tax pay-

The use of most of Pescia's direct taxes in the sixteenth century to pay directly for provincial expenditures was most likely related to administrative developments initiated by the Medici grand dukes with a view to strengthening local support for their rule; and the size of transfer payments in the form of indirect taxes was related to Florentine policies toward the development of regional economies.

Finally, to understand the expenditures of Pescia's government also requires an awareness of the changing functions of local government in the course of the Renaissance. For the size of total expenditures and the relation between local and transfer payments was as much the product of local forces as of Florentine policies. Not least among the former was the government's ability to raise revenues.

REVENUES

The government of Pescia had two principal sources of revenues: gabelles and direct taxes. Throughout most of the Renaissance these were sufficient to meet the expenditures of the commune. Yet such was the situation during the first decades of the fifteenth century and again at the end of the century that neither gabelles nor direct taxes could yield sufficient revenues to cover the expenditures of local administration and the fiscal obligations imposed by Florence.

Gabelles

The government of Pescia imposed a variety of gabelles on the population of the town. In addition to a gate tax, there were taxes on the slaughter and sale of meat, on the retail sale of wine, oil, and bread, on contracts, fishing rights, and so forth. Of these the most important in the fourteenth and early fifteenth century were the gabelles on meat and wine sold at retail as well as the gate gabelle.

---

ments. After a few years these privileges expired but things went on as usual, with no one noticing until 1564 when the matter came to the attention of the *Pratica Segreta,* which commented: "La Pratica ha visto la prima e antica loro capitulatione et si meraviglia che non sia stata prorogata, ma crede fusse lasciata per inadvertentia . . . ," ASF, *Pratica Segreta,* 7, ins. 31.

Table 4–5. Revenues from the principal gabelles, 1374–1442 (in lire)

Year	Gate	Meat	Wine	Total
1374	1,020	696	1,880	3,596
1376	960	360a	2,040	3,360a
1387	960	348	1,992	3,300
1414	864	468	732	2,164
1415	1,020	420	n.a.	n.a.
1416	744	418	522	1,504
1427	612	432	480	1,522
1428	516	450	426	1,392
1429	672	384	366	1,342
1438	744	516	498	1,758
1439	828	456	432	1,716
1440	624	468	432	1,524
1441	708	444	394	1,546
1442	600	456	456	1,512

n.a. = not available.
a Based on partial data. The full amount was larger.

Sources: ASPe, Del., 7, fols. 44r–v; 8, fol. 177r; 10, fols. 38r, 129r; 12, fol. 138r; 17, fols. 59r–6or, 181v–191v; 21, fols. 20r–22v; 120r–121v, 148v–149v; 24, fols. 20r–22r, 73r–75v, 131r–133r, 203v–206v, 284v–286v.

Lack of data about the gabelles as well as about total government revenues and expenditures precludes a very accurate estimate of the importance of gabelles in the last half of the Trecento. If the scattered data shown in Table 4–5 are representative, we can estimate that revenues from the principal gabelles amounted to approximately 3500 lire annually. Prior to the rapid growth of transfer payments to Florence in the late Trecento, this sum represented approximately one-third of the estimated minimum annual expenditures of the commune, not including expenditures for the salt tax.[85]

By the second decade of the fifteenth century, receipts from the four principal gabelles had declined to less than half of what they had been in 1374, 1376, and 1387. They continued to de-

85. Expenditures for the salt tax were not included because the data are not available. The remaining expenditures have been estimated on the following basis: 4000 lire for administration and local expenses, 3100 lire for salaries of soldiers and castellans, 2400 lire for the ordinary tax. Total = 9500 lire. Payments in kind and labor services were unavailable.

cline throughout the 1420s and by 1429 they had reached a low
of 1,342 lire. Not taking into account the salt tax, Pescia needed
at least eight times this amount to cover local expenditures and
obligations to Florence. The wars against Milan and Lucca, resumed in 1424, and the imposition of higher taxes by Florence
had helped to weaken the already precarious economy of Pescia
as they had also weakened the economy of Florence.[86] In Pescia
as in the dominant city deteriorating economic conditions contributed to the decline of gabelle revenues.[87] Thus, just at a time
when revenues were most needed to meet rising Florentine obligations, the government of Pescia saw its revenues from gabelles
dwindle.

The resumption of peace and the relaxation of Florentine obligations after 1435 were accompanied by a slight improvement
in gabelle revenues. By the 1480s and 1490s the average annual
revenue from the gabelles was 2,155 lire, which was approximately one-third the amount needed to cover annual expenditures before the closing years of the century. Not even the disruptions caused by the French invasions and the war for the
reconquest of Pisa had much impact on gabelle revenues. The
economy as we have noted earlier was much sounder. While the
military campaigns of the end of the century reduced the share
of total communal revenues derived from gabelles, the reason
for this was that total communal revenues had increased rapidly
as a result of government efforts to meet war-related expenditures. Despite the war, however, the buyers of the gabelles apparently felt that the prospects of making a profit remained
unchanged.

With the exception of this interlude at the end of the fifteenth
century, the relation between gabelle revenues and the revenues
needed to meet communal expenditures remained unaltered for
most of the sixteenth century. By the 1520s the annual revenues
from the principal gabelles averaged over 4000 lire and by the
closing decades of the century they had reached 7600 lire. Both

86. As in most other Italian cities, the right to collect the gabelles was sold
    to the highest bidders. As a result, the revenues collected were directly
    related to the tax farmers' estimates of economic conditions.
87. For a discussion of declining gabelle revenues and the economic conse-
    quences of war in Florence, see Molho, *Public Finances*, pp. 45-49,
    125-52.

of these amounts constituted over one-third of communal revenues during those periods.

Direct Taxes

The major source of revenues at Pescia during the Renaissance was direct taxes. Lacking communal budgets, it is for us impossible to determine the annual amounts collected before the last quarter of the Quattrocento. The infrequency with which other sources of revenues are discussed in communal deliberations before the late 1380s suggests, however, that before that time direct taxes in conjunction with gabelles were usually sufficient to meet communal expenditures. Since these, not including the salt tax, amounted to an estimated 9500 lire annually, direct taxes may have brought in approximately 6000 lire annually, or two-thirds of the revenues needed to cover expenditures.

By the late 1380s communal deliberations reveal a greater concern for the government's ability to meet expenditures that were rapidly rising as a result of larger transfer payments to Florence. Direct taxes had always consisted of two kinds of impositions, one was an *ad valorem* tax on property, and the other a head tax originally imposed on males between the ages of eighteen and seventy, excluding foreigners residing in the town for less than ten years. In September 1390, the head tax was extended to all males above the age of fourteen, including foreigners residing at Pescia for more than one year.[88] These traditional direct taxes, however, proved increasingly inadequate to meet growing expenditures. The government might impose direct taxes but it could not collect them from people who did not have the money to pay.[89] Attempts to coerce the local population into paying their debts to the commune failed. Not even the prospect of incarceration elicited payments from communal debtors.[90] Furthermore these measures eroded the tax base. As we have seen,

---

88. ASPe, *Del.,* 11, fols. 132r–133v.
89. Petitions for exemption from taxes because of poverty increased. For several examples, see ASPe, *Del.,* 18, fol. 183v; 20, fol. 77r.
90. In 1428 the city council elected nine men whose job was to collect revenues from communal debtors and who had the authority to jail anyone who refused to pay. Judging by subsequent difficulties in raising revenues, this move appears to have failed. ASPe, *Del.,* 21, fol. 180v.

in the early years of the fifteenth century, Pescia was becoming depopulated partly because people sought to escape the taxes that
were being levied with greater and greater frequency. In order to
alleviate the problem, the city council ordered that the descendants of banished Ghibellines should be allowed to return to
Pescia.[91] Nevertheless, the ranks of the taxpayers apparently did
not grow sufficiently to solve Pescia's mounting fiscal problems.
Increasingly, transfer payments to Florence were late and the
town incurred the threat of heavy fines.[92]

The situation worsened with the renewed Florentine aggres-
sions against Lucca in the 1420s. Pescia unwillingly found itself
the center of the battlefield. In July 1430 a siege by Lucchese
troops was successfully repelled, but the price of victory was high.
Many of the houses outside the town walls were destroyed, fields
were burned, and famine, the frequent companion of war, soon
made itself felt.[93] In the face of such calamities it is not surprising that Pescia's payments to Florence became more infrequent.
Representatives of the town pleaded with the dominant city to
scale down their fiscal obligations, but their moving pleas fell on
deaf ears.[94] By 1435, unable to make further payments, Pescia
owed Florence over 4300 florins.[95]

The cancellation of most of this debt, the reduction of Florentine transfer obligations, and the resumption of peace in the
Valdinievole after 1435 undoubtedly improved the government's

91. BCatPe, *Memorie Galeotti*, p. 146.
92. Although Florence sent numerous letters to the officials of Pescia threat-
   ening fines and punishment if payment were not forthcoming, many of
   Pescia's payments were late and no fines were exacted. For several examples of this frequent event, see ASF, *CC*, 1, fols. 21v, 28v; 22, fols. 31r,
   37r; 23, fols. 23r, 41r.
93. Some of the damage was done by soldiers in the Florentine army. ASPe,
   Del., 22, fols. 23v, 33r, 96v, 115r.
94. In November 1431, the priors instructed the city council of Pescia to
   send ambassadors to Florence to beg for a tax reduction, explaining:
   "Cum comunitas piscie iam diu multas et infinitas expensas substulerit
   et infinite dapne in servitium M. comunitas Florentine et maxime in hac
   guerre que ut clare videtur non solum terram Piscie iam desolavit sed
   totum universum comitatum florentie. Et cum comunitas Piscie se re-
   periat maxima quantitates debiti involute per modum quod nunquam
   erit possibile dicte comunitate dicte debiti finire et consumare . . . ,"
   ASPe, *Del.*, 22, fol. 117v.
95. ASF, *Monte*, 1098, fol. 24.

ability to meet its fiscal obligations once more with revenues derived from gabelles and direct taxes. By the 1480s and early
1490s direct tax revenues averaged 4,135 lire annually, again two-
thirds of the revenues needed to cover communal expenditures.[96]

This felicitous state of affairs was temporarily interrupted in
1494 by the French invasion and the Florentine war for the reconquest of Pisa. Despite increased revenues from direct taxes, expenditures outpaced the regular sources of revenue, and the government once more sought alternative sources of funds. Difficulties
in obtaining larger revenues by means of direct taxes in the late
1490s were probably aggravated by plague and food shortages in
1496 and 1497, and again in 1499 and 1500, when Pisan troops
running over Pescia's countryside made it impossible for the
peasants to plant the following year's food crop.[97] As in the 1420s
Pescia's payments began to be in arrears. By 1500 the debt
reached 1,016 florins.[98] The fiscal problems of the 1490s, however, do not seem to have reached the proportions of the earlier
crisis. By 1512 the town had managed to repay two-thirds of its
debt, and the remainder was cancelled by the newly returned
Medici regime.[99] Although communal budgets do not survive for
the first decade of the sixteenth century, there is no evidence that
any efforts were made either before or during that period to
secure outside sources of funds to pay Florence. This raises doubts
about the seriousness with which the town tried to meet its fiscal
obligations. Florence was greatly weakened during this period.
Pisa, Arezzo, and Montepulciano had revolted against Florentine
rule, and Pistoia was contemplating following suit. It is quite
possible that Pescia, taking advantage of Florentine weaknesses,
was not trying very hard to fulfill fiscal obligations that would
have been difficult for the dominant city to collect.

By 1515 payments to Florence had been resumed, and direct
taxes with few exceptions once more covered two-thirds of the
annual obligations of Pescia's government until the 1630s. Under
normal circumstances, therefore, direct taxes and gabelles were
sufficient to meet the fiscal needs of the commune. But when
these two sources were inadequate, as they were especially be-

96. See Appendix 7.
97. BCatPe, *Memorie Galeotti*, p. 189.
98. ASF, *Monte*, 1106, fol. 91.
99. ASF, *Monte*, 1107, fol. 96.

tween the late 1380s and 1435, the government of Pescia was compelled to find at least temporary if not always desirable alternatives.

Forced Loans, Moneylenders, and Florentine Bankers

In addition to direct and indirect taxes, the government could force loans from the population of Pescia and borrow from outside sources. Of the two, the first was the preferred expedient because it was the most advantageous politically. Forced loans could be manipulated so that a disproportionate share fell on those who were considered political enemies. Accordingly, forced loans were frequently levied on Ghibellines, who had no legal means of redress because they had no political rights.[100]

The earliest references to forced loans in the surviving communal deliberations date to the 1370s. The amounts borrowed, however, were usually small and were repaid within a short period of time. By the late 1380s, when Florentine fiscal obligations began to increase rapidly, the imposition of forced loans became a more common occurrence and one that touched heretofore untapped segments of the population. The first installment of the new lance tax in 1386 was paid with a loan from the *operari* of the churches of Pescia, two more forced loans were levied in January of 1387, a third in August, and a fourth in December of that year.[101] By 1391 even the candle lit at the cathedral of Florence in honor of St. John, a ritual obligation symbolic of Pescia's subjection to Florence, was bought with money from a forced loan.[102]

The size of revenues collected in this manner is not known but the frequency with which forced loans were imposed suggests that in the last decade of the fourteenth and the first three decades of the fifteenth century they accounted for a larger share of communal revenues than in any other period of Pescia's history. After the last quarter of the Quattrocento when communal budgets give a better indication of the importance of forced loans, it is clear that they were no longer a significant portion of communal revenues. They were levied infrequently and usu-

---

100. ASPe, *Del.*, 11, fols. 185r–v.
101. ASPe, *Del.*, 9, fol. 211r; 10, fols. 23r, 26r, 79r–80r, 98v–99v.
102. ASPe, *Del.*, 11, fol. 196r.

ally for very small amounts in times of military crisis such as the
French invasion, when they accounted for more than 10 percent
of annual revenues.[103] The infrequency of war after 1434, combined with the smaller size of transfer payments to Florence and
the improved tax base resulting from a wealthier economy, must
have reduced the usefulness of forced loans as a fiscal device.

But even in the early fifteenth century, when they were most
frequent, the usefulness of forced loans was limited because like
direct taxes they were restricted by the wealth of the local economy and by political resistance to increased taxes so that they
could not yield sufficiently large revenues to solve the fiscal problems of the commune. Funds borrowed from outside sources did
not pose this problem, and the government of Pescia in the early
Quattrocento increasingly resorted to borrowing from non-Pesciatine sources.

One of these sources was the officials of the Florentine government. The *podestà* of Pescia, for example, provided the funds to
pay Florence for the third installment of the lance tax in 1386.[104]
The following year, the distinguished humanist and chancellor
of the Florentine republic, Coluccio Piero Salutati, who was
born in nearby Stignano, lent Pescia's government 45 florins plus
"meritus" so that it could pay the lance tax once again.[105] In
1419, one year after serving as vicar of the Valdinievole, Ridolfo
Peruzzi, a partner in the Peruzzi bank, paid for part of Pescia's
ordinary tax obligation to Florence.[106] The interest rates charged
by these officials are not known, but the opportunity of supple-
menting their salaries with income from private loans may have
been an added incentive to office holding in the Florentine bureaucracy.

In addition to loans from local officials, revenues were sought
among Jewish and Gentile moneylenders, who were invited to
settle in the Florentine dominion as subject areas found themselves unable to raise the revenues demanded by Florence.[107] As

103. See Appendix 7.
104. ASPe, *Del.*, 10, fol. 26r.
105. ASPe, *Del.*, 10, fols. 82r, 83r.
106. ASF, *Monte*, 1094, fol. 207.
107. Anthony Molho, "A Note on Jewish Moneylenders in Tuscany in the
    Late Trecento and Early Quattrocento," in *Renaissance Studies in Honor
    of Hans Baron*, A. Molho and John Tedeschi, eds. (De Kalb, Ill., 1971),
    pp. 99–119. Jewish moneylenders were also called in at Venice in the

early as 1391 the city council of Pescia tried to find a Jewish moneylender to settle in the town. Its efforts, however, were not immediately successful since two years later they were borrowing from a Florentine moneylender residing at Pescia.[108] By 1402 the Jewish firm of Agnolo di Abramo had settled in Pescia and was apparently doing a brisk business with the government as well as the townspeople. Between 1402 and 1415 Agnolo and his partners were doing well enough to pay Florence an annual tax of 200 florins for the privilege of being allowed to lend money within the Florentine dominion. This was considerably above the median taxable wealth of Pesciatine households.[109] Jewish moneylenders remained at Pescia until the expulsion of the Jews from the Florentine state in 1428—a departure that caused local authorities much grief.[110]

Loans from Jews were supplemented during the first decades of the Quattrocento by loans from Florentine bankers. In March 1417, the city council owed the Florentine firms of Orlando Guccio and Piero Velluti more than 254 florins and was searching for some way to finance another loan so as to pay Florence a sum owed for the previous year's special tax.[111] In 1418 the government also owed Francesco Ridolfi of Florence the sum of 100 florins and Puccio Leonardi 540 florins. The latter also advanced an additional 163 florins so that Pescia could pay its ordinary tax obligation.[112]

These foreign creditors enabled Pescia to tap larger revenues than were available within the local economy. It was with these borrowed funds that transfer payments to Florence continued to

---

1380s so that citizens could meet their tax payments. R. Mueller, "Les prêteurs juifs de Venise au moyen age," *Annales E.S.C.*, 30 (1975), 1277–1302.

108. ASPe, *Del.*, 12, fol. 132r.

109. ASF, *Monte*, 1090, fols. 103, 105, 158; 1091, fols. 224, 229, 233, 236; ASPe, *Statuti*, 4 unnumbered folios. For data on wealth see Ch. 3. In 1417 another partnership of Jewish moneylenders replaced that of Agnolo di Abramo. This second company paid Florence an annual tax of 240 florins. It also owned property at Pescia. ASF, *Monte*, 1093, fol. 248; 1094, fol. 101; 1096, fol. 240; 1103, fol. 191; ASF, *Notarile*, Stefano Onesti, O–20, I, fols. 85r–86r.

110. The city council complained about the problems of not having a local moneylender and asked Florence to provide one. ASPe, *Del.*, 21, fol. 173r.

111. ASPe, *Del.*, 17, fol. 187r.

112. ASPe, *Del.*, 18, fol. 33r.

be made. In the short run this expedient worked, but it was a mere palliative, and in the long run it may have contributed to Pescia's fiscal crisis. The essential problem was that local revenues could not keep pace with fiscal obligations. While loans provided funds on a temporary basis the town had to repay them at interest and this, judging from the evidence of other towns in the same plight as Pescia, could run as high as 20 to 30 percent annually.[113] Attempts at repayment therefore contributed to the reduction of Pescia's wealth.

As communal indebtedness grew, the government was no longer searching for loans to pay the Florentine government but for loans to repay previous loans.[114] In September 1418 the heir of the Florentine banker Puccio Leonardi petitioned for repayment of 470 florins and the money was secured by means of a loan from Piero Rucellai. When a year later Rucellai and other creditors asked for their money back, the funds to do so were borrowed from Roberto Spini and from the *podestà*.[115]

By October 1419, communal indebtedness had become so acute that Pescia's payments to the Florentine Monte officials were made directly by Florentine bankers. Between the end of 1419 and February 1422 the Peruzzi and Velluti banks paid the Monte 1,528 florins.[116] This amounted to four-fifths of Pescia's fiscal obligations to the Monte during that period. The gravity of the situation coupled with the social pressures resulting from Pesciatine marriage customs prompted the priors to consider raising revenues by licensing a brothel.[117] If revenues could not be obtained by appealing to the civic virtues of the population, they might be obtained by trading on their private vices.

Whatever the success of this measure, it hardly solved the problem. The Peruzzi bank continued to make some of Pescia's transfer payments to Florence.[118] The payments, however, were not large enough to cover the town's fiscal obligations and beginning in 1424 Pescia began to default in its payments to Florence. By

113. Molho, *Public Finances,* pp. 38–41; *idem,* "Jewish Moneylenders in Tuscany," pp. 102, 107–8.
114. Pescia did not have a funded debt as did Florence. All references to communal indebtedness refer to a floating debt.
115. ASPe, *Del.,* 18, fols. 103v, 104v.
116. ASF, *Monte,* 1094, fols. 207, 244, 357.
117. ASPe, *Del.,* 18, fols. 210v, 211v.
118. ASPe, *Del.,* 24, fol. 18v; ASF, *Monte,* 1095, fols. 226, 257.

the end of the decade, the ordinary and lance obligations were 940 florins in arrears.[119] By the following year, instead of making payments into the Monte, the priors were asking the Monte officials to lend them the money to pay the vicar's salary.[120] Communal indebtedness had come full circle. Florence which was supposed to be the recipient of Pescia's payments was now being asked to pay Pescia's obligations.

At no other time in its history did Pescia face a fiscal crisis of such magnitude. The heavy reliance on Jewish moneylenders and Florentine bankers was unknown after mid-fifteenth century. Never again did the government have such serious difficulties in raising revenues derived from the local economy and population.

Underlying the problem of communal indebtedness was not only the problem of the increased size of communal expenditures and obligations, but the problem of the burden of taxes. The crisis of the 1420s and early 1430s, like no other moment in Pescia's fiscal history, raises the question of the incidence of taxation and the degree to which Pescia's population could support the fiscal demands imposed by its government and by the government of Florence.

THE BURDEN OF TAXES

During the first years of Florentine domination, when government expenditures at Pescia did not include transfer payments to Florence, the per capita tax payments must have been very light. If total expenditures did not much exceed the estimated 2500 lire for routine administration and fell on a population of approximately 2500, the per capita tax payments may have been close to 1 lira.

The demographic decline of mid-fourteenth century, coupled with the rapid growth of transfer payments to Florence did much to increase per capita tax payments. By 1427 and for the next few years, fiscal obligations and expenditures had risen to at least 12,700 lire, of which 8,760 lire were obligations to Florence.[121]

119. ASF, *Monte*, 1096, fols. 305, 322.
120. ASPe, *Del.*, 22, fol. 6r.
121. Estimated expenditures have been derived as follows: local administration, 4000 lire; salt tax, 1600 lire; salaries of soldiers at local fortifications, 3100 lire; ordinary tax, 2400 lire; lance tax, 550 lire; special tax, 1,050 lire; Total 12,700 lire.

Since Pescia had 1800 people, payment should have resulted in
an annual per capita tax of 7 *l.* 1 *s.* of which 4 *l.* 17 *s.* would have
constituted transfer payments to Florence. Thus, in just fewer
than one hundred years, the per capita tax obligation had risen
more than seven-fold, two-thirds of which could be attributed to
the fiscal demands made by Florence. Although by defaulting on
their Florentine tax obligations, Pesciatines reduced their per
capita tax payments to 6 *l.* 15 *s.*, the burden of taxes was still substantial.

The per capita payment of taxes and presumably the burden
as well were considerably reduced after mid-fifteenth century
both because population and wealth were rising and because
government expenditures until mid-sixteenth century were lower
than before. Yet even the rise in expenditures after mid-sixteenth
century did not result in as high per capita tax payments as in
the early Quattrocento. The government's average annual expenditures of 20,275 lire in the last years of the Cinquecento (half
of which constituted transfer payments to Florence) necessitated
per capita tax payments of 3 *l.* 5 *s.* on the part of Pescia's 6,192
inhabitants. Both the per capita tax payments and the share going to Florence had declined by half since the fiscal crisis of the
1420s. If in addition we recall the effects of inflation, per capita
tax payments in real terms were less than one-fourth of what they
had been a century and a half earlier.[122] Without then even taking into account the growing wealth of Pesciatines in the sixteenth century, it would be safe to conclude that the per capita
burden of taxes at Pescia and the amount going to Florence had
both declined by more than 75 percent since the 1420s.

A fall in the per capita payment of taxes imposed by the subject cities of Florence as well as by Florence itself may not have
been an unprecedented occurrence during the last half of the
Renaissance. More studies of the public finances of Tuscan communes will have to be made before determining whether this
was the general trend, but the case of at least one town, San
Gimignano, parallels that of Pescia.[123]

It remains to be seen, however, to what extent the rising per

122. One-half of the reduction is accounted for by a decline in per capita
    tax payments in money terms, and one-fourth more is accounted for by
    changes in the general level of prices.
123. Enrico Fiumi, *Storia economica e sociale di San Gimignano* (Florence,
    1961), p. 191.

capita burden of taxes in the first century of our study and the declining per capita burden in the following two centuries paralleled similar movements in Florence itself. More precisely, to what extent were the citizens of Pescia shouldering a larger per capita burden of taxes than their Florentine counterparts; and if the burden was heavier in the subject city, could it be attributed to the fiscal demands of the dominant city? In short, to what extent were the fiscal relations between Florence and Pescia exploitative of the subject city?

The problem of fiscal exploitation and of comparative rates of taxation is one of the most difficult and controversial in Renaissance historiography. Although in the last two decades a number of scholars challenged traditional theories of the exploitation of the *contado* and district, until recently most had argued that Florence like other Italian cities built its prosperity and financed its territorial expansion upon the ruthless and exploitative fiscal exactions imposed on oppressed subject areas.[124] Usually implicit in this thesis was the belief that both the per capita payment and the burden of taxes were heavier in subject areas than in Florence itself. A comparison between Pescia and Florence suggests that perhaps the opposite was true.

In the mid-1420s Florentine expenditures exceeded the revenues collected from the rest of the state by about 614,717 florins annually.[125] This amount represents a minimum estimate of what the government collected from the roughly forty thousand residents of Florence.[126] On a per capita basis then, Florentines paid

124. See the Introduction.
125. Data were derived from Molho, *Public Finances*, table 4, for the years 1424, 1426, and 1427, for which information is available. The figure cited was obtained by subtracting the average of contado revenues and half of all gabelle revenues from the average total expenditures for those years. Although Molho treats gabelle revenues as collected on city residents only, Herlihy and Klapisch correctly point out that the inhabitants of the rest of the state contributed as well (*Les Toscans*, p. 22). The share collected from the city is not known so I have arbitrarily chosen one-half. The effect of this is to minimize the taxes paid by Florentines thus making it more difficult to argue that they were paying a high share of taxes compared to others.
126. Another method of estimating the amounts paid by Florentines is to add half of all gabelle revenues collected by the government to the revenues collected from forced loans and catasti. The average for these years comes to 682,916 florins. Data derived from Molho, *Public Finances*, tables 4 and 5.

the government 61 *l.* 10 *s.* each year, a sum almost nine times greater than the per capita obligation of 7 *l.* 1 *s.* owed by Pesciatines and larger yet than the actual per capita payments of 6 *l.* 15 *s.* actually made at Pescia after defaulting on various taxes.[127]

But what does this really tell us about the comparative burden of fiscal exactions? After all, Florentines were on average much wealthier; they could afford to pay more. A more accurate assessment of the burden of taxes can be obtained by looking at the share of taxable wealth that these payments constituted. Turning to this measure of taxation it seems that Florentines paid the government yearly between 8 and 9 percent of their taxable wealth.[128] Pesciatines paid only 3.5 percent.[129] The difference between tax burdens in Florence and Pescia are thus much smaller than it first appears. Still, we are left with the startling conclusion that Florentines were shouldering two and a half times the fiscal burden of Pesciatines.

Part of the explanation for this may lie in the system of forced loans imposed on Florentine residents as opposed to the direct taxes collected from the rest of the state. When the Florentine government needed funds, it ordered the payment of interest-bearing loans by Florentine residents and only those who could not pay the assessed amount paid a direct tax for a portion of the

127. This per capita estimate of tax payments at Florence is very conservative. Herlihy and Klapisch estimate that, not counting gabelles between 1423 and 1427, Florentines paid 68 *l.* annually. Certain gabelles were also higher at Florence than elsewhere. Whereas in the late 1420s Pesciatines were paying 17 *s.* 10 *d.* per capita for salt; Florentines were paying 28 *s.* Herlihy and Klapisch, *Les Toscans,* pp. 19, 21.

128. The taxable wealth of Florence in 1427 was 7,665,068 florins. So as to make wealth data comparable for all of Tuscany, this amount is already adjusted to exclude the per capita exemptions allowed only in the city and not the rest of the state. Data on wealth are from Herlihy and Klapisch, *Les Toscans,* p. 243. The per capita payment of taxes as a share of taxable wealth was calculated as follows:

$$\frac{614{,}717 \text{ fl.} \times 100}{7{,}665{,}068 \text{ fl.}} = 8.0\%;$$

alternatively:

$$\frac{682{,}916 \times 100}{7{,}665{,}068} = 8.9\%.$$

129. Pescia's total taxable wealth in 1427 was 339,332 lire and tax obligations came to 12,700 lire annually.

assessment.[130] This makes it difficult to make exact comparisons of the tax burdens since there were different fiscal systems at work, one for Florence and one for the rest of the state. But assuming that only half of Florentine payments were in the form of direct taxes, this still means that Florentines were shouldering a higher fiscal burden, not only compared to Pescia but to the rest of the state.[131] On the eve of the introduction of the catasto, Florentines believed that the inhabitants of the dominion did not bear a fair share of the fiscal burden.[132] The evidence for Pescia suggests that they were correct.

Whether the subsequent pattern of fiscal relations changed the balance between subjects and rulers must await further work by scholars on Florentine public finance in the late Renaissance. Most probably the balance did not change to the detriment of subject areas. If on the one hand certain taxes were introduced to favor some Florentine industries, on the other, after the establishment of the Medici principate, government efforts in the fiscal realm were aimed at creating a unified Tuscan state under grand-ducal hegemony. To the extent that the Medici did this by currying the favor of rural areas and weakening Florence, the seat of strongest opposition to the principate, the fiscal burden of subject areas must have become relatively lighter. Indeed, one scholar has suggested that the fiscal policy of the grand dukes toward subject areas was guided primarily by the desire to have allies outside the narrow circle of the Florentine oligarchy.[133]

130. On the system of forced loans see Molho, *Public Finances*, ch. 4. The principal and interest on these loans were not redeemable in cash. Interest was paid as a credit on future loan assessments. Those unable to pay the full assessment paid half to one-third as a direct tax. The number of people taking this option seems to have grown in the early fifteenth century. In one neighborhood of Florence between 1381 and 1406 the proportion of people paying the full amount of the loan declined from about one-half to one-sixth, which suggests that most of the revenues collected were in the form of direct tax payments (*ibid.*, p. 68).

131. In the mid-1420s residents of the *contado* and dominion had 53.8 percent (4,127,344 florins) as much taxable wealth as Florentines. On the other hand they paid only 26.8 percent (164,845 florins) as much taxes as Florentines did to the Florentine government. Data are based on Herlihy and Klapisch, *Les Toscans*, p. 243, and Molho, *Public Finances*, table 4.

132. Herlihy and Klapisch, *Les Toscans*, p. 21.

133. Antonio Anzilotti, *La crisi costituzionale della Repubblica fiorentina*

Whatever its policies over the dominion compared to the dominant city itself, it is at least incontrovertible that, with regard to Pescia, the Florentine government did not pursue a fiscal program aimed at obtaining an ever increasing share of the subject city's wealth.[134] The escalating fiscal obligations of the late fourteenth and early fifteenth century did constitute an onerous and growing burden on the community, but this was due to the necessities of war which fell on Florentines as well. Thereafter they did not grow in proportion to the increasing size and wealth of the town. Had Florentine policy in the Renaissance been motivated primarily by the desire to acquire an ever greater share of dominion wealth, fiscal obligations at Pescia should have been increasing in the course of the sixteenth century. Instead, as we have noted, the per capita fiscal obligations in real terms as well as the burden of taxes were reduced after mid-fifteenth century.

Neither can it be said that the administration of Florentine fiscal policy at Pescia was characterized by increasing strictness on the part of the Florentine government.[135] Although fiscal demands were at times accompanied by ominous warnings about the consequences of noncompliance, the records of the Florentine Camera and the Monte are replete with instances of payments that were months and years in arrears and for which no fines or other penalties were ever exacted. Furthermore, as we have seen, what Pescia was supposed to pay Florence and what was in fact paid were not always one and the same. When the town's debts to the dominant city reached major proportions, the obligations

---

(1912, reprinted, Rome 1969), pp. 118, 129, 61. Unfortunately, the development of policies and institutions under the duchy has been a much neglected field. My own findings on the political economy of Cosimo I, in a book-length study underway, confirm the importance of this area. It is interesting to note in this connection that, when Cosimo reduced the burden of military expenses by reorganizing the armed forces, he did not allow Florentines to enter the military. Clearly, he was afraid of rearming them.

134. The thesis that Florence attempted to obtain increasing shares of the wealth of the district and *contado* has been most recently advanced by Marvin Becker. Becker, *Florence in Transition*, 2:73.

135. Marvin Becker has argued that Florentine policy was increasingly rigorous after mid-fourteenth century and that the dominant city began to exercise tight controls over the countryside as its own fiscal needs grew in the last half of the Trecento. Becker, *Florence in Transition*, 2:74.

were reduced. In short, the administration of Florentine fiscal policy was not nearly as inflexible as the law might suggest.

This is not to say that all of Pescia's requests for tax reductions were granted or that it was always easy to meet fiscal obligations. Indeed, the economic effects of Florentine fiscal policy may at times have made it more difficult to meet fiscal obligations. In the early fifteenth century, the heavy demands made by Florence probably encouraged the depopulation of Pescia, thereby placing a heavier tax burden on the remaining inhabitants.

Yet the economic effects of Florentine fiscal policy were not all negative. High taxes may have discouraged economic development in the early fifteenth century but they did not bring about the demise of once flourishing industries. Commercial and industrial activity had been limited at Pescia even before Florentine domination, and while taxation may have drawn capital away from investment, there was nothing inherent in Florentine policies to prohibit the development of commerce and industry. On the contrary, the development of the paper and printing industries as well as the development of commercial agriculture testifies to the fact that economic development in general was significant under Florentine rule. Moreover, to the extent that Florence promoted the abolition of trade barriers within the Florentine state, its fiscal policy encouraged the development of Pescia's economy. The city's wine, silk, paper, and books were actively traded within the Florentine dominion, and by the end of the sixteenth century Pescia's flourishing economy had come to be fully integrated into a Tuscan regional economy dominated by the Florentine market.

In conclusion, what can be said about the factors that influenced the fiscal relations between Florence and its subject city? Possibly the most apt interpretation, advanced by Anthony Molho, is that the Florentine attitude toward the fiscal policy to be imposed was ambivalent and "hardly characterized by a singleness of purpose."[136] To begin with, in the late fourteenth and early fifteenth century policy was influenced by the Florentine desire to finance its territorial expansion with revenues derived in part from its subject areas. At the same time, the revenues obtained were used not only to finance Florentine territorial ambitions but to protect

136. Molho, *Public Finances,* p. 32.

the Florentine state from the territorial encroachments of other Italian powers.

Second, Florentine officials must surely have been aware that, no matter how much they wanted to squeeze funds out of subject areas, compared to what they could obtain from the city of Florence the possibilities were rather limited. The total wealth of a town like Pescia in 1427 (339,333 lire = 85,000 florins) was less than the value of the estate of several of the richest Florentine families. Pescia's ordinary tax, which at its maximum came to 652 florins, seems a paltry sum next to the 1300 florins per annum paid to the state by Francesco Datini in the early 1400s, the 430 florins paid each year by Matteo Palmieri between 1428 and 1433, or the 787 florins paid yearly by Filippo Strozzi in the late 1480s and 1490s.[137] With a tax base like this within its own walls, why would Florence bother trying to squeeze any more out of Pescia?

Third, the Florentine desire for revenues was counterbalanced at times by the exigencies of political developments within the city, and especially by the needs of new regimes to consolidate their power. This task could be facilitated by the development of cordial relations between the new rulers and subject areas. One of the most obvious ways of achieving that goal was to reduce the fiscal obligations of subject areas. Not only was the threat of revolt thereby reduced, but the grateful subjects would presumably actively support their benefactors. It is not coincidental that the two instances when Pescia's fiscal obligations were reduced occurred just after the arrival of new Medici regimes in Florence, first in 1434 and again in 1512.

A fourth factor influencing fiscal relations between the two cities was the emergence of a more efficient administration of the Florentine state. Florentine administrative reforms, as Marvin Becker has pointed out, were frequently aimed at centralizing the administration of the Florentine dominion.[138] But in the Valdinievole, where communities had a strong tradition of au-

---

137. These are the net amounts paid by Datini, Palmieri, and Strozzi, i.e., the total amount paid to the state as forced loans minus interest and partial reimbursements on the capital. *Ibid.*, pp. 94–98; Richard Goldthwaite, *The Building of Renaissance Florence: An Economic and Social History* (Baltimore, 1980), p. 59.
138. Becker, *Florence in Transition*, 1:200.

tonomy, administrative reform and centralization occurred at a
slower pace than elsewhere.[139] Centralized control of the fisc appears limited until mid-sixteenth century. In a dispute with the
Five on the Contado, the Tuscan magistracy that oversaw dominion affairs, Pesciatine officials claimed that up to 1549 their
city council had always been responsible for the collection and
expenditure of public funds and that the accountants hired by
the council as well as the vicar of the Valdinievole who periodically examined the books never saw any irregularities or grounds
for objection.[140] Probably the books had also been examined and
routinely approved by the Five on the Contado for the previous
35 years, but it is only in 1549 that this magistracy began to assert
itself.[141] Henceforth no extraordinary expenditures could be made
without the prior consent of the Five.

This change in policy points toward centralization. On the
other hand, in the management of provincial revenues, Florentine
administrative reform in the sixteenth century points in the opposite direction—that is, most revenues collected in the Valdinievole
were not sent to Florence but were spent in the region.

Not unrelated to these types of administrative reform were efforts to curb fiscal abuses. At Pescia, as elsewhere, the dominant
city was careful to limit unnecessary fiscal exactions imposed by
unscrupulous Florentine officials. This was true even in the
Quattrocento when Florentine exactions were at their highest.[142]
Under the grand dukes this policy became part of a design to extend their own political power and control by reserving for themselves the ultimate authority to redress fiscal injustices committed
by government officials. In the eyes of many of their subjects the
Medici thus became the protectors of the people's fiscal rights.[143]

If many of these factors tended to limit the share of Pescia's
wealth obtained by Florence, the long-term benefits to the dominant city outweighed any short-term disadvantages. By not fleec-
ing Pescia or other subject areas the Florentine government

139. Chittolini, "La formazione dello stato regionale," pp. 58–63.
140. The dispute arose because the Five on the Contado objected to past
    expenditures for building a slaughterhouse. ASF, *Pratica Segreta,* 159,
    fols. 138r–139v.
141. It was the Five on the Contado who argued that Pescia had been for-
    warding its books for that length of time (*ibid.*).
142. *Capitoli,* 2:36; 2:32; ASF, *Diplomatico,* Pescia, 23 February 1385.
143. Anzilotti, *La crisi,* p. 129.

helped to encourage the development of flourishing economies.
Both the Florentine economy and the Florentine government
derived many advantages as a result. Pesciatine silk, for example,
supplied the Florentine silk cloth industry and Pesciatine paper
supplied the Florentine printing industry. The increased level
of commercial exchange provided additional tax revenues to the
Florentine government. By pursuing a moderate fiscal policy after
mid-fifteenth century the Florentine government ensured the
survival and facilitated the development of a profitable source of
revenues for the Florentine state.

5

The Patriciate

The economic and fiscal integration of Pescia into a larger regional framework was accompanied by a strengthening of social and cultural ties. To some extent these were the inevitable by-products of closer economic contacts but in the sixteenth century they were also enhanced by deliberate grand-ducal efforts to create a new class of subjects—a class of Tuscan administrators with an unshakable allegiance to the central government. As a result, Pescia, and probably other parts of the dominion, experienced a significant transformation in its social structure. A patriciate class with a new mentality, new habits, and new political, social, and economic bonds began to emerge in the sixteenth century. This class had a profound impact on Pescia's economy and society. It also constituted a major link between Florence and its subject town.

POLITICS

The establishment of the duchy in 1532 irrevocably altered the political balance of power within Tuscany. The Florentine patriciate, though never totally replaced in the administration of the state, found itself frequently bypassed by the Medici, who in consolidating their own authority relied either on less prominent Florentines or on the old established families of the dominion, some of whom had on earlier occasions been of service to the

Medici.[1] The idea was to identify people who had been relatively powerless under the old regime and who had no independent source of political support, and to tie their fortunes to those of the Medici and the state. By filling many top bureaucratic posts with leading men from the dominion, the Medici moreover assured themselves of having not only loyal but also trained administrators. For the personnel of the efficient and bureaucratized grand-ducal administration were highly educated, especially in law, and previously had acquired years of experience in local administration.[2]

Training, most notably in law or the notarial arts, became *de rigeur* with the sons of many Pesciatine families in the late Renaissance. Even those who pursued an ecclesiastical career often had a legal education.[3] The importance placed on this kind of training is apparent in the financial support offered for it by Messer Giulio Turini of Pescia, who maintained several students on scholarship at the University of Pisa. Giuliano Lorenzo Ceci, one of those students, tells us that in 1551, when he was there, there were twelve other Pesciatines attending the university.[4]

1. Anzilotti, *La crisi*, p. 62. Although the Florentine patriciate was never totally replaced in the administration of the Florentine state, Cosimo I in consolidating his own authority attempted to employ both non-patricians and non-Florentines in the nascent bureaucracy; R. Burr Litchfield, "Office-holding in Florence after the Republic," *Renaissance Studies in Honor of Hans Baron,* eds., A. Molho and J. Tedeschi (Dekalb, 1971), pp. 531–56.

2. The importance of lawyers in the republican period is analyzed by Lauro Martines, *Lawyers and Statecraft in Renaissance Florence* (Princeton, 1968).

3. A definitive list of university trained Pesciatines, of course, cannot be obtained. The Florentine archives, however, do contain the notebooks of 55 Pesciatine notaries for the sixteenth century, compared to 32 for the fifteenth. In addition, various lists of illustrious Pesciatines and family histories have yielded the names of 42 other sixteenth-century men with law degrees and 14 who were doctors of medicine. Some of them, such as Mons. Lorenzo Cecchi, Elpidio Berrettari, and Pietro Nucci, became well-known scholars, teachers, and administrators at various universities. The basis for these surveys are: Ansaldi, *Cenni biografici;* Cecchi and Coturri, *Pescia ed il suo territorio;* BComPe, I.A.90, B. Buonvicini, *Memorie di famiglie, 1699;* I.B.7, P. Buonvicini, *Memorie di Pescia, 1692;* I.A.3, F. Galeotti, *Stemmi e alberi genealogici di famiglie pesciatine;* I.B.22, *Memorie e ritratti di pesciatini illustri;* I.A.91, O. Galeotti, *Famiglie pesciatine, 1658;* I.B.24, *Famiglie, memorie a alberi genealogici.*

4. BComPe, I.B.52, *Libro di ricordi di Lorenzo di Giuliano Ceci,* fols. 3r–3v.

Because of their education and the political expertise acquired in local politics, a number of Pesciatine families found themselves thrust into prominent positions in the Grand Duchy of Tuscany. The Pagni, who had distinguished themselves in military service against Pisa in the 1490s as well as in Pesciatine politics, were perhaps the most visible. After obtaining a law degree Lorenzo Andrea Pagni pursued a career in local administration in the 1520s and then joined the ducal bureaucracy, eventually becoming secretary to Cosimo I in 1537. One of his most important tasks was to negotiate with foreign princes, especially Emperor Charles V. Lorenzo's brother Bernardino served in the ducal armies as overseer of all Tuscan fortifications. A cousin, Monsignor Cristiano Luca Pagni, served as secretary to Duke Cosimo I in addition to being apostolic protonotary.[5]

But the Pagni were not the only ones to find rewarding careers under a succession of Medici grand dukes. The Turini, Onesti, Galeotti, Cecchi, Mainardi, and others all occupied a variety of important posts, ranging from director of the treasury (*Luogotenente della Camera Fiscale*) to auditor of the *Otto di Pratica,* one of the most important magistracies of the state.[6]

The bond between the notable families of the dominion and the Medici helped to strengthen the bond between these families and the papacy. Although a few brilliant but isolated examples of ecclesiastical advancement by provincials such as the Pesciatine Cardinal Jacopo Ammannati can be found in the fifteenth century, it is with the election of Cardinal Giovanni de' Medici as Pope Leo X in 1513 that ecclesiastical careers opened up for Pescia's patriciate.[7] Leading the way in this direction was the Turini family. Baldassare Turini, Jr. had been in the service of Cardinal Giovanni de' Medici when the latter was taken captive at the battle of Ravenna in 1512. To reward this faithful service through his ordeal, Giovanni made Baldassare the papal datary when he became pope. After the pope's death in 1522, Baldassare

In his will, Giuseppe Albertini also made provision for a scholarship fund at Pisa. Cecchi and Coturri, *Pescia ed il suo territorio,* p. 198.

5. Information on the Pagni was culled from the sources cited in n. 3.

6. *Ibid.*

7. Ammannati was a favorite of Pope Pius II who heaped many honors on him. See Calamari, *Il confidente di Pio II: Cardinale Jacopo Ammannati,* 2 vols., Rome/Milan, 1932.

continued to work for his successors. He was secretary first to another Medici pope, Clement VII and then to Paul III. Baldassare's
brother Andrea was also employed by these three popes as their
physician. Lorenzo di Giulio Turini, a grandnephew of these
papal servants, held many titles in the Papal States, including
governor of Todi, vice-legate in the Romagna, governor of
Spoleto, and governor of Ascoli. Before the family became extinct in mid-seventeenth century, one other member, Giulio di
Piero, a nephew of Lorenzo, also had a chance to advance his
career in the papal bureaucracy. In Rome he was *auditore generale* of the Campagna Marittima and subsequently a fiscal ad-
visor to Cardinal Acquavicia, and he ended his days as governor
of Palo in the territory of Bari.[8]

Professional advancement in public administration was the
most important but by no means the only avenue by which the
ruling house of Tuscany tied local families to its own destiny.
There were other rewards as well. Some were material, such as
the villas confiscated from political opponents among the Florentine patriciate and given to the new servants of the regime. This
is how Lorenzo Pagni obtained the villa that had belonged to
Francesco Valori.[9] Other rewards were honorary but nonetheless
of great value in a society where rank and privilege were becoming increasingly significant. Many inhabitants of the dominion
were granted Florentine citizenship in recognition of their loyal
service, especially during the war against Siena when Cosimo I
sought to bolster the allegiance of subjects who were being asked
to contribute heavily to the war effort.[10] Among the Pesciatine

---

8. The ecclesiastical careers pursued by the Turini and other Pesciatine
families were culled from the sources cited in n. 3.

9. Spini, "Architettura e politica nel principato mediceo," p. 828.

10. ". . . the duke extended Florentine citizenship to many and in 1555
wanted to extend it even among the inhabitants of the district. The
taxes imposed to sustain the war and the necessity of keeping the people
well disposed in such dangerous circumstances moved him to grant some
sign of favor. With his own hand on 9 August, declaring that he was
pleased for the aid given him by the cities and towns of the district and
because of the faith they constantly maintained in him, wishing to grant
them a sign of benevolence, he ordered that each [town and city] could
grant Florentine citizenship to those families judged most worthy of this
honor . . ." Riguccio Galluzzi, *Istoria del Granducato di Toscana* (Florence, 1781), I:364.

families to receive this honor at that time were those of Francesco, Michelangelo, and Girolamo Orlandi, Antonio di Luca Pagni, and Lorenzo d'Andrea Pagni. They and their legitimate male descendants could now enjoy the rights and privileges of Florentine citizenship without having to reside or build a house in Florence as was customarily expected of other Florentine citizens.[11]

Membership in the Order of Santo Stefano was also a coveted prize for loyalty and good service. Created in 1562 by Cosimo I "to honor God, defend the Catholic faith, secure the Mediterranean from infidels, and ornament his posterity," the order was inspired by the chivalric ideals of the Crusades.[12] But it must also be seen as an effort by the new Medici dynasty to gain prestige among other European ruling houses and to integrate important

11. ASF, *Senato de' 48*, 15, pp. 200–202, 238; 16, ins. 23. The rights and privileges of Florentine citizenship are not well defined. In the fourteenth and early fifteenth century, a number of legists addressed this issue with special emphasis on determining the status of naturalized citizens (*cives ex privilegio*). While their opinions strengthened the naturalized citizens' theoretical claims to equal treatment, the nativist impulses of the Florentine population drove a wedge between their legal equality and the actual benefits conferred upon them by specific grants of citizenship. New citizens, for example, if allowed to hold public office, were usually required to wait many years before they could do so. This disparity diminished after 1404, as eligibility for public office, heretofore the most significant attribute of citizenship, was drastically curtailed even among native citizens. But the most severe blow to the real, if not the honorific, advantages of citizenship must have come from the altered function of public offices after the fall of the republic. The meaning of citizenship in the republican period is discussed in Julius Kirshner, "Paolo di Castro on 'Cives ex Privilegio': A Controversy over the Legal Qualifications for Public Office in Early Fifteenth-Century Florence," in *Renaissance Studies in Honor of Hans Baron*, eds. A. Molho and J. Tedeschi, pp. 227–64; Kirshner, "*Civitas Sibi Faciat Civem*: Bartolus of Sassoferrato's Doctrine on the Making of a Citizen," *Speculum*, 48 (1973), 694–713; Kirshner, "'Ars Imitatur Naturam': A Consilium of Baldus on Naturalization in Florence," *Viator*, 5 (1974), 289–333; Peter Riesenberg, "Citizenship at Law in Late Medieval Italy," *Viator*, 5 (1974), 333–46. There are no similar studies for the period of the principate.
12. Remark made by Francesco Settimanni, cited in Samuel Berner, "The Florentine Patriciate in the Transition from Republic to the Principato, 1530–1610," Ph.D. diss., University of California, Berkeley, 1969, p. 236. The Order of Santo Stefano is discussed by G. Guarnieri, *Storia della Marina Stefaniana* (Leghorn, 1935).

Tuscan families into the recently established duchy.[13] From its
creation to the early 1630s thirteen Pesciatines were admitted to
the order, among them members of the Orlandi, della Barba,
Cecchi, Ducci, Forti, Marchi, and Orsucci families.[14]

The efforts of the Medici dynasty had their intended effect.
The patriciate of dominion towns like Pescia came to identify
with the ruling house. It is no coincidence that the Medici coat
of arms was readily displayed by these families either on the
façades or in the interior of their palaces.[15] The Medici emblem
was a visible sign of political loyalty as well as a reminder to
family, friends, and neighbors of the most important source of
political power and social connections.[16] In recognition of this
loyalty, the painted representations of the principal towns of the
realm, which Cosimo I commissioned for the Florentine palazzo
vecchio, include a depiction of Pescia with the title *Piscia oppidum adeo fidele.*

As the leading families of Pescia became identified politically
ever more closely with the central administration of the state they
sought to consolidate their political power within Pescia itself.
In the sixteenth and early seventeenth century political participation was not possible for a large proportion of the growing
immigrant population of the town. Starting in the sixteenth century, immigrants had to wait fifty years to obtain citizenship,
compared to only ten in the mid-fourteenth and early fifteenth
century.[17] No amount of pleading or bribing was likely to aid

13. *Ibid.*
14. ASF, *Manoscritti,* 656, Ruolo Generale de Cavalieri di S. Stefano, fols.
    197–98.
15. The household inventory of Pietro Meo Nucci, for example, includes
    the "coats of arms of the duke and duchess of Florence"; ASF, *Notarile
    Moderno,* 2883, Francesco Filippo Bonagrazia, fols. 12r–13r. Similarly,
    among the household goods of Bonagrazia Matteo Bonagrazia one could
    find a cloth coat of arms of the grand duke. ASF, *Notarile Moderno,*
    7382, Girolamo Orlandi, fols. 74r–74v. The display of the Medici coat
    of arms in small towns of the dominion has been noted by Spini, *Architet-
    tura e politica da Cosimo I a Ferdinando I,* p. 28.
16. The Turini palace in Rome goes even farther in its glorification of the
    Medici. The program of the frescoes in the *salone* was an elaborate
    allegorical praise of the Medici family. A detailed analysis may be found
    in David R. Coffin, *The Villa in the Life of Renaissance Rome* (Prince-
    ton, 1979), pp. 262–65.
17. ASF, *Miscellanea Medicea,* 308, ins. 1. At Pescia citizenship was a require-
    ment for political participation.

Figure 5-1. "Pescia with the Nievole and Pescia rivers, with many mul-
berries produced there, a spider, and a silk bud; with a standard on
which is the red dolphin, the emblem of that place; also painted is
Pescia from life with the following words under the picture: 'Piscia
oppidum adeo fidele.'" (Giorgio Vasari, *Ragionamenti*, in *Le opere di
Giorgio Vasari* (Florence, 1832–38), 2:1406.) *Source:* Gab. Fotografico,
Soprintendenza beni artistici e storici, Florence.

the immigrants' cause. Many, according to the city council, tried
these methods to no avail.[18] The growing frustration of those excluded from political power came to a head in the late 1500s
when Giorgio and Vincenzo di Dioneo Campioni, inhabitants of

18. ". . . altre volte dalli medessimi et da altri ancora per ottenere questo
    privilegio di cittadinanza è stato offerto assai somma di denari a facere del
    Publico cosa che non si fà da quelle persone . . ." (*ibid.*).

Pescia for thirty years but still denied citizenship by the city council, appealed to the Nine on the Contado. When it ordered the
Pescia city council to grant them citizenship, so great was the
commotion and the danger of an upheaval by the ruling class,
that the city council appealed to the grand duke who ended the
affair by denying citizenship to the Campioni. The city council
feared that if citizenship were granted in this case "it would open
up the field to those others who have not been able until now to
obtain what they asked for."[19]

The relative narrowing of the political system is also apparent
from a scrutiny of local office-holders. If we examine the lists of
top posts, priors and Capitani di Parte Guelfa, for three separate
decades, the 1480s, 1525–1534, and 1569–1578, the ratio of office-
holders to offices remains constant, despite the growth in population that occurred during this period.[20] In any decade, an office-
holder would on the average occupy either of these two posts
about one and a half times, and in addition he took repeated
turns on the larger city council.

Perhaps even more important is the domination of the political system by the same families. To be sure, office was not the only
vehicle for exercising political influence. The number of posts
occupied by members of one kinship group could vary significantly according to the number of adult male kinsmen and the
vagaries of professional careers that could take them out of town
for lengthy periods. Nonetheless, the Orlandi, the Pagni, the

19. *Ibid.*
20. These decades were selected for the following reasons. The 1480s were
    the last peaceful years before the political upheavals of the late fifteenth
    and early sixteenth century. The years 1525–34 straddle the transition
    from republic to duchy. It was therefore possible to look for changes in
    the office-holding class that might be related to partisan loyalties. In
    fact, however, no such changes were observed, thus supporting the long-
    held contention by Pesciatine scholars that, though generally sympathetic
    to the Medici, Pesciatines tried to minimize possible damage from either
    side by remaining neutral. Cecchi and Coturri, *Pescia ed il suo territorio*,
    pp. 150–61. The period 1569–78 was selected because it spans the Pescia-
    tine political conflicts of 1572 (see p. 185) so that once more observations
    might be made regarding changes in the office-holding class. Again, none
    were found. It should also be noted that the total number of offices re-
    mained unchanged in all periods. There were 6 priors and 4 captains of
    the Parte Guelfa elected every two months, making a total of 60 offices
    open each year and 600 each decade.

Fantozzi, and a few others recur with amazing regularity. In each of the three decades examined approximately 20 percent of priorates and captaincies were held by six families and about 30 percent were held by twelve families.[21]

The frequency with which some families appear in the roster of office holders is perhaps best illustrated by the prolific Orlandi in the decade of the 1480s. Members of this large kinship group occupied the posts of prior and captain thirty-four times. In just one decade, Gherardo Baldassare Orlandi was both a prior and a captain twice, while his sons took altogether seven turns as priors and four as captains. This adds up to fifteen posts occupied by one father and his sons in one decade alone.[22]

In the 1490s the base of the political system was narrowed by a new procedure for selecting office-holders. The names of those eligible for political office were placed in pouches by the ten *riformatori,* as in the past. But now the *riformatori* were to be selected from families who had paid property and other taxes at Pescia for at least 100 years.[23] The system was further closed when in 1543 it was decided that two of the ten *riformatori* had to be members of the Orlandi and the Pagni families.[24]

The criteria used by the *riformatori* for placing a name in a pouch were never spelled out, but it is clear from the lists of office holders that bringing in new blood was not what the *riformatori* had in mind. When this became apparent to many, an attempt was made in 1572 to circumvent the system by asking the vicar to push for an increase in the number of *riformatori* to twelve and relaxation of the rule requiring a record of tax payments for the previous hundred years. The proposal was vehemently denounced

21. In the 1480s the top six families held 19.17 percent of posts and the top twelve families held 29 percent. In 1525–34 the figures are 19.8 percent and 33.8 percent respectively, and in 1569–78 they are 20.2 percent and 35 percent.
22. Gherardo Baldassare Orlandi was elected prior in May 1480 and March 1488, and captain in November 1484 and September 1489; Niccolò Gherardo Orlandi and Benedetto Gherardo Orlandi were elected priors in March 1382 and May 1484 respectively; Jacopo Gherardo was elected prior in March 1483 and May 1487, and captain in September 1485 and January 1486; Francesco Gherardo was elected prior in January 1485, November 1486, and May 1489, and captain in September 1485 and September 1488.
23. Statute of 3 June 1493, cited in ASF, *Pratica Segreta,* 9, ins. 41.
24. *Ibid.;* Salvagnini, *Pescia,* p. 29.

by the priors of Pescia and the issue was brought before the grand duke's closest advisors, the Pratica Segreta.[25] Not surprisingly, they and the grand duke ruled against the proposed change because, among other things, "any change could cause disorder."[26] The Medici knew where the basis for their support lay and they were not about to rock the boat, at least not when it came to substantive issues, although they were willing to make concessions toward the less powerful in matters involving honor.[27]

Thus, the Pesciatine patriciate forged ever closer political bonds with the Medici and the influential administrators of Tuscany while divorcing themselves from the rest of Pesciatine society. In the social realm, too, similar developments took place.

SOCIETY

By means of their political and professional connections the leading families of Pescia were able to integrate themselves into an emerging Tuscan elite. Their social world was becoming richer, more cosmopolitan, and more separate from the rest of Pesciatine society. In the course of the sixteenth century a full fledged patriciate began to emerge—a patriciate that closed its political and social world to the rest of the Pesciatine population.

The political bonds with the Medici court and the nascent aristocracy of Tuscany were reinforced by bonds of marriage with

25. The vicar wrote to the grand duke in favor of these changes "atteso che il populo era augmentato et molti facevono instantia d'essere uno del numero delli riformatori." The priors of Pescia denied this and accused the vicar of trying to obtain favors for his friends. ASF, *Pratica Segreta,* 9, ins. 41.

26. The Pratica recommended "relassar questo negotio ne medessimi termini, sanza innovare o alterare cosa alcuna, perchè ogni mutatione poterebbe causar disordine et si contrafarebbe allo statuto predetto . . ." (*ibid.*).

27. That same year a dispute arose regarding the order in which the priors should walk in processions. According to Pesciatine law, if the *proposto* of the priors was a *minore,* he had to walk behind the priors who were *maggiori.* This irked the *minori,* many of whom were increasingly not agricultural laborers or manual workers as had once been the case but professionals of high standing and wealth. The grand duke and his advisers resolved the dispute by ruling that if a *proposto* who was a *minore* was a "Dottore, Cavagliere, Capitano, o Nottaio," he should precede all other priors so that "si darebbe occasione a ciascuno di acquistarsi honori et dignità." ASF, *Pratica Segreta,* 9, ins. 44.

other prominent families of the grand duchy. Marriage in the Renaissance had always been regarded as a vehicle for useful political and economic alliances. What was new in the sixteenth century was the increased ability of Pescia's leading families to conclude these alliances with prominent Florentine and Tuscan families. Undoubtedly this reflects the wider political, social, and economic world which these families inhabited. In the fifteenth century, when Pescia was relatively self-contained, the possibility of a wider set of social networks was very limited. To be sure there were a few isolated marriages with good Florentine families such as the marriage between Michele Guerrieri Orlandi to Piera di Antonio Naldino Altoviti, a marriage that was possible because Michele's branch of the Orlandi family had temporarily settled in Florence.[28] But in the sixteenth and early seventeenth century these alliances became more common.[29]

The Turini family of Pescia illustrates what occurred in several of the leading houses (see Figure 5.1). The Turini were an old and prominent family, active in Pesciatine politics since the fourteenth century. The catasto shows them to be the third wealthiest household in Pescia. Some of the family's wealth was used to educate its members in law and medicine as well as to introduce the paper industry to the town. Yet despite their wealth, education, and local political influence, the Turini did not make any brillant matches in the fifteenth century. Instead, they entered into marriages with prominent local families such as the Orlandi, the Cecchi, and the Onesti. All this changed in the next few generations. Andrea Turini, Pope Leo X's physician, developed a two-pronged strategy toward the marriage of his offspring which was followed by the next several generations. The daughters were married to prominent Pesciatine or provincial families, the sons to prominent Florentines. The plan was ideally suited to increasing the prestige and widening the social networks of the family while at the same time minimizing the cash outlay for dowries. Hence, Andrea's two daughters married into the Galeotti, Gherardi, and Buonvicini families of Pescia, while his son Giulio married Ginevra Gualterotti of Florence. Giulio's two sons Piero and Turino married respectively a Ginori and an

28. Cecchi and Coturri, *Pescia ed il suo territorio,* pp. 278–88; ASF, *Catasto,* 69, fol. 171v.
29. Based on an examination of 134 marriages.

Ottavanti of Florence. His daughter married a Panciatichi of Pistoia. In turn Piero's son Baldassare married Maria di Lorenzo Bonsi of Florence and his daughter Alfonsina married Francesco Gatteschi of Pistoia. The only exception to the pattern was Clarisse, the daughter who married Ulisse Bardi of Florence.[30]

The marriage strategies that aimed at the creation of kinship networks with the best families of the state also had the effect of narrowing the openings at the lower end of the patriciate. In the marriages recorded for sixteenth- and early seventeenth-century families, the old names are generally linked with each other. The Galeotti marry the Cecchi, the Cecchi marry the Onesti, the Buonvicini, and the Pagni. These in turn marry the Ricci, the Galeotti, the Turini, and so on. A few alliances were made with new blood when money or connections outside of Pescia overcame the taint of humble social origins. Two notable examples involved the Cappelletti and the Puccinelli. The Cappelletti, it will be recalled, were a new family in the sixteenth century, having arrived only in 1520. By the 1580s, thanks to the efforts of Cristofano Simone Cappelletti, the family had acquired wealth, a position at the court of Ferdinand I, and the right to operate Pescia's first water-powered silk throwing mill. As a consequence, Cristofano was able to marry into the Oradini family, an old and not particularly wealthy Pesciatine family but one which had recently established impeccable credentials of loyalty and service to the Medici. Captain Giovanni Oradini, Cristofano's father-in-law, had been employed by Giovanni de' Medici dalle Bande Nere. Later on he commanded a troop of infantry sent by Cosimo I to aid Charles V in Flanders, and also military companies in San Sepolcro, Arezzo, and Siena in the 1550s. Having married into a family of good name and with a solid footing in the new regime, Cristofano proceeded to marry his two daughters to a family of equally good name at Pescia and one with economic advantages. Anna and Benedetta Cappelletti both married into the Galeffi with whom Cristofano had several business partnerships.[31]

30. BComPe, I.A.3, Galeotti, *Famiglie pesciatine*. Alliances with prominent Florentines were also made by the Ducci, Galeotti, Pagni, and others. Two members of the Mainardi family also married into the Medici; Cecchi and Coturri, *Pescia ed il suo territorio*, p. 260.

31. Cecchi and Coturri, *Pescia ed il suo territorio*, pp. 220-21, 277; ASF, *Notarile Moderno*, 4035, Vincenzo Piero Gialdini, fols. 5r, 79r.

Figure 5-2. Selective genealogy of the Turini

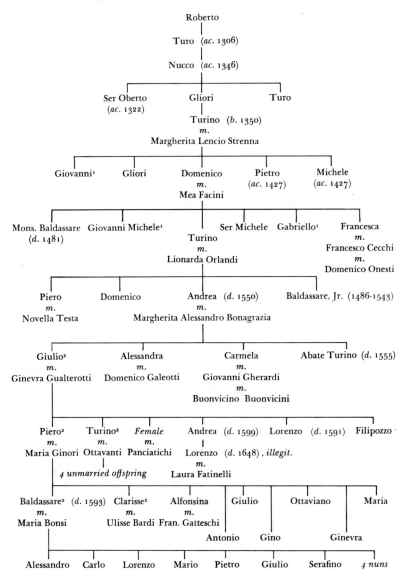

1. Branch dies out within two generations and identity of spouses is unknown.
2. Married to a Florentine.

The other new family that entered into the ranks of the Pesciatine patriciate were the Puccinelli. Like the Cappelletti, this family arrived in the 1520s. Gismondo Puccinelli had a distinguished
military career under Cosimo I, who in recompense asked the
Pesciatine government to allow members of the family to become
citizens and be eligible for the highest offices and honors of
the town. With this kind of backing, it is not surprising that
Gismondo was able to marry Caterina di Filippo Antonio Cardini,
a daughter of one of the wealthiest and most prestigious families
in Pescia.[32]

These two instances reveal that blood considerations never
completely obliterated other concerns; marriage had economic
and political dimensions as well. But the rarity of marriage alliances between the old established families of Pescia and the large
number of new families that settled in the town after the fifteenth
century does suggest that family name, that is, lineage, was of
overwhelming importance. It also suggests that family name,
wealth, and political power most often went hand in hand. It
was not until the catastrophic events of 1631 that Pescia's patriciate was forced of necessity to open up its ranks to families like
the Magnani who until then had been kept out of the upper
reaches of the social order.

The importance of the family name in the late Renaissance is
evident from several of the arrangements that Pesciatine families
made to preserve it. We have already noted how the Cardini,
about to become extinct, passed their wealth to one branch of the
Orlandi to whom they were related by marriage, on condition
that the Orlandi adopt the Cardini name and coat of arms.[33]

The Turini were also forced to make special arrangements to
preserve the family name. Baldassare Pio Turini probably thought
he was doing all he could to ensure the preservation of his family
when he and his wife, Maria Bonsi, brought forth into the world
seven male and four female offspring all of whom survived child-
hood. As a prudent *capofamiglia,* he placed all four daughters in
a convent so as not to squander the family fortune in dowries,
and chose a clerical career for one of his sons. That still left him
with six males to carry on and extend the family name and for-

32. Cecchi and Coturri, *Pescia ed il suo territorio,* p. 300.
33. See Ch. 2, n. 25.

tune. But fate dealt him a cruel blow. Two sons, Alessandro and Carlo, died while pursuing their studies, Lorenzo was killed in a brawl at Parma, Mario was killed in battle at Milan, Pietro was murdered at Pescia, and Giulio died before he had a chance to marry. Knowing that the family name would become extinct with the death of his only remaining son, Fra Serafino, Baldassare bequeathed the family patrimony and name to Lorenzo, an illegitimate child of his paternal uncle Andrea who had been provost of the churches of Pescia.[34] The Turini name, however, seemed destined not to survive, for Lorenzo, who had married Laura Fatinelli of Lucca, did not have any children. Consequently, he too adopted an heir, Filippo di Giovanni Buonvicini, who in order to inherit the Turini patrimony was obligated either to drop his family name for that of Turini or use the two names in hyphenated fashion, a custom adopted by several Pesciatine families. Filippo chose the latter course rather than forgo a large inheritance.[35]

The family coat of arms also served as a sign of distinction by which the patriciate established separate identities. These symbols of the dynastic family are ubiquitous in the façades of Pesciatine palaces erected in the sixteenth and seventeenth centuries and they also appear among the household inventories of the time as objects that were prominently displayed inside the family domicile.[36]

The preservation of the family name and insignia went hand in hand with attempts to maintain the integrity of the family patrimony. The Turini, the Buonagrazia, the Rosellini, and others of their class, imposed a *fideicommissum* on their legacies so that not only the name itself but the ancestral holdings would set the family apart from the mainstream of Pesciatine society. The inalienability of property outside the family was one of the

---

34. BComPe, I.A.3, Galeotti, *Famiglie pesciatine.* Similar provisions were made by Filippo Alessandro Buonagrazia, who states in his will that in the event that direct male descendants should become extinct, the family patrimony should go to the male descendants of his niece on condition that they adopt the Buonagrazia name and coat of arms. ASF, *Notarile Moderno,* 4330, Antonio Giovanni Forti, fols. 8r–12r.

35. BComPe, I.A.3, Galeotti, *Famiglie pesciatine.* Other families using hyphenated names include the Galeffi-Cappelletti and the Cecchi-Martini.

36. ASF, *Notarile Moderno,* 7382, Girolamo Orlandi, fols. 74r–74v; 10649, Stefano Pierfrancesco Simi, fols. 151r–152v.

strategies by which the Pesciatine patriciate sought to keep others from encroaching on their position in the social hierarchy.[37]

The aristocratic mentality that appears to be forming in the sixteenth century also made itself felt in matters of social conduct. Membership in the Order of Santo Stefano placed some of Pescia's patriciate not only among a group of individuals who were loyal to the grand dukes but also among a group whose actions had to accord with certain aristocratic codes. As one historian put it, "members of the Order were forbidden to engage in manual trade on pain of exclusion; they had a highly developed sense of their own importance and made certain that they were separated from other segments of Florentine society; and they were required to prove their 'nobility' for entrance and to establish fixed incomes."[38] The Orlandi, the della Barba, the Ducci, and other knightly families of Santo Stefano could not and were not expected to behave like others.

Nowhere is this more apparent than in the habits of conspicuous consumption that Pescia's patriciate displayed in the sixteenth and early seventeenth century. The most visible form of liberal spending was palace building—an activity that occupied many Pesciatine families in the late Renaissance. Unfortunately, no building accounts or contracts survive to shed light on this important aspect of local life, but the physical evidence is itself a reminder of its significance for the town. The domestic palace was a special object of family pride and display. Although it may have belonged to only one branch of a family, it was a focus for family solidarity and dynastic pride. Domenico Stefano Rosellini, canon of the Church of Santa Maria Maggiore of Pescia, exhibited these kinds of feelings toward the Rosellini palace when he bequeathed it to his nephew with the obligation "to maintain and hold open the house where the testator presently lives and in that house he must live continually and hold it open and honorably for friends and kinsmen [amici et parenti] just as the testator had it during his own lifetime."[39] The palace was a place where the family could come together no matter what their differences

37. BComPe, I.A.3, Galeotti, *Famiglie pesciatine*; ASF, *Notarile Moderno*, 4330, Antonio Giovanni Forti, fols. 8r–12r; 4035, Vincenzo Piero Gialdini, fols. 91v–97r.
38. Berner, "The Florentine Patriciate" (Ph.D. diss.), p. 236.
39. ASF, *Notarile Moderno*, 4035, Vincenzo Piero Gialdini, fols. 91v–97r.

and make a show of unity toward the outside world. It was here that the honor of the family could be maintained.

Because it was a showpiece, the Pesciatine domestic palace of the late Renaissance was designed with considerable attention to architectural detail. The Turini palace, of which only the richly ornamented façade remains, was redesigned by Giuliano di Baccio d'Agnolo.[40] Among other palaces, the della Barba, said to have been designed by Pompeo della Barba's friend Raphael, also shows signs of thoughtful planning, even if it is not to be attributed to the great artist himself.[41] In many of these buildings the owners were obviously trying to emulate the fashions and styles of grander palaces in Florence. The rusticated windows of the Cardini palace are copied from buildings designed by Ammannati, those of the Ricci palace are influenced by Buontalenti. The rusticated stone first used in the Medici palace in the fifteenth century is imitated in the late sixteenth-century constructions on Pescia's Piazzetta Ducci. Often these attempts were not very successful. The Florentine-style window brackets on the Palazzo Cecchi, for example, look small and stunted when reduced to fit the more modest scale of a provincial palace. The building efforts of a provincial aristocracy could not compete with those of the capital. But this is of little consequence. What is more important is that the Pesciatine patriciate displayed its wealth by aping the fashions of more cosmopolitan and wealthier Florence.[42]

40. Salvagnini, *Pescia*, p. 85. The same architect was asked by his patron Baldassare Turini to design the impressive family chapel in the Pesciatine cathedral. Baldassare Turini's interest in building had begun in Rome when he asked his friend Raphael to oversee construction of his palace, now called Villa Lante. After Raphael's death in 1520, Giulio Romano and others supervised the project until its completion several years later. (Vasari's attribution of the entire design to Giulio Romano has been convincingly refuted by recent scholars. Coffin, *The Villa in Renaissance Rome*, pp. 261–62.) Well-known artists were also at work on the interior decorations. Giovanni da Udine was responsible for the *stucchi* in the loggia and Polidoro da Caravaggio executed a number of the frescoes. Renato Lefevre, "Il Gianicolo di Baldassare Turini," *L'osservatore romano*, 31 July 1976, p. 4.
41. Salvagnini, *Pescia*, p. 85.
42. This was a common though little studied phenomenon throughout the dominion. See C. Sodini, "Architettura e politica a Barga: 1527–1569," in G. Spini, ed., *Architettura e politica da Cosimo I a Ferdinando I*, pp. 164–83.

Figure 5-3. Cecchi Palace, an example of patrician building emulating Florentine architectural styles (see text).

Habits of conspicuous consumption did not stop at the palace door. In their furniture, clothes, and other material trappings the Pesciatine patriciate differentiated itself more and more from their social inferiors. Sixteenth-century inventories reveal a more lavish life style than at earlier times. The newly built or redecorated palaces were furnished with a profusion of high-quality objects: beds and chests of drawers with delicate inlaid woodwork, brass washbasins with enamel and silver decorations, majolica dishes, silverware, crystal salt-cellars, tooled leather hangings worked with gold and silver, and so on. On their persons too, upper-class Pesciatines indulged their taste for opulence. Property settlements and dowries now included a larger amount of jewelry: silver hair-nets, coral crowns, gold buttons, mother-of-pearl belts, and diamonds and sapphires set in gold.[43]

The cultural impact of this change in life style cannot be underestimated. The Pesciatine patriciate did not simply invest old material culture with new glitter, they actually brought new forms of culture to Pescia. In the decoration of interior spaces new genres were introduced alongside the crucifixes and madonnas characteristic of earlier times. Sculptured effigies of notable Pesciatines, framed canvas paintings, some of them containing portraits and other secular themes, slowly made their way into the artistic patrimony of the town.[44] Occasionally even pagan subjects were introduced. In the house of Abdon Jacopo Marini we find appropriately enough paintings depicting the birth of Adonis, Venus falling in love, and Adonis's death.[45] But even religious works such as the lovely martyrdom of St. Dorothy, commissioned from the court painter Jacopo Ligozzi for the church of San Francesco, have a new quality about them. The St. Dorothy, with its portrait of Andrea Turini and emphasis on the rich dress of the subjects as well as on the leaves and flowers for which the painter was justly famous, is a work that glorifies the secular world of the sixteenth century.[46]

The introduction of works by well-known Renaissance artists such as Raphael, Ligozzi, and others may have contributed to the birth of modest native artistic efforts.[47] The first Pesciatine

---

43. For several examples, see ASF, *Notarile*, G-20, Antonio Galeotti, ins. 90; *Notarile Moderno*, 2767, Piero Antonio Gialdini, fols. 106r–106v, 158r–160v; 10649, Stefano Pierfrancesco Simi, fols. 29r–32v; 2883, Francesco Filippo Bonagrazia, fols. 12r–13r; BComPe, I.B.19, *Libro di Ricordanze di Ottavio Galeotti*, fols. 37r, 42r.

44. Portraits are mentioned in several inventories, e.g., ASF, *Notarile Moderno*, 10649, Stefano Pierfrancesco Simi, fols. 29r–32v, 151r–152v. Noteworthy for its ambition, though not necessarily for its excellence, is also the tomb sculpture of Baldassare Turini in his family chapel, attributed to Pierino da Vinci, a nephew of Leonardo, Salvagnini, *Pescia*, p. 131.

45. ASF, *Notarile Moderno*, 10649, Stefano Pierfrancesco Simi, fols. 29r–32v.

46. E. Nucci, *Piccola guida storica artistica della chiesa di San Francesco in Pescia* (Pescia, 1915), pp. 18–19. On Jacopo Ligozzi, see Joan Nissman and H. Hibbard, *Catalogue of Florentine Baroque Art from American Collections*, The Metropolitan Museum of Art (New York, 1969), p. 20.

47. The impetus for building the Turini chapel came from Baldassare Turini's purchase of a Madonna by Raphael. The painting was bought by Ferdinand de' Medici in 1697 and taken to the Pitti palace. I. Ansaldi,

painter to have attracted any notice was Benedetto Pagni, a disciple of Giulio Romano. After a sojourn in Mantua in which he
helped Romano with the Palazzo del Tè, he returned to Pescia
where he painted numerous works, including a self-portrait and a
fresco of Vulcan in a palace on the main piazza. Other Pesciatine painters active from mid-sixteenth through the early seventeenth century include Mariano Graziadei, a disciple of Ridolfo
Ghirlandaio, Alessandro Bardelli, Fioravanti Sansoni, Domenico
Soldini, and Luca Vanni. These were not by any means artistic
geniuses. Most of them did not achieve reputations beyond the
local confines. But they were artists who were aware of the major
trends in larger artistic circles, and they found enough demand
for their work at Pescia and its surroundings to allow them to
pursue their artistic careers.[48]

In the realm of letters too there is a noticeable change beginning in the sixteenth century. At Pescia as elsewhere, books were
in greater evidence. One inventory includes as many as seventy
books "of various types, part in print, part by hand, part in
vulgare and Latin and Greek."[49] Interest in books and book
collecting led to the creation of Pescia's first public library in
mid-seventeenth century, begun with the collection amassed by
Mons. Romualdo Cecchi (d. 1648) and bequeathed by him to the
cathedral chapter expressly for public use.[50]

The well-to-do and well-educated patriciate of Pescia expressed
its interest in literature not only through reading but through
writing and other scholarly activities as well. As we have already
seen, the printing ventures of mid-sixteenth century included the
works of local literati such as the poet and member of the Florentine Academy Simone della Barba and his brother Pompeo.[51]

---

*Descrizione delle sculture, pitture, ed architetture della città e diocesi di
Pescia,* 2d rev. ed. (Pescia, 1816), pp. 12–13.

48. Salvagnini, *Pescia,* pp. 131–35.

49. ASF, *Notarile Moderno,* 4040, Vincenzo Piero Gialdini, fols. 198v–110r;
Notarile, G-20, Antonio Galeotti, ins. 90.

50. Cecchi and Coturri, *Pescia ed il suo territorio,* p. 229.

51. In addition to translating some of Cicero's works, Simone della Barba
wrote *Della vera nobilità,* dedicated to Giulio dei Medici. Pompeo della
Barba's printed works include: *Discorsi filosofici sopra il sogno di Scipione,
Dialogo delle arme e delle lettere, Dell'immortalità dell'anima secondo
gl'accademici e peripatetici, De secretis natura,* and *Della sobrietà del
vivere e dell'esercitio* (dedicated to S. Carlo Borromeo). He also left vari-

The Pesciatine humanist and lawyer Filippo Albertini also wrote several books as did his brother Giuseppe. Several prominent Pesciatines, among them Tommaso Onesti and Stefano Simoni, became well-known Greek and Latin scholars and taught at the University of Bologna. Such others as Pietro Nucci, Giovanbattista Onesti, and Elipidio Berrettari wrote and pursued their careers at the University of Pisa.[52] Though away from Pescia for lengthy periods of time these men nonetheless retained their Pesciatine connections. They corresponded with friends and family, they returned for visits, and often came back to die or be buried in their native soil. Their travels and employment in faraway places exposed them to a broader cultural world than that from which they came and they brought part of it back with them.[53] In cultural terms, the artists, writers, and scholars of Pescia together with the friends and kinsmen who made up their audience brought the Renaissance to their native town.

The emergence of a patriciate class that was closely linked to the highest political and social circles of Tuscany thus had wide repercussions for Pesciatine society. Its influence made itself felt in the realms of culture, economics, politics, and society. The patriciate narrowed the cultural gap between Pescia and the leading centers of learning and art. It also introduced such activities as paper making, printing, and silk throwing that helped transform the Pesciatine economy. And this was not coincidental, for it was this group that had the capital to engage in these efforts. The learning and interest in literature of men like the Turini and the della Barba led them to invest in printing, and their

---

ous medical treatises in manuscript form, of which one deals with the baths of Montecatini.

52. The works and careers of these men are discussed in Cecchi and Coturri, *Pescia ed el suo territorio*, pp. 198, 213, 216, 267, 275–76, 313, and *passim*.

53. The strength of ties to Pescia is readily seen in the lives of men like Baldassare Turini, Jr., who despite his high connections and lengthy stay in Rome nonetheless worked hard to improve the lot of his native town. It was through his efforts that Pescia was removed from the diocese of Lucca and made a *prepositura* directly under papal jurisdiction. Like many others of his class, he was buried at Pescia in his family chapel. Among those who achieved fame or fortune elsewhere but either retained strong ties or came back to Pescia during their last years were Clemente Marco and Marc'Antonio Cardini, Romualdo Bastiano Cardini, Lorenzo Francesco Cecchi, and Lorenzo Giulio Turini.

political connections at court, led men like Simone Cappelletti to seek licenses for the operation of large silk processing firms. Finally the patriciate's habits of conspicuous consumption helped support the growing ranks of Pesciatine artisans.

If the price for these changes was a more closed political system and an aristocracy with habits and ideas not very congenial to the democratic sensibilities of the modern world, Pesciatine culture and society nevertheless profited from the innovations introduced by the patriciate and from the links it helped forge with the rest of the Florentine state.

Conclusion

The history of Pescia in the Renaissance is part of the larger transformation of European society from medieval self-sufficiency to modern interdependency. Indeed, what distinguishes the evolution of Pescia from that of several other towns such as San Gimignano, which had flourished during the Middle Ages only to languish in picturesque decay in subsequent centuries, is precisely the town's ability to adjust to this new reality. Increasingly, communes previously autonomous would have to accommodate politically, economically, and socially to the needs of a regional and European framework.

Pescia's ability to adjust is most obvious in its demographic development. After more than a century of population decline which in its major outlines conformed to that of other European societies but which was aggravated locally by Florentine fiscal policies, the town began to recover after mid-fifteenth century. Stimulated by sustained high birth rates, lower mortality rates, and, above all, immigration, Pescia's population increased more than four-fold. Not only was it possible for a subject town to grow in the course of the Renaissance, but it was possible to do so more rapidly than the ruling city.

The demographic expansion that took place was in large measure related to the gradual transformation of the structure of the economy. People went to Pescia because the economic opportunities there were better than in most of Tuscany. By the early sixteenth century Pescia had begun to establish new production patterns based on regional specialization and long-distance trade. These patterns involved a more efficient use of labor, an increase in trade with larger urban centers, and an expansion of employment both in agricultural by-occupations and in the non-agricultural sectors. In contrast with most towns of its size which had vigorous economies in the medieval period, Pescia did not seek to compete with cities like Florence or Lucca—a competition which it would certainly have lost—but rather it sought to specialize in those activities that catered to the needs of larger economies and that linked it to a regional and European framework. In this as in its noteworthy population growth Pescia was part of a pattern that affected many parts of Europe at this time. The European economy began to emerge as a series of interconnected regional economies that were increasingly differentiated from each other and that left those areas unable to adjust farther and farther behind.

What made possible Pescia's transformation? Why did it succeed and other towns of the Florentine state fail? Ultimately it was local initiative that brought about change. To be sure, when Francesco Buonvicino introduced the white mulberry he did not foresee an agricultural revolution. But his neighbors who planted the tree throughout their properties and their descendants who gratefully acknowledged their debt to Buonvicino by painting his portrait in the communal palace certainly recognized a good thing when they saw it. The people of Pescia themselves, more than anyone else, were responsible for the changes that brought about a higher level of prosperity. The introduction of sericulture, of paper manufacturing, and of silk throwing was all the work of native entrepreneurs who understood how to exploit Pescia's competitive advantages.

Local initiative, however, should not obscure the role of Florence in this transformation. The new Pesciatine economy was unmistakably oriented toward the dominant city. Florence provided the conditions without which economic growth could not have taken place: military protection from other territorial states, a large trading area relatively free of tariff barriers, a market for Pescia's products, and access to economic networks that linked Pescia to the rest of Europe via the economic institutions developed by Florentine businessmen.

The integration of Pescia into this larger economic world was given a substantial boost after the establishment of the Medici principate. Cosimo I and his descendants sought to transcend the relatively narrow economic concerns of the city of Florence and to tighten the economic bonds linking all parts of the state. Their many attempts to revitalize the economy of Pisa, their rulings in favor of certain dominion industries against the interests and complaints of Florentine guilds, their extension of corporate jurisdictions from the gates of Florence to the boundaries of Tuscany, were all aimed at the creation of a more unified economic state.[1] It was as part of this policy that the Valdinievole's road system was altered to favor Pescia, that a rotating system of free fairs was established in the area, and that Pesciatine capitalists were granted patents to establish silk throwing mills.

The political administration of the state also became more unified during the Renaissance so that gradually a regional state emerged. Efforts in this direction began as early as mid-fourteenth century, but they were strengthened after the fall of the republic because of the grand dukes' determination to free themselves from the control of the city of Florence. One aspect of grandducal policy as we have seen was the establishment of a Tuscan bureaucracy staffed with functionaries from towns like Pescia and Colle di Valdelsa. Another aspect was the attempt to bring all subjects, whether Florentine or not, under a single system of justice emanating from the person of the prince.[2] This policy is evident in the 1543 abolition of privileges allowing local areas to have jurisdiction over crimes such as homicides and a variety of other violent acts. The justification given was that the duke wanted such serious crimes "punished equally in the city as in all his dominion, so that everyone may live in the same fear of the law."[3] This movement toward legal and administrative equalization, though haphazard and far from complete, raised the status

1. Galluzzi, *Istoria*, I:150–51. Conflicts between the Florentine wool industry and that of the countryside are cited by Maurice Carmona, "La Toscane face à la crise de l'industrie lanière: techniques et mentalités économiques aux XVIe et XVIIe siècles," in *Produzione, commercio e consumo dei panni di lana (nei secoli XII–XVIII)*, ed. Marco Spallanzani (Florence, 1976), pp. 154–56. The guild statutes of the Florentine *medici e speziali*, for example were extended to the entire state in mid-sixteenth century.
2. Danilo Marrara, *Studi giuridici sulla Toscana Medicea: Contributo alla storia degli stati assoluti in Italia* (Milan, 1965), pp. 33–34.
3. ASF, *Senato dei 48*, 13, ins. 90.

and political power of the dominion with respect to Florence and
provided professional opportunities that had hitherto been denied
to Pesciatines and other subjects of the Florentine state.

The price for this integration into a Tuscan regional framework was, aside from the initial loss of political autonomy, the
exaction of tribute by Florence and the attempt, after mid-
sixteenth century, to impose a number of proto-mercantilist
measures. These efforts by the dominant city undoubtedly drew
some capital away from economic development but, as we have
seen, the payment of tribute was relatively light after the first
century of Florentine rule and the barriers to effective governmental regulation of the economy were formidable. On the
whole the balance of economic returns seems to have outweighed
the economic costs of integration into the Florentine territorial
state.

The returns, however, were not the same for everyone in Pesciatine society. If on the one hand the gradual emergence of a truly
regional economic and political system brought about greater
equalization between Florentines and subject citizens, on the
other, this same transformation widened the economic and political disparities within Pescia. The gap between rich and poor
probably grew as did that between the political power holders
and those who were systematically excluded from political participation in the life of the town. Pescia's integration into a larger
territorial framework encouraged the inequalities among various
segments of Pesciatine society. A new aristocracy emerged that
was best able to take advantage of the opportunities made possible by Florentine rule. And within limits, the Tuscan government promoted these divisions, seeing in this class a source of
support for its own policies. The new aristocracy felt a growing
sense of kinship with the ruling circles of the Florentine state
and the courts of the new European monarchies of the sixteenth
century. While they brought a more cultured and cosmopolitan
outlook to Pescia they also created a more hierarchical society.
Within Pescia itself its status as a Florentine dependency exac-
erbated the social, cultural, and political differences between
subjects and rulers at a time when these differences were becoming less pronounced between the ruling city and its subject towns
in the dominion.

Appendices

1. THE CATASTO AND THE
DECIMA GRANDUCALE

The catasto of 1427 was compiled by the Florentine government in order to provide a rational basis for taxation in the city, *contado,* and district of Florence. It consists of declarations by all houeholds regarding their wealth and the number, ages, sex, and relationships of all members of the household. Thorough descriptions of the catasto and critical analyses of the problems it raises for demographic and economic historians have been provided by Elio Conti, *I Catasti agrari della Repubblica Fiorentina* (Rome, 1966), and David Herlihy and Christiane Klapisch-Zuber, *Les Toscans et leurs familles: Une étude du catasto florentin de 1427* (Paris, 1978).

Although these discussions will not be repeated here, several comments are appropriate. Like all records compiled for fiscal purposes, the catasto poses a number of problems for demographic historians. First, many of the propertyless, the indigent, and in general the poorest and most physically mobile members of society were able to evade the catasto administrators. Based on a comparison of notarial and other types of records with the catasto, Conti estimates that for the entire countryside of the Florentine state, about 10 percent of all households were not listed.[1] My own comparison of the names of agricultural workers listed in the declarations of Pescia's landowners with the names of heads of households who submitted tax declarations, yielded a lengthy list of unaccounted for names. Many of these agricultural workers may have been listed as dependents in households headed by others, some may have lived or filed tax declarations in neighboring communities, but the list is too long (over one hundred names) to be attributed solely to these possibilities. Undoubtedly many agricultural tenants and sharecroppers escaped the tax officials.

A second problem lies in the under-reporting of dependents within households for which tax declarations were filed. Since the catasto was to be the basis for a poll tax as well as an *ad valorem* tax, and since information about dependents would in all likelihood be used for collecting other taxes such as the salt

1. Elio Conti, *I catasti agrari della Repubblica fiorentina* (Rome, 1966), p. 99.

tax (usually levied on all persons above a certain age), there was good reason, at least in the subject areas of Florence, to try to conceal the number of dependents. (In the city of Florence itself, a 200-florin exemption per dependent provided an incentive to report accurately.) The extent of underreporting is especially obvious in the case of female infants and children. At birth the male-female ratio should be about 105 to 100, yet in Pescia's catasto the ratio is 143 to 100. While lower, the ratio at ages 0–4 is still distorted: it stands at 110 to 100.

A third difficulty in using the catasto arises from the inaccurate reporting of ages. As in most pre-modern populations, ages ending in zero and five were favored especially. The least favored ages were those ending in one, three, seven, and nine. If ages were reported accurately, these should account for 40 percent of all ages. In Pescia, as in most other parts of the Florentine state, they account for barely more than 20 percent.

A fourth problem is that fiscal residence and actual residence do not coincide. At Pescia, for example, 2.2 percent of all individuals listed lived outside of Pesciatine territory. Presumably the resultant error in estimating the total population is offset by the probability that a roughly equal number of individuals residing at Pescia filed their declarations elsewhere.

Finally, religious institutions seldom declared the number of persons affiliated with them. Although these institutions were required to file a declaration of their holdings, they were exempt from taxes and did not have to provide information about their members. A few did. At Pescia out of twenty-one religious institutions only the following listed their personnel: the Monastery of S. Michele (11 nuns, 5 *conversi*); church of S. Maria Maggiore (presumably the 24 priests who share the Easter meal); church of S. Stefano and three of its chapels (2 priests, 3 chaplains); church of S. Andrea and S. Bartolomeo (1 priest); chapel of S. Jacopo and S. Filippo in the Church of S. Filippo (1 priest, 1 chaplain); and the Spedale of S. Maria Nuova (4 friars). The non-secular population thus amounted to over fifty-two persons.

From the economic point of view the catasto also raises some questions primarily because it has some features of an income and a property tax, without being one or the other. Each head of a household was required to list all his real and personal property, stocks, business investments, and so on. Average annual business profits and returns on agricultural investments for the three years previous to the catasto were capitalized at a rate of 7 percent. The sum of such capitalizations became the taxpayers' taxable wealth. In the case of agricultural properties, the returns on farms worked by the taxpayer himself were calculated by taking the average annual yield, multiplying it by a constant that approximated the price of that particular commodity (e.g., 12 s. per barrel of wine, 12 s. 6 d. per libbra of oil), dividing the product by half, to compensate for labor inputs, and then capitalizing it at 7 percent. If the property was leased, the same procedure was used on the share or rent accruing to the landowner, except that, for obvious reasons, there was no compensation to the owner for labor inputs.

According to Conti, the formula was a fairly good estimate of the value of properties and of returns on business investments. The only problem with it was that there was a tendency to declare smaller returns than were actually received. On the whole, he estimates that the figures in the catasto represent about three- to four-fifths of the actual returns.[2]

Another problem for using the catasto as a basis for determining such questions as extent of cultivated area in a community or the total wealth of a community, is that persons having property or investments in one place could declare them elsewhere if their residency did not coincide with the site of their investment. In the case of Pescia, this does not appear to be an insurmountable difficulty. Because it was impossible to consult several hundred catasto volumes in search of such holdings, it was assumed that the percentage of Pesciatine lands declared elsewhere, with the exception of Florence, was roughly equal to that of non-Pesciatine lands declared at Pescia. This came to about 6 percent of all land holdings.[3] The city of Florence, on the other hand, deserved special treatment because of the argu-

2. *Ibid.*, p. 58. There is no agreement yet on what items were underreported the most. Raymond de Roover stressed the evasions possible with easily concealed movable property. Herlihy and Klapisch on the other hand, argue that the catasto weighed most heavily on movable property and investments in the funded debt. Cf. Raymond de Roover, *The Rise and Decline of the Medici Bank 1397–1494* (New York, 1963), p. 25; and Herlihy and Klapisch, *Les Toscans*, p. 67.

3. Since almost all parcels listed in the catasto were identified by place name, it was possible to determine the amount of non-Pesciatine lands by means of place-name analysis. Most of non-Pesciatine landholdings were actually located in neighboring communities.

ment that one of the manifestations of Florentine economic imperialism was the massive purchase of land by Florentine citizens.[4] If this had been true at Pescia it would have meant that
large segments of Pescia's arable would have gone unrecorded in
the town's catasto. Yet an investigation of the tax returns of half
of the *gonfaloni* of Florence, including several located in the
quarters of Santo Spirito and Santa Maria Novella, which are in
the direction of Pescia, reveals that Florentine ownership at Pescia was negligible.[5]

Finally, the catasto in one out of five cases does not contain information on the size of land parcels declared. To compensate
for this, when crops and land valuations were known, it was
necessary to find the linear equation that best expressed the relation between these variables and then to substitute the appropriate A and B constants into the linear prediction equation. It
was thus possible to use the two known variables—land valuation
and crop—to estimate the third and unknown variable—size.[6]
For each type of crop or crop mix, size was regressed on valuation, in a linear equation of the form $Y' = A + Bx$, where $Y' =$
size, and $x =$ valuation. The resulting values for A and B (see
Table A–1) were then employed to obtain values for Y'.

To analyze the agricultural economy of Pescia it is useful to
compare data from the catasto with that of the *Decima* of 1535.
This document, however, which surveys the properties of local
residents, is in many respects different from the catasto so that
some discretion must be used.[7]

4. Purchases of land by Florentines occurred at San Gimignano and Pisa;
   Fiumi, *San Gimignano*, pp. 214–16; Michael Mallett, "Pisa and Florence
   in the Fifteenth Century: Aspects of the Period of the First Florentine
   Domination," in *Florentine Studies*, ed., N. Rubinstein, pp. 432–41. The
   more general problem of investment in rural land by urban dwellers is
   treated by Pinto, "Ordinamento colturale."
5. Among the five Florentine residents who declared property at Pescia, the
   only substantial amount was declared by Michele del Maestro Guerrieri
   [Orlandi] from Pescia, who had nine parcels valued at 320 florins. All five
   declarations were from the quarter of Santa Croce, which was not in the
   direction of Pescia.
6. Tenure systems were not included in the equation because they were
   not significant in determining valuations. See pp. 93–99.
7. For a description of the Decima see G. F. Pagnini del Ventura, *Della
   decima e di varie altre gravezze imposte dal comune di Firenze. Della*

Table A–1. Relation between size and land valuations, catasto 1427

Crop	Constant A	B	*t*-value	No. of plots
Woods	1.4147	0.3116	4.87	169
Cereals	1.0003	0.2352	21.99	1,042
Olives	0.6103	0.0195	10.17	123
Vineyards	0.8927	0.0369	20.21	631
Olives and vineyards	1.1326	0.0489	21.50	423
Vineyards and cereals	2.8611	0.0364	6.74	32
Pasture, fallow	1.1495	0.2461	8.02	117
Any 3 crops combined	2.3048	0.0899	11.59	31
Unknown	1.7158	0.1517	15.88	75

Note: a Durbin-Watson statistic was not derived to test for auto-correlation because the cases were not ordered.

To begin with, although the Decima was presumably a 10 percent tax on annual income from property, we do not really know how the valuations in the Decima were arrived at. There is much evidence of a sizeable discrepancy between the figures reported and actual income.[8] Consequently, for many analytical purposes the catasto and the Decima cannot be compared directly with each other, but must be used as two internally consistent but independent sources.

With the Decima, as with the catasto, there was also the possibility that much land might go undetected if it were owned by non-residents. An attempt, therefore, was made to search for names of non-Pesciatine landowners among the names mentioned by taxpayers when they identified their property by listing contiguous owners. Obviously, this is not a very "scientific" method but it should ferret out any major foreign property owners. As with the catasto, however, it appears that most of Pescia's land in 1535 was in the hands of Pesciatines.[9]

This is not surprising. To the extent that Florentines invested in Tuscan lands, they probably found it easier to buy up vast

moneta e della mercatura dei Fiorentini fino al secolo XVI (Lisbon and Lucca, 1765–1766).

8. Berner, "The Florentine Patriciate" (Ph.D. diss.), pp. 394–401.

9. This procedure was developed by Herlihy in his study of Santa Maria Impruneta, where he detected a growing number of holdings in Florentine hands. Herlihy, "Santa Maria Impruneta," pp. 256–60.

tracts in the newly reclaimed lowlands around Pisa and Altopascio. Yet even there, Florentine incursions were minor until
the late sixteenth and early seventeenth century. During this
later period, Florentine names still seldom appear in Pesciatine
estimi and notarial records. The Medici did own two farms in
the vicarate of Pescia which were part of the Altopascio properties they acquired in 1584. But on the whole, Pescia was just
enough out of the way and into the hills that it remained un-
touched by the Florentine sweep westward.[10]

A more significant omission from the Decima is that of ecclesiastical holdings, which were exempt from the survey. Using the
same procedure as was employed for foreign landowners, it was
determined that approximately one-fifth of all parcels were in
the hands of ecclesiastical institutions. In calculating changes in
the size of the cultivated area this omission had to be taken into
account. But the task was facilitated by the fact that at least
those parcels that were listed almost invariably contained data
on size.

10. For an analysis of the generally later date of this movement than has
    heretofore been believed, see Paolo Malanima, "La proprietà fiorentina
    e la mezzadria nel contado pisano," in *Contadini e proprietari nella Tos-
    cana moderna,* Mario Mirri, *et al.,* eds. (Florence, 1980), pp. 345–76. The
    history of Altopascio has been examined by McArdle, in *Altopascio.*

2. BAPTISMS

Pescia's baptismal registers, housed in the Archivio della Parrochia della Cattedrale di Pescia, are among the oldest in Italy. Starting with the year 1487, the series continues (with some interruptions) through the seventeenth century. The first six volumes contain the name and patronym of each infant and its parents (family names are infrequent), and the date of baptism. The bad state of preservation of the registers, however, makes them impossible to read for many years. The series is legible and appears complete for the years 1488–1501. Thereafter, either because of missing pages or faded ink, it is possible to count only the number of annual baptisms for a few years. Even this is done with some risk of miscalculation because of the faded ink. Since the names are illegible the count depends on counting the number of lines made across the page by the officiating priest in order to separate entries. It is assumed that each line separated one baptism. Consequently, other than a rough yearly consistency for the series as a whole and a comparison of the number of baptisms at certain times against known total population figures, there is no way of analyzing the reliability of the series. On both these counts, however, the registers appear fairly reliable. The data derived from them are summarized in the table that follows.

Annual Baptisms

Year	Male	Female	Total	Year	Total
1488	72	63	135	1554	217
1489	75	61	136	1555	178
1492	76	75	151	1556	190
1493	68	58	126	1557	233
1494	64	65	129	1558	193
1495	81	69	150	1559	252
1496	54	48	102	1560	258
1497	56	66	122	1562	250
1498	73	78	151	1563	217
1499	66	57	123	1565	230
1500	71	58	129	1569	285
1501	89	78	157	1570	244
1533			174	1574	302
1534			185	1575	229
1536			227	1577	294

Year	Total	Year	Total
1578	264	1608	275
1579	258	1609	306
1580	342	1610	297
1586	307	1611	297
1587	285	1612	289
1588	299	1613	324
1589	303	1614	295
1590	291	1615	289
1591	314	1616	340
1592	334	1617	353
1593	279	1618	344
1594	284	1619	266
1595	333	1620	312
1596	247	1621	303
1597	304	1622	254
1598	240	1623	326
1599	227	1624	285
1600	326	1625	303
1601	266	1626	281
1602	245	1627	279
1603	254	1628	281
1604	255	1629	250
1605	260	1630	256
1606	184	1631	152
1607	303	1632	227

3. AGE STRUCTURE AT PESCIA, 1427

Age	Male	Female	Total	Age	Male	Female	Total
0	33	23	56	46	5	2	7
1	31	30	61	47	3	2	5
2	27	35	62	48	3	3	6
3	35	27	62	49	0	0	0
4	17	14	31	50	38	40	78
5	10	9	19	51	1	0	1
6	15	8	23	52	4	4	8
7	13	18	31	53	0	0	0
8	11	8	19	54	9	6	15
9	8	10	18	55	12	14	26
10	12	5	17	56	6	5	11
11	17	1	18	57	2	1	3
12	17	15	32	58	3	2	5
13	13	8	21	59	2	0	2
14	11	17	28	60	21	41	62
15	19	14	33	61	0	1	1
16	8	7	15	62	6	0	6
17	9	3	12	63	3	1	4
18	10	11	21	64	2	1	3
19	4	2	6	65	7	9	16
20	16	24	40	66	4	4	8
21	4	4	8	67	2	2	4
22	12	8	20	68	3	4	7
23	8	8	16	69	0	0	0
24	11	15	26	70	31	28	59
25	6	11	17	71	0	0	0
26	13	13	26	72	8	4	12
27	12	7	19	73	4	3	7
28	9	10	19	74	5	1	6
29	3	2	5	75	9	3	12
30	16	23	39	76	8	1	9
31	1	0	1	77	4	0	4
32	7	4	11	78	5	1	6
33	6	3	9	79	2	0	2
34	7	4	11	80	16	10	26
35	10	15	25	81	0	0	0
36	17	19	36	82	0	0	0
37	2	2	4	83	0	0	0
38	0	10	10	84	0	1	1
39	1	0	1	85	2	0	2
40	21	30	51	86	0	0	0
41	2	0	2	87	1	0	1
42	8	3	11	88	1	0	1
43	3	0	3	89	0	0	0
44	3	6	9	90	2	3	5
45	12	18	30	Missing	42	22	64

4. SOME COMMODITY PRICES AT PESCIA
(in soldi di piccioli)

	Wine[a]		Oil[b]	
	Price	Observations	Price	Observations
1475	25	7	—	–
1476	35	8	14	4
1477	20	2	14	2
1478	20	2	—	–
1479	25	2	—	–
1480	25	2	—	–
1481	40	3	16	2
1494	50	1	—	–
1496	45	1	—	–
1501	30	2	—	–
1503	30	1	—	–
1504	35	1	22	1
1505	25	1	—	–
1508	45	1	—	–
1531	59	3	37	2
1539	52	1	—	–
1543	—	–	22	1
1544	37	3	21	2
1549	65	1	39	1
1550	—	–	28	1
1551	—	–	33	1
1552	—	–	36	2
1553	—	–	33	2
1554	58	2	—	–
1564	40	1	—	–
1590	50	1	44	1

a Per barrel.
b Per libbra.

Sources: ASPi, *Conventi Soppressi,* 667, 681, 677, 684, 723; ASF, *Libro Commercio,* 305; BComPe, I.B.52.

	Reeled Silk[a]	
	Price	Observations
1450s	250	1
1489	220	1
1497	200	1
1500	200	1
1501	200	1
1503	215	1
1504	210	2
1507	250	1
1524	220	1
1525	223	1
1526	200	1
1527	200	1
1541	230	1
1543	180	1
1544	200	1
1545	240	1
1549	225	2
1550	222	3
1551	225	3
1552	221	4
1553	230	1
1554	274	1
1556	286	1
1564	286	1
1567	300	3
1568	275	2
1570	234	1
1590	385	1
1595	440	1
1596	475	3
1597	455	5
1599	478	4

[a] Per libbra.

Sources: F. de Roover, "Andrea Banchi"; ASPi, *Conventi Soppressi,* 723;
BComPe, *Libro Creditori e Debitori A. Galeotti;* ASPe, 1188, *Registro Spedale
S. Maria Nuova;* BComPe, I.B.8; I.B.52; I.B.63; BNF, *Archivio Capponi,* 33;
ASF, *Libro Commercio,* 305; ASF, *Archivio Cerchi, Fondo Galli.*

5. SOURCES FOR THE STUDY OF
PUBLIC FINANCE

The abundance of documentation, such as governmental budgets, deliberations, and statutes, has provided much of the impetus for recent studies of medieval and Renaissance public finance in Tuscany.[1] The most important sources for a study of the public finances of Pescia, in chronological order, are the records of the Florentine Camera del Comune, the records of the Florentine funded debt, the Monte, and the communal budgets of Pescia. Between 1384 and 1433 the *provveditori* of the Florentine treasury, the Camera del Comune, attempted to present a synopsis of the city's financial standing by recording summaries of annual debits and credits.[2] Among the payments recorded are the direct taxes paid to Florence by Pescia and the other towns of the district. An examination of the entries recorded reveals, however, that after the first years of the fifteenth century the records of the *provveditori* do not contain complete information.[3] Beginning in 1405 there are a few omissions, and the gaps become larger with the years. By 1419 the books provide no information at all on Pescia, and this was not because the town had stopped its payments.

The records of the Camera can be supplemented by the use of documents from the administrators of the Monte. Since a growing portion of Florentine revenues was used for payment of interest to Monte creditors, these revenues probably began to be

1. Some of the most recent works on the subject include, Marvin Becker, "Problemi della finanza pubblica fiorentina della seconda metà del Trecento e dei primi del Quattrocento," *Archivio storico italiano,* 123 (1965), 433–66; William Bowsky, *The Finance of the Commune of Siena* (Oxford, 1970); David Herlihy, "Direct and Indirect Taxation in Tuscan Urban Finance, 1200–1400," *Finances et comptabilité urbaines du XIIIe au XVIe siècle* (Brussels, 1964), pp. 385–405; Molho, *Public Finances;* de la Roncière, "Gabelles."
2. The series is entitled, *Camera del Commune—Provveditori—Entrata e Uscita.*
3. There is some disagreement regarding the completeness of the Camera records. Charles de la Roncière claims that they show only the funds channeled through the Camera. Anthony Molho, on the other hand, claims that the above mentioned series contains a complete summary of all public funds. See de la Roncière, "Gabelles," p. 163, n. 1; Molho, *Public Finances,* pp. 195–97.

channeled directly through the Monte rather than the Camera. Consequently, taxes from the towns of the district were paid to the officials of the Monte so that they in turn could repay communal creditors. This may explain the gaps in the Camera records and the appearance at about the same time of payments by Pescia and other district towns in the records of the Monte. It may also explain why the city council of Pescia refers to the Monte officials as the recipients of the town's tax payments to Florence.[4] Accordingly, beginning in 1405 and over the next two centuries Pescia's annual direct tax obligations as well as actual payments are recorded in a series entitled *Provveditori del Monte—Entrata e Uscita del Camarlingho per la Diminuzione del Monte.*

The completeness and reliability of the Monte records with reference to regular annual tax obligations is beyond doubt.[5] There is less certainty, however, about the extent to which special taxes were also recorded. As their name implied, special or extraordinary taxes were imposed sporadically, and because of this there is no foolproof way to ascertain if all of them were entered in the books of the Monte officials. For the period preceding 1434, when the Monte records can be compared to the incomplete Camera records, there is evidence that two special taxes went unrecorded, probably because they were used directly to pay extraordinary military expenditures.[6] For the period between the end of 1433 and the beginning of 1471, there is no comparable series of documents with which to test the accuracy of data from the Monte. This is probably the weakest part of the series with respect to our knowledge about special taxes. None are recorded by the Monte officials, and there is evidence that at least one such tax was imposed on Pescia.[7]

The most complete and accurate information on the public finances of Pescia can be found in the communal budgets, which were single ledgers that summarized the numerous revenues and

4. ASPe, *Del.*, 18, fols. 104v, 162r.
5. It should be noted that one volume in the Monte series, covering the years 1522–37, is missing.
6. The first such tax was imposed in 1407 and the second in 1413. ASF, *CC*, 22, fols. 31r; 23, fols. 22r, 23r; 25, fols. 30v, 41v; 26, fols. 23v, 29v.
7. The deliberations of the city council of Pescia discuss the imposition of a five-year special tax imposed in 1441. ASPe, *Del.*, 24, fols. 250r, 255r.

expenditures of Pescia's government. The entries are recorded in two consecutive sections, *Entrate* and *Uscite,* that were balanced and audited every six months. Within each section entries were listed in categories according to their precise nature, such as revenues from direct taxes, revenues from fines, expenditures for communal salaries, expenditures for the chancery, and others. Although from year to year there was no complete uniformity in the number or nature of the categories, the ledgers usually provide sufficient detail to allow the assignment of most entries to consistent functional categories. It is therefore possible to trace the public finances of Pescia with considerable accuracy over a period of more than one century.[8]

The records of the Florentine Camera, the Monte, and the budgets of Pescia form three overlapping series that provide most of our information on communal revenues and expenditures from 1384 to 1630. Additional information, especially for the period preceding the first of our series, can be found in the deliberations of the city council and in the statutes of Pescia. It should be noted, however, that none of these sources provides systematic information on transfer payments to Florence in the form of gabelles. Since these were usually sold to tax farmers, Florentine officials recorded only the total revenues received from these sales rather than the amounts collected from single communities or individuals. Yet this omission is of little consequence because gabelles accounted for a very small percentage of communal expenditures (see 3. *Gabelles,* in *Transfer Payments to Florence* section of Chapter 4).

8. The budgets of Pescia form a series entitled *Saldi e Bilanci della Comunità.* The volumes for the years 1502–14 and 1548–60 are missing.

6. PESCIATINE GOVERNMENT EXPENDITURES, 1410–1419 (in lire)

Year	Local payments			Transfer payments to Florence				
	Adminis-tration[a]	Labor services	Payments in kind	Salt tax[a]	Fortifi-cations[a]	Ordinary tax[b]	Lance tax[b]	Extraor-dinary tax[c]
1410	4,000	n.a.	n.a.	1,400	3,100	2,767	—	—
1411	4,000	n.a.	n.a.	1,400	3,100	2,767	—	—
1412	4,000	n.a.	n.a.	1,400	3,100	2,767	244	—
1413	4,000	n.a.	n.a.	1,400	3,100	2,767	733	—
1414	4,000	n.a.	n.a.	1,400	3,100	2,767	976	1,158
1415	4,000	n.a.	n.a.	1,400	3,100	690	—	—
1416	4,000	n.a.	n.a.	1,400	3,100	1,796	977	1,158
1417	4,000	n.a.	n.a.	1,400	3,100	2,400	733	—
1418	4,000	n.a.	n.a.	1,400	3,100	865	733	—
1419	4,000	n.a.	n.a.	1,400	3,100	2,445	—	—

n.a.: not available

Sources: [a] Estimated expenditure, see ch. 4.
[b] ASF, *Monte* 1091, 1093, 1094.
[c] ASF, *CC*, 25, fols. 30v, 41v; 26, fols. 23v, 19v.

7. REVENUES AND EXPENDITURES OF THE PESCIATINE GOVERNMENT, 1484–1499 (in lire)

| | Revenues | | | | Expenditures | | | | |
| | | | | | Local | Transfer payments to Florence | | | |
Year	Indirect taxes[a]	Direct taxes	Loans	Total	Administration	Labor services	Provincial expenditures	Direct taxes	Total
1484	1,549	4,970	628	7,147	4,813	692	497	1,116	6,118
1485	2,160	3,324	—	5,484	3,359	—	333	1,752	5,444
1486	2,308	3,703	396	6,407	4,196	329	169	1,719	6,421
1487	2,336	5,075	—	7,411	5,839	—	195	1,283	7,317
1488	2,188	4,365	—	6,553	3,739	40	331	2,082	6,192
1489	2,231	3,519	—	5,750	3,633	—	51	2,049	5,733
1490	2,262	3,811	—	6,073	3,899	—	—	2,174	6,073
1491	2,261	4,080	—	6,341	4,407	—	—	2,170	6,577
1492	2,088	3,962	—	6,050	4,290	—	—	2,090	6,380
1493	2,142	4,538	—	6,680	3,315	—	61	2,061	5,437
1494	2,004	4,469	460	5,591	3,565	286	—	2,043	5,894
1495	2,272	5,272	1,420	8,964	6,146	1,166	—	2,209	9,521
1496b	2,183	4,376	—	6,561	6,297	—	—	247	6,544
1498	1,854	4,672	—	6,526	5,249	—	—	1,481	6,730
1499	2,484	5,791	764	9,039	6,170	276	—	2,308	8,754

a This represents gross income from the four principal gabelles: gate, meat, wine, bread.

b Information for 1497 is incomplete.

Source: ASPe, Saldi e Bilanci della Comunità, 683. The annual amounts for each column represent aggregates for many items so that specific folio references cannot be given.

8. REVENUES AND EXPENDITURES OF THE PESCIATINE GOVERNMENT, 1580–1589
(in lire)

	Revenues				Expenditures				
					Local	Transfer payments to Florence			
Year	Indirect taxes[a]	Direct taxes	Loans	Total	Administration	Labor services	Provincial expenditures	Direct taxes	Total
1580	7,204	9,165	—	16,396	8,576	—	5,819	2,700	17,165
1581	6,452	11,168	—	17,620	13,878	18	3,543	2,644	20,083
1582	6,780	12,175	—	18,955	8,926	104	7,531	2,635	19,196
1583	6,816	16,097	—	22,913	15,536	309	3,292	2,643	21,780
1584	6,836	14,097	—	20,933	9,543	297	9,285	1,689	20,814
1585	7,284	11,215	—	18,499	11,518	396	5,463	2,640	20,017
1586	7,308	10,721	—	18,029	9,422	—	8,115	2,590	20,127
1587	7,578	12,960	—	20,538	12,257	172	5,879	2,117	20,425
1588	7,979	15,447	—	23,426	10,117	686	8,027	2,761	21,591
1589	7,620	14,798	—	22,418	9,500	313	7,975	4,300	22,088

[a] This represents gross revenues from the three principal gabelles: gate, meat, bread.
Source: ASPe, Saldi e Bilanci della Comunità, 688, 689. The annual amounts for each column represent aggregates of many items so that specific folio references cannot be given.

9. INVENTORY OF THE PROPERTY OF ABDON JACOPO MARINI

In Dei nomine amen. Anno a Nativitate Domini millesimo sex-
centesimo quinto, indictione tertia, die trigesimaprima mensis
Iulii. . . . Actum Pisciae et domi ubi vitam agebat Abdon de
Marinis. . . .

Cum sit quod alias de presenti mense Iulii et anni Abdon
quondam Iacobi Abdonnis de Marinis de Piscia ex hac vita de-
cesserit, relictis post se et adhuc hodie viventibus Cesare et Iacobo
eius filiis legitimis et naturalibus, eiusque haereditas de iure et
ex forma statutorum terrae Pisciae devoluta sit dictis Caesari et
Iacobo eius filiis praedictis . . . ideo constituti personaliter co-
ram me notario et testibus suprascriptis dicti Caesar et Iacobus,
et . . . presens inventarium de bonis, rebus et iuribus dicti Abdonnis et hodie eius hereditatis in hunc modum et formam facere
procuraverunt et fecerunt. . . . Et primo bona immobilia sunt
infrascripta videlicet. . . .

. . . Item unam domum, positam in terra Pisciae, luogo detto
la via delli Orlandi. . . . In qua quidem domo reperta fuerunt
infrascripta mobilia, superlectiles, iura, instrumenta, libri et rationes infrascriptae, vulgari sermone descripta pro maiori eorum
intelligentia videlicet. Et prima, in cantina, due botte di tenuta
di barili venti l'una, tre botte di tenuta di barili dodici l'una,
due botte di tenuta di sei barili l'una in circa, cinque botte di
tenuta di quattro barili l'una. In ciglieri di detta casa, tre pille
da grano murate, di tenuta di staia sesanta di grano per ciasche-
duna, tre coppi da olio di tenuta in tutto di libbre sesanta alla
grossa. In sala una tavola di noce lavorata, co' i piedi a lione, et
sua cornice intorno, di braccia cinque in circa; uno tavolino di
noce, di braccia due in circa; quindici sgabelli di noce, con sue
spalliere; quattro seggiole di Pistoia, usate; otto quadri grandi,
di braccia due et mezzo l'uno, con cornice di noce et pitture, ne'
quali è dipinto et descritto la Nascita d'Adone, l'Inamoramento
di Venere, la Vita et la Morte di detto Adone; quattro arme dipinte in tela; braccia ventitre per lunghezza et braccia quattro
per altezza di corami d'oro inargentati, usati, per ornamento di
detta sala, computatoci cinque portiere di corame d'oro della medesima sorte; due alari di ferro, paletta, molle et forcina con
palle d'ottone. Nella camera di detta sala, a man ritta verso la

via, braccia ventisette di corami d'oro della medesima sorte et
altezza che sono quelli di sala. Nell'anticamera di detta sala dui
letti d'albero con il suo materasso, pagliariccio et guanciale lun-
gho di piuma per letto, uno paviglione bianco et uno altro listrato di turchino, usati; due casse di noce usate, uno forzieri
d'albero vecchio, uno tavolino di gesso usato, uno armadio vecchio, uno cassone vecchio per tenervi pannine. Item nella detta
anticamera braccia diciotto per lunghezza et braccia due et dui
terzi per altezza di panno di più colori per spalliere, uno quadro
piccolo dipintovi un San Francesco. Nella camera buia in su
detta sala a man sinistra verso la corte, uno letto d'albero con
due materassi, pagliariccio et guanciale lungo con il suo paviglione [di] lino bianco et ruggine, vecchio, due casse di noce
usate, uno tavolino di castagno, uno armadio di castagno, braccia diciotto di lunghezza et braccia due et dui terzi per altezza di
panni di più colori per spalliere per uso di detta camera, quattro
quadretti di tela dipinti di più sorti, uno attaccacappe di noce
et uno d'albero. Item in detta camera buia ventitre libbri com-
putatovi i giornali di debitori et creditori, cantanti parte d'essi
in Adonne di Gherardo Marini et Iacopo Marini suo figliuolo,
segnati [di] lettera A, B, C et come segue per alfabato, coperti di
carta pecora con sue fibbie et correggie, vecchi; uno altro libbro
con suo giornale, coperti di cuoio giallo, vecchi, con tre correggie
per ciascheduno, segnati di lettera M, cominciati l'anno 1571,
cantanti in detto Iacopo Marini camarlingo della magnifica
Comunità di Pescia l'anno 1593, con alcuni quadernucci [di] ri-
ceute attenenti a detto libbro; Q. coperto di carta pecora vecchia, di ricordi d'allocationi di case et possessioni, et altro co-
minciato da Iacopo d'Adonne Marini l'anno 1572 et seguito da
detto Adonne suo figliuolo fino a l'anno 1588; . . . Item in
detta camera buia, in una cassa di noce sei tovaglie line usate,
lunghe braccia sei et sette l'una in circa, diciotto mantiluzzi usati,
dieci salviette usate, dieci canovacci, dodici lenzuola usate, quattro grembiuli lini, uno paviglione lino listrato di bianco con suo
tornaletto, usati, due sargie dipinte gialle et nere, da letto, due
coperte di lana bianche, usate, uno copertoio bianco di lino im-
bottito, otto coltelli con maniche d'osso nero, otto forcine della
medesima sorte, sei forcine d'argento a zampa di bue, sei cuchiai
d'argento uno de' quali serve per forcina et cuchiaio. Item l'instrumento del lodo dato nella divisione fra Adonne Marini et

Marino suo fratello, rogò ser Giuseppe Orlandi, due instrumenti
di compre di terre, fatte nel Comune di Monte Carlo fino de
l'anno 1569 sotto dì 29 di Novembre, et l'altro sotto dì dua di
maggio 1575, . . . Item molte scritture et altre fede di più et diverse persone attenenti ad alcune pretensioni di detto Adonne,
come si dice, contro Marino suo fratello et sua heredi. Item uno
instrumento di pagamento di scudi trecento, fatto da detto Adonne
Marini, come si dice mallevadore di Giovanni di Berto Berti a
madonna Giulia, moglie al presente di Salvestro di Piero Galeotti
da Pescia, et per lei ad altri, come in detto instrumento sotto dì
19 di maggio 1599, rogò ser Pio Ceci. . . . dui tapeti usati, im-
pegnati al Monte di Pietà di Pescia per lire trentacinque; uno
paro di calzoni con casacca di velluto a opere, usati, di detto
Adonne, con uno paio di calzette fatte a ago, di filaticcio, nero,
con sue nappe di taffetta, et capello di feltro, usati; una zimarra
di velluto nero con pelo, di sua moglie, quale è in pegno al
Monte di Pistoia per lire cinquantasei; tre anelli d'oro, uno con
pietra verde, l'altro a uso d'agnus deo, da una faccia il Volto
Santo, dall'altra uno San Giovanni, il terzo con crugnola rossa
entrovi due figurine; una medaglia d'oro entrovi uno volto d'ala-
bastro. Nella cucina, sesanta pezzi di stagno fra piccoli et grandi;
tre bacini d'ottone, due lucernine d'ottone, due brocche, due ca-
tini di ramo [sic] cioè uno piccolo et uno grande, due teglie, dui
testi, una caldaia, due paiuolini, tutti di ramo; quaranta piatti di
terra di più sorte con più pentole et mestolini per uso della cucina; uno armadio di castagno, usato, per uso della cucina; quattro lucernine di ferro stagnate con manicho, due padelle, uno
scardaletto [sic] di ramo, uno mortaro con suo pestello, una ca-
tena dal fuoco, dui stidioni, una paletta, molle, uno schizzo d'ottone, una grattugia. In una stanza grande sopra la sala, dui
forzieri vecchi, voti. Nella camera della via di dietro, uno letto
d'albero con dui sacconi et due materassi et uno tornaletto bianco; item uno altro letto d'albero con una coltrice vecchia et
sacchone et tornaletto di tozzi, una cassa di Venetia, usata, vota,
uno forzieri piccolo, usato, uno tamburo coperto di cuoio vecchio, una spera vecchia, uno tavolino di noce di lunghezza di
braccia due in circa, una portiera di tozzi usata. Nella stanza sopra alla cucina, uno arcile vecchio da fare il pane, uno forzieri
vecchio, uno saccone con i legnami d'albero a uso di lettiera, uno
paro d'alari di ferro piccoli, uno tavolino di castagno usato, due

conche piccole, uno coppo da olio vecchio. Nella stanza a tetto, due botte da aceto di tenuta di barili cinque in circa l'una, dui archoni da grano montanini di tenuta di staia sesanta di grano in circa, in tutto; item uno tappeto di più colori, vecchio. . . .

Io Ceseri d'Adonne Marini da Pescia ho fatto questo inventario di tutti i beni et cose che si trovano nella heredità di detto Adonne mio padre, et in fede di ciò mi sono sottoscritto di propria mano detto dì in Pescia, in presentia di ser Stefano Simi et di detti testimoni. . . .

Io Iacopo d'Adonne Marini da Pescia ho fatto questo inventario di tutti i beni et cose che si trovano nell'heredità di detto Adonne mio padre, et in fede di ciò mi sono sottoscritto di mia mano propria detto dì in presentia di ser Stefano Simi et di detti testimoni. . . .

Bibliography

MANUSCRIPT SOURCES

Archivio Capponi, Florence. IV.2.24. Bocche della Valdinievole, 1591.
Archivio di Stato di Firenze:
> *Camera del Comune*
> *Camera Fiscale*
> *Capitoli*
> *Catasto 1427*
> *Decima 1535*
> *Diplomatico*
> *Miscellanea Medicea*
> *Libri di Commercio*
> *Monte*
> *Notarile*
> *Notarile Moderno*
> *Pratica Segreta*
> *Statuti dei Comuni Soggetti*

Archivio di Stato di Lucca:
> *Estimi di Pescia*
> *Gabella Maggiore*

Archivio di Stato di Pescia:
> *Deliberazioni*
> *Opere e Luoghi Pii*
> *Saldi e Bilanci*
> *Sanità*

Archivio di Stato di Pisa:
> *Conventi Soppressi*

Biblioteca della Cattedrale di Pescia:
    Memorie di Pescia raccolte da Francesco Galeotti nel 1659
    Battesimi

Biblioteca Comunale di Pescia:
    Fondo Sismondi
    Libri di Creditori e Debitori
    Libri di Ricordi
    Riformatori delle Gabelle. 11. 1503.
    Statuti
    Stradario

Biblioteca Nazionale Centrale di Firenze:
    Archivio Capponi
    Magliabechi

SECONDARY SOURCES

Almagià, Roberto, ed. Le regioni d'Italia. Turin, 1964.

Ansaldi, Giuseppe. *Cenni biografici dei personaggi illustri della città di Pescia e dei suoi dintorni.* Pescia, 1872.

———. *La Valdinievole illustrata.* Pescia, 1879.

Ansaldi, Innocenzio. *Descrizione delle sculture, pitture, ed architetture della città et diocesi di Pescia.* 2d rev. ed. Pescia, 1816.

Anzilotti, Antonio. *La costituzione interna dello stato fiorentino sotto il Duca Cosimo I de' Medici.* Florence, 1910.

———. *La crisi costituzionale della Repubblica fiorentina.* 1912. Reprint, Rome, 1969.

Anzilotti, P. *Storia della Val di Nievole dall'origine di Pescia fino all'anno 1881.* Pistoia, 1846.

Arias, Gino. *I trattati commerciali della repubblica fiorentina.* Florence, 1901.

Baldasseroni, P. O. *Istoria della città di Pescia e della Valdinievole.* Pescia, 1784.

Barclay, George. *Techniques of Population Analysis.* New York, 1962.

Barbiere, Giuseppe. *La Toscana. Le regioni d'Italia.* Edited by G. Barbiere. Vol. 8. Turin, 1964.

Bayley, Charles C. *War and Society in Renaissance Florence: The De militia of Leonardo Bruni.* Toronto, 1961.

Bec, Christian. *Les Marchands ecrivains à Florence, 1375–1434.* Paris, 1967.

Becker, Marvin. *Florence in Transition.* 2 vols. Baltimore, 1968.

———. "Problemi della finanza publica fiorentina della seconda metà del Trecento e dei primi del Quattrocento." *Archivio storico italiano,* 123 (1965), 433–66.

Becker, William. "Imperialism." In *Encyclopedia of American Economic History*. Edited by Glenn Porter. New York, 1979.

Berengo, Marino. *Nobili e mercanti nella Lucca del Cinquecento*. Turin, 1965.

Berkner, Lutz K. "The Stem Family in the Development Cycle of the Peasant Household: An Eighteenth-Century Austrian Example." *American Historical Review*, 77 (1972), 398–418.

Berner, Samuel. "The Florentine Patriciate in the Transition from Republic to Principato: 1530–1610." Ph.D. diss., University of California, Berkeley, 1969.

———. "The Florentine Patriciate in the Transition from Republic to Principato." *Studies in Medieval and Renaissance History*, 9 (1972), 3–15.

———. "Florentine Society in the late Sixteenth and Early Seventeenth Centuries." *Studies in the Renaissance*, 18 (1971), 203–46.

Biagi, Guido. *In Valdinievole, guida illustrata*. Florence, 1913.

Bishop, M. W. H. "Aging and Reproduction in the Male." In *Reproduction and Aging*. Edited by Andrós Balázs et al. New York, 1974.

Blum, André. *On the Origins of Paper*. New York, 1934.

Bogue, Donald J. *Principles of Demography*. New York, 1969.

Bowsky, William. *The Finance of the Commune of Siena*. Oxford, 1970.

Braudel, Fernand. *Capitalism and Material Life, 1400–1800*. New York, 1967.

———, and F. Spooner. "Prices in Europe from 1450 to 1750." In *The Cambridge Economic History of Europe*. M. Postan and H. J. Habakkuk, eds. Vol. 9. Cambridge, 1967.

Briquet, Charles M. *Les Filigranes: Dictionnaire historique des marques du papier dès leurs apparitions vers 1280 jusq'en 1600*. 1923. Reprint, New York, 1966.

Brown, Judith, and J. Goodman. "Women and Industry in Renaissance Florence." *Journal of Economic History*, 40 (1980).

Brucker, Gene. *The Civic World of Early Renaissance Florence*. Princeton, 1977.

Bueno de Mesquita, D. M. "The Place of Despotism in Italian Politics." In *Europe in the Later Middle Ages*. Edited by John R. Hale. London, 1965.

Buhler, C. *The Fifteenth Century Book*. Philadelphia, 1960.

Caggese, Romulo. *Classi e comuni rurali nel medioevo italiano*. 2 vols. Florence, 1907–08.

———. *Firenze dalla decadenza di Roma al risorgimento d'Italia*. Florence, 1912.

Calamari, Giuseppe. *Il confidente di Pio II: Cardinale Jacopo Ammannati*. 2 vols. Rome/Milan, 1932.

————. "La lega dei comuni di Valdinievole e la loro pace con Firenze (1328–1329)." *Bulletino storico pistoiese,* 28 (1926), 3–18.

————. "Leghe e arbitrati tra i comuni della Valdinievole nel secolo XIII." *Bollettino di ricerche e di studi per la storia di Pescia e di Valdinievole,* 1 (1927), 6–9; 2 (1928), 20–29.

————. *Lo statuto di Pescia.* Florence, 1928.

Cantini, Lorenzo. *Legislazione toscana, 1532–1775.* Florence, 1800–1808.

Carlsson, G. "The Decline of Fertility: Innovation or Adjustment Process." *Population Studies,* 20 (1966), 140–60.

Carmona, Maurice. "La Toscane face à la crise de l'industrie lanière: techniques et mentalités économiques aux XVIᵉ et XVIIᵉ siècles." In *Produzione, commercio e consumo dei panni di lana (nei secoli XII–XVIII).* Edited by Marco Spallanzani. Florence, 1976.

Cecchi, M., and E. Coturri. *Pescia ed il suo territorio nella storia, nell'arte e nelle famiglie.* Pistoria, 1961.

Chappell, Warren. *A Short History of the Printed Word.* New York, 1970.

Cherubini, Giovanni. "La mezzadria toscana delle origini." In *Contadini e proprietari nella Toscana moderna: atti del Convegno di studi in onore di Giorgio Giorgetti,* vol. 1. Edited by Mario Mirri et al. Florence, 1979.

————. "La proprietà fondiaria nei secoli XV–XVI nella storiografia italiana." *Società e storia,* 1 (1978), 9–33.

Cheung, S. N. *The Theory of Share Tenancy.* Chicago, 1969.

Chittolini, Giorgio. "La crisi delle libertà comunali e le origini dello stato territoriale. *Rivista storica italiana,* 82 (1970), 99–120.

————. "La formazione dello stato regionale e le istituzioni del contado: ricerche sull'ordinamento territoriale del dominio fiorentino agli inizi del secolo XV." In *Egemonia fiorentina ed autonomie locali nella Toscana nord-occidentale del primo Rinascimento: vita, arte, cultura.* 7th International Congress, Centro Italiano di Studi di Storia e d'Arte, Pistoia. Bologna, 1978.

Chojnacki, Stanley. "Dowries and Kinsmen in Early Renaissance Venice." *Journal of Interdisciplinary History,* 5 (Spring, 1975), 571–600.

Cipolla, Carlo M. *Le avventure della lira.* Milan, 1958.

————. *Cristofano and the Plague: A Study in the History of Public Health in the Age of Galileo.* Berkeley and Los Angeles, 1973.

————. *Public Health and the Medical Profession in the Renaissance.* New York, 1976.

Coale, Ansley J., and Paul Demeny. *Regional Model Life Tables and Stable Populations.* Princeton, 1966.

Coffin, David R. *The Villa in the Life of Renaissance Rome.* Princeton, 1979.

Cohen, Benjamin J. *The Question of Imperialism: The Political Economy of Dominance and Dependence.* New York, 1973.

Conti, Elio. *I catasti agrari della Repubblica fiorentina.* Rome, 1966.

Corradi, Alfonso. *Annali delle epidemie occorse in Italia dalle prime memorie fino al 1850.* Bologna, 1865.

Corti, Gino, and J.-Gentil da Silva. "Note sur la production de la soie à Florence au XVe siècle." *Annales, E.S.C.,* 20 (1965), 309-11.

Coturri, Enrico. "Le pievi della Valdinievole alla fine del secolo X." *Bullettino storico pistoiese,* 3, ser. 3 (1968), 20-30.

Dallington, Robert. *A Survey of the Great Dukes State of Tuscany.* London, 1605.

Damsholt, Torben. "Some Observations on Four Series of Tuscan Corn Prices, 1520-1630." *Scandinavian Economic History Review,* 12 (1964), 145-64.

Davidsohn, Robert. *Geschichte von Florenz.* Berlin, 1896-1927. Italian translation, *Storia di Firenze.* Florence, 1956-65.

De la Roncière. *See* La Roncière.

Del Panta, Lorenzo. *Una traccia di storia demografica della Toscana nei secoli XVI-XVIII.* Florence, 1974.

Demeny, P. "Early Fertility Decline in Austria-Hungary: A Lesson in Demographic Transition." *Daedalus,* 97 (1968), 502-22.

De Roover, F. Edler. "Andrea Banchi, Florentine Silk Manufacturer and Merchant in the Fifteenth Century." *Studies in Medieval and Renaissance History,* 3 (1966), 221-86.

———. "Cost Accounting in the Sixteenth Century: The Books of Christopher Plantin, Antwerp Printer and Publisher." *Accounting Review,* 12 (1937), 226-37.

———. "Lucchese Silks." *Ciba Review,* 80 (1950), 2902-32.

———. "Per la storia dell'arte della stampa in Italia." *Bibliofilia,* 55 (1953), 107-15.

De Roover, Raymond. *The Medici Bank: Its Organization, Management, Operations and Decline.* New York, 1948.

———. *The Rise and Decline of the Medici Bank, 1397-1494.* Cambridge, Mass., 1963.

De Vries, Jan. *The Dutch Rural Economy in the Golden Age, 1500-1700.* New Haven, 1974.

Dini, Francesco. *Le cartiere in Colle di Valdelsa.* Castelfiorentino, 1902.

Doria, Giorgio. *Uomini e terre di un borgo collinare dal 16 at 18 secolo.* Milan, 1968.

Duncan, F., and L. Scott. *Metropolis and Region.* Baltimore, 1960.

Fanfani, A. "La preparation intellectuelle et professionnelle à l'activité economique in Italie du XVe au XVIe siècle." *Le Moyen Age,* 57 (1951), 327-46.

Ferretti, Jolanda. "L'organizzazione militare in Toscana durante il governo di Alessandro e Cosimo I de' Medici." *Rivista storica degli archivi toscani*, 1 (1929), 248–75; 2 (1930), 58–80, 133–52, 211–19.

Fieldhouse, D. K. *Economics and Empire, 1830–1914.* London, 1973.

Fiumi, Enrico. "Economia e vita privata dei fiorentini nelle rilevazione statistiche di Giovanni Villani." *Archivio storico italiano*, 91 (1953), 207–41.

———. *Storia economica e sociale di San Gimignano.* Florence, 1961.

———. "Sui rapporti economici fra città e contado." *Archivio storico italiano*, 94 (1956), 18–68.

Flinn, M. W. *British Population Growth, 1700–1850.* London, 1970.

Fumagalli, Giuseppe. *Dictionnaire géographique d'Italie pour servir à l'histoire de l'imprimerie dans ce pays.* Florence, 1905.

Galleotti, A. *Le monete del Granducato di Toscana.* 2nd ed. Bologna, 1971.

Gallerani, Anna Maria, and Benedetta Guidi. "Relazioni e rapporti all'Ufficio dei Capitani di Parte Guelfa." In *Architettura e polifica da Cosimo I a Ferdinando I.* Edited by Giorgio Spini. Florence, 1976.

Galli, Nori A. *La grande Valdinievole.* Florence, 1970.

Gambutti, A. "L'architettura del primo Rinascimento nella Toscana nord-occidentale: influssi fiorentini e caratteristiche locali." In *Egemonia fiorentina ed autonomie locali nella Toscana nord-occidentale del primo Rinascimento: vita, arte, cultura.* Centro Italiano di Studi di Storia e d'Arte, Pistoia. Bologna, 1978.

Galluzzi, Riguccio. *Istoria del Granducato di Toscana.* Florence, 1781.

Giorgetti, Giorgio. "Contrati agrari e rapporti sociali nelle campagne." In *Storia d'Italia*, 6:1. Turin, Giulio Enaudi, 1973.

Goldthwaite, Richard. *The Building of Renaissance Florence: An Economic and Social History.* Baltimore, 1980.

———. "I prezzi del grano a Firenze nei secoli XIV–XVI. *Quaderni storici*, 28 (1975), 5–36.

———. *Private Wealth in Renaissance Florence.* Princeton, 1968.

———. "Schools and Teachers of Commercial Arithmetic in Renaissance Florence." *The Journal of European Economic History*, 1 (1972), 418–33.

———. "The Florentine Palace as Domestic Architecture." *The American Historical Review*, 77 (1972), 977–1012.

Goodman, Jordan. "The Florentine Silk Industry in the Seventeenth Century." Ph.D. diss., University of London, 1977.

Goubert, Pierre. *Beauvais et le Beauvaisis de 1600 à 1730.* Paris, 1960.

Guarnieri, G. *Storia della Marina Stefaniana.* Leghorn, 1935.

Guasti, C., and A. Gherardi. *I capitoli del comune di Firenze: inventario e regesto.* Florence, 1866–93.

Guicciardini, Francesco. *Selected Writings.* Edited and introduced by Cecil Grayson. London, 1965.

Guidi, Pietro. *Rationes decimarum Italiae nei secoli XIII et XIV, Studi e Testi.* Vatican City, 1932.

Habakkuk, H. J. *Population Growth and Economic Development Since 1750.* Leicester, 1971.

Hafez, E. S. E. "Reproductive Senescence," *Aging and Reproductive Physiology.* Ann Arbor, 1974.

Helleiner, Karl F. "The Population of Europe from the Black Death to the Eve of the Vital Revolution." In *The Cambridge Economic History of Europe.* M. Postan and H. J. Habakkuk, eds. Vol. 6. Cambridge, 1967.

Henry, Louis. "The Population of France in the Eighteenth Century." In *Population in History.* Edited by D. V. Glass and D. E. C. Eversley. London, 1965. ,

Herlihy, David. "Direct and Indirect Taxation in Tuscan Urban Finance, 1200–1400." In *Finances et comptabilité urbaines du XIIIe au XVIe siècle.* Brussels, 1964.

———. *Medieval and Renaissance Pistoia: The Social History of an Italian Town, 1200–1430.* New Haven, 1967.

———. "Population, Plague, and Social Change in Rural Pistoia, 1201–1430." *Economic History Review,* 18, 2d ser. (1965), 225–44.

———. "Santa Maria Impruneta: A Rural Commune in the Late Middle Ages." In *Florentine Studies: Politics and Society in Renaissance Florence.* Edited by Nicolai Rubinstein. London, 1968.

———. "Some Social and Psychological Roots of Violence in the Tuscan Cities." In *Violence and Civil Disorder in Italian Cities, 1200–1500.* Edited by Lauro Martines. Berkeley, 1972.

———. "Urbanization and Social Change." In *Four "A" Themes:* [papers delivered at the] *Seventh International Economic History Congress.* Edinburgh, 1978.

———. "Viellir à Florence au Quattrocento." *Annales E.S.C.,* 24 (1969), 1338–52.

———, and Christiane Klapisch-Zuber. *Les Toscans et leurs familles: une étude du catasto florentin de 1427.* Paris, 1978.

Hirsch, R. *Printing, Selling and Reading, 1450–1550.* Wiesbaden, 1967.

Hollingsworth, T. H. "The Importance of the Quality of the Data in Historical Demography." In *Population and Social Change.* Edited by D. V. Glass and R. Revelle. London, 1972.

Hoover, E. *An Introduction to Regional Economics.* New York, 1971.

Hunter, D. *Paper Making Through Eighteen Centuries.* New York, 1930.

Imberciadori, Ildebrando. *Campagna toscana nel'700.* Florence, 1953.

Jones, P. "From Manor to Mezzadria: A Tuscan Case-Study in the

Medieval Origins of Modern Agrarian Society." In *Florentine Studies: Politics and Society in Renaissance Florence.* Edited by Nicolai Rubinstein. London, 1968.

―――. "Per la storia agraria nel medioevo: lineamenti e problemi." *Rivista storica italiana,* 76 (1964), 287–384.

―――. "Review of D. Herlihy, *Medieval and Renaissance Pistoia.*" *Economic History Review,* 24, 2d ser. (1971), 512–17.

Kent, Francis W. *Household and Lineage in Renaissance Florence: The Family Life of the Capponi, Ginori and Rucellai.* Princeton, 1977.

Kirshner, Julius. "Paolo di Castro on 'Cives ex Privilegio': A Controversy over the Legal Qualifications for Public Office in Early Fifteenth-Century Florence." In *Renaissance Studies in Honor of Hans Baron.* Edited by A. Molho and J. Tedeschi, Florence, 1971.

―――. "*Civitas Sibi Faciat Civem:* Bartolus of Sassoferrato's Doctrine on the Making of a Citizen." *Speculum,* 48 (1973), 694–713.

―――. "'Ars Imitatur Naturam': A Consilium of Baldus on Naturalization in Florence." *Viator,* 5 (1974), 289–333.

Kirshner, Julius, and Anthony Molho. "The Dowry Fund and the Marriage Market in Early *Quattrocento* Florence." *Journal of Modern History* 50:3 (Sept. 1978), 403–38.

Klapisch, C., and Michel Demonet. "A uno pane et uno vino. Structure et développement de la famille rurale toscane (debut du XVe siècle)." *Annales E.S.C.,* 27 (1972), 873–901.

Koebner, Richard, and Helmut Schmidt. *Imperialism: The Story and Significance of a Political Word, 1840–1960.* Cambridge, 1964.

Landes, David S. "The Nature of Economic Imperialism." *Journal of Economic History,* 21 (1961), 497–512.

La Roncière, Charles de. *Florence: Centre economique regional au XIVe siècle.* Aix-en-Provence, 1976.

―――. "Indirect Taxes or 'Gabelles' at Florence in the Fifteenth Century." In *Florentine Studies.* Edited by Nicolai Rubinstein. London, 1968.

Lefevre, Renato. "Il Gianicolo di Baldassare Turini." *L'osservatore romano,* 31 July 1976.

Leggett, William F. *The Story of Silk.* New York, 1949.

Le Roy Ladurie, Emmanuel. "Démographie et 'funestes secrets': Le Languedoc (fin XVIIIe–début XIXe siècle." *Annales historiques de la Revolution française,* 37 (1965), 385–400.

―――. *Montaillou: The Promised Land of Error.* New York, 1979.

Licata, Baldassare. "Il problema del grano e delle carestie." In *Architettura e politica da Cosimo I a Ferdinando I.* Edited by Giorgio Spini. Florence, 1976.

Lisini, A. "I segni delle cartiere di Colle." *Miscellanea storica della Valdelsa,* 5 (1897), 247–50.

Litchfield, R. Burr. "Office-holding in Florence after the Republic." In *Renaissance Studies in Honor of Hans Baron.* Edited by A. Molho and J. Tedeschi. De Kalb, Ill., and Florence, 1971.

Luzzatto, Gino. *An Economic History of Italy from the Fall of the Roman Republic to the Beginning of the Sixteenth Century.* Translated by P. J. Jones. London, 1962.

McArdle, Frank. *Altopascio: A Study in Tuscan Rural Society, 1587–1784.* Cambridge, 1978.

Machiavelli, Niccolò. *The Discourses.* Modern Library Edition. New York, 1950.

Magnani, E. *Cartiere Toscane.* Pescia, 1960.

Malanima, Paolo. "La proprietà fiorentina e la mezzadria nel contado pisano." In *Contadini e proprietari nella Toscana moderna.* Edited by Mario Mirri *et al.,* Florence, 1980.

Mallett, Michael. *Mercenaries and Their Masters: Warfare in Renaissance Italy.* Totowa, N.J., 1974.

———. "Pisa and Florence in the Fifteenth Century: Aspects of the Period of the First Florentine Domination." In *Florentine Studies: Politics and Society in Renaissance Florence.* Edited by Nicolai Rubinstein. London, 1968.

Marrara, Danilo, *Studi giuridici sulla Toscana Medicea: Contributo alla storia degli stati assoluti in Italia.* Milan, 1965.

Martines, Lauro. *Lawyers and Statecraft in Renaissance Florence.* Princeton, 1968.

———. *Power and Imagination: City-States in Renaissance Italy.* New York, 1979.

Mazzi, C. "La mensa dei priori di Firenze nel secolo XIV." *Archivio storico italiano,* 20 (1897), 336–68.

Melis, Federigo. "Note sulle vicende storiche dell'olio d'oliva (secoli XIV–XVII)." In *Dell'olio e della sua cultura.* Florence, Cassa di Risparmio di Firenze, 1972.

———. "Vini medievali delle colline lucchese e della Valdinievole che ritornano alla ribalta." *Vini d'Italia,* 9 (1967), 167–71.

Molho, Anthony. "A Note on Jewish Moneylenders in Tuscany in the Late Trecento and Early Quattrocento." In *Renaissance Studies in Honor of Hans Baron.* Edited by A. Molho and John Tedeschi. De Kalb, Ill., and Florence, 1971.

———. *Florentine Public Finances in the Early Renaissance, 1400–1433.* Cambridge, Mass., 1971.

Morelli, Roberta. *La seta fiorentina nel Cinquecento.* Milan, 1976.

Moreni, Domenico. *Annali della tipografia fiorentina di Lorenzo Torrentino.* 2nd ed. Florence, 1819.

Mueller, R. "Les prêteurs juifs de Venise au moyen age." *Annales E.S.C.*, 30 (1975), 1277–1302.

Montaigne, Michel de. *Journal du voyage*. Paris, 1906.

Nissman, Joan, and H. Hibbard. *Catalogue of Florentine Baroque Art from American Collections*. The Metropolitan Museum of Art. New York, 1969.

Noonan, John T., Jr., *Contraception: A History of Its Treatment by the Catholic Theologians and Canonists*. Cambridge, Mass., 1965.

Nucci, E. *L'arte della seta in Valdinievole*. Pescia, 1917.

————. *Piccola guida storica artistica della chiesa di San Francesco in Pescia*. Pescia, 1915.

Pagnini del Ventura, G. F. *Della decima e di varie altre gravezze imposte dal comune di Firenze. Della moneta e della mercatura dei Fiorentini fino al secolo XVI*. Lisbon and Lucca, 1765–66.

Parenti, Giuseppe. *Prezzi e mercato del grano a Siena (1546–1765)*. Florence, 1942.

————. *Prime ricerche sulla rivoluzione dei prezzi a Firenze*. Florence, 1939.

Pazzagli, Carlo. *L'agricoltura toscana nella prima metà dell'800*. Florence, 1973.

Pedreschi, Luigi. "L'industria della carta nelle provincie di Lucca e di Pistoia." *Rivista geografica italiana*, 70 (1963), 149–76.

Pinto, Giuliano. "Il personale, le balie e i salariati dell'ospedale di San Gallo di Firenze negli anni 1395–1406: Note per la storia del salariato nelle città medievali." *Ricerche storiche* (1974), 114–61.

————. "Ordinamento colturale e proprietà fondiaria cittadina nella Toscana del tardo medioevo." In *Contadini e propietari nella Toscana moderna: atti del Convegno di studi in onore di Giorgio Giorgetti*. Siena, 11–13 March 1977. Florence, 1980.

Plesner, J. "Una rivoluzione stradale nel Dugento." *Acta Jutlandica*, 10 (1938), 3–101.

Poni, Carlo. "Archaeologie de la fabrique; la diffusion des moulins de soie 'alla bolognese' dans les Etats venetians du XVIe au XVIIIe siècles," *Annales: E.S.C.*, 27 (1972).

————. *Gli aratri e l'economia agraria nel bolognese dal XVII al XIX secolo*. Bologna, 1963.

Pollak, M. "Production Costs in Fifteenth Century Printing." *Library Quarterly*, 39 (1969), 318–30.

Puccinelli, Maria. "La Valdinievole." *Memorie della Società Geografica Italiana*, 29 (1970), 3–130.

Reid, Joseph D., Jr. "Sharecropping in History and Theory." *Agricultural History*, 49 (1975), 426–40.

Repetti, Emmanuele. *Dizionario geografico, fisico, storico della Toscana*. Vol. 4. Florence, 1841.

Ridolfi, R. *La stampa in Firenze nel secolo XV.* Florence, 1958.

Riesenberg, Peter. "Citizenship at Law in Late Medieval Italy." *Viator,* 5 (1974), 333–46.

Roscoe, William. *The Life of Lorenzo de' Medici Called the Magnificent.* 10th rev. ed. London, 1872.

Romano, Ruggiero. "La storia economica dal secolo XIV al Settecento." In *Storia d'Italia.* Vol. 2. Edited by G. Einaudi. Turin, 1974.

Rossiaud, Jacques. "Prostitution, jeuneusse et société dans les villes de Sud-Est au XVe siècle." *Annales, E.S.C.,* 31 (1976), 289–325.

Rubinstein, Nicolai. "Florence and the Despots: Some Aspects of Florentine Diplomacy in the Fourteenth Century." *Transactions of the Royal Historical Society* (1952), 21–46.

Salvagnini, Gigi. *Pescia, una città: proposta metodologica per la lettura di un centro antico.* Florence, 1975.

Salvemini, Gaetano. "Un comune rurale nel secolo XIII." In *Opere di Gaetano Salvemini.* Edited by Ernesto Sestan. Milan, 1961.

———. *Magnati e popolani in Firenze dal 1280 al 1295.* Florence, 1899.

Schevill, Ferdinand. *Medieval and Renaissance Florence.* New York, 1963.

Schultz, Theodore W. *Transforming Traditional Agriculture.* New Haven, 1964.

Simonde de Sismondi, Jean. *Tableau de l'agriculture toscane.* Geneva, 1801.

Skinner, Quentin. *The Foundations of Modern Political Thought.* 2 vols. Cambridge, 1978.

Sodini, C. "Architettura e politica a Barga: 1527–1569." In *Architettura e politica da Cosimo I a Ferdinando I.* Edited by Giorgio Spini. Florence, 1976.

Spini, Giorgio, ed. *Architettura e politica da Cosimo I a Ferdinando I.* Florence, 1976.

———. "Architettura e politica nel principato mediceo del Cinquecento." *Rivista storica italiana,* 83 (1971), 792–845.

———. "Questioni e problemi di metodo per la storia del principato mediceo e degli stati toscani del Cinquecento." *Rivista storica italiana,* 53 (1941), 76–93.

Stiavelli, Carlo. *La storia di Pescia nella vita privata del secolo XIV al XVII.* Florence, 1903.

———. *Saggio di una bibliografia pesciatina.* Pescia, 1900.

Tagliaferri, Amelio. *L'economia Veronese secondo gli estimi dal 1409 al 1635.* Milan, 1966.

Targioni Tozzetti, G. *Relazioni d'alcuni viaggi fatti in diverse parti della Toscana.* Bologna, 1971; original edition, Florence, 1773.

Torrigiani, Antonio. *Le castella della Val di Nievole.* Florence, 1865.

Touring Club Italiano. *Guida d'Italia: Toscana.* Milan, 1959.

Vermeulen, A., R. Rubens, and L. Verdonck. "Testosterone Secretion and Metabolism in Male Senescence." In *Reproduction and Aging.* Edited by Andrós Balázs *et al.* New York, 1974.

Villani, Giovanni. *Cronica di Giovanni Villani.* Florence, 1823.

Waley, Daniel. "The Army of the Florentine Republic from the Twelfth to the Fourteenth Century." In *Florentine Studies: Politics and Society in Renaissance Florence.* Edited by Nicolai Rubinstein. London, 1968.

Witt, Ronald. "Coluccio Salutati and the Political Life of the Commune of Buggiano." *Rinascimento,* 17 (December 1966), 27–55.

Wrigley, E. A. "Family Limitation in Pre-Industrial England." *Economic History Review,* 19, 2d ser. (1966), 82–109.

———. "Mortality in Preindustrial England." In *Population and Social Change.* Edited by D. V. Glass and R. Revelle. London, 1972.

———. *Population and History.* New York, 1969.

Index